A Daybook
for March
In Yellow Springs, Ohio

A Memoir in Nature
and an Almanac with Applications
for the Lower Midwest, the Middle Atlantic Region
and the Eastern States,
Being a Personal Narrative and Synthesis of
Common Events in Nature between 1981 and 2023
in Southwestern Ohio,
on the Cusp of 21st Century Climate Change
at the Beginning of the Sixth Great Extinction,
with Weather Guidelines
and a Variety of Natural Calendars,
Reflections by the Author
and Seasonal Quotations
from Ancient and Modern Writers

By

Bill Felker

A Daybook for the Year in Yellow Springs
Volume 3: March

Cover from a watercolor by Libby Rudolf

Copyright 2022 by Bill Felker

Published by the Green Thrush Press
Box 431, Yellow Springs, Ohio
Printed in the United States of America

ISBN-13: 978-1544631202
ISBN-10: 1544631200

For my uncle, the Rev. Bill Keefe, and my grandfather, Henry Keefe, who taught me about the moon

No one suspects the days to be gods.

Ralph Waldo Emerson

Introduction

Here are no stories told you of what is to be seen at the other end of the world, but of things at home, in your own Native Countrey, at your own doors, easily examinable with little travel, less cost, and very little hazard. This book doth not shew you a Telescope, but a Mirror, it goes not about to put a delightful cheat upon you, with objects at a great distance, but shews you yourselves.

Joshua Childrey, 1660

This memoir is a record of everyday walks in fields and woods, an exploration of what it means for me to live in in southwestern Ohio. I have gathered here quotations about time and nature, essays from my column in the local newspaper, meteorological commentary made up from my lengthy obsession with tracking the weather, notes about common events in nature, syntheses of these events, and astronomical information based on my years of writing almanacs. Although I have organized my work on a scaffolding of back-yard natural history and observation, I am not a naturalist and have had no training in the natural sciences. All of what is contained in the *Daybook* is the result of my search for myself and for meaning.

This particular aspect of my search began in 1972 with the gift of a barometer. My wife, Jeanie, gave the instrument to me when I was succumbing to graduate school stress in Knoxville, Tennessee, and it became not only an escape from intense academic work, but the first step on the road to a different kind of awareness about the world.

From the start, I was never content just to watch the barometric needle; I had to record its movement, then graph it. I was fascinated by the alchemy of the charts that turned rain and Sun into visible patterns, symbols like notes on a sheet of music, or words on a page.

From my graphs of barometric pressure, I discovered that the number of cold fronts each month is more or less consistent, and that the Earth breathes at an average rate of about once every three to five days in the winter, and once each six to eight days at the peak of summer.

A short apprenticeship told me when important changes

would occur and what kind of weather would take place on most any day. That information was expressed in the language of odds and percentages, and it was surprisingly accurate. Taking into consideration the consistency of certain patterns in the past, I could make fairly successful predictions about the likelihood of the repetition of such paradigms in the future. As Yeats says, the seasons "have their fixed returns," and I found points all along the course of the year which appeared to be fixed moments for change. The pulse of the world was steadier than I had ever imagined.

My graphs also allowed me to see the special properties of each season. August's barometric configurations, for example, are slow and gentle like low, rolling hills. Heat waves show up as plateaus. Thunderstorms are sharp, shallow troughs in the gentle waves of the atmospheric landscape. Autumn arrives like the sudden appearance of a pyramid on a broad plain. By the end of September, the fronts are stronger; the high-pressure peaks become taller; the lows are deeper, with almost every valley bringing rain. By December, the systems loom on the horizon of the graph like a range of mountains with violent extremes of altitude, sometimes snowcapped, almost always imposing and sliced by canyons of wind.

From watching the weather, it was an easy step to watching wildflowers. Identifying plants, I saw that flowers were natural allies of my graphs, and that they were parallel measures of the seasons and the passage of time. I kept a list of when each wildflower blossomed and saw how each one consistently opened around a specific day, and that even though a cold year could set blooming back up to two weeks, and unusual warmth accelerate it, average dates were quite useful in establishing sequence of bloom which always showed me exactly where I was in the progress of the year.

In the summer of 1978, Jeanie and I took the family to Yellow Springs, Ohio, a small town just beyond the eastern edge of the Dayton suburbs. We bought a house and planned to stay. I began to write a nature almanac for the local newspaper. To my weather and wildflower notes I added daily sunrise and sunset times, moonrise and moonset, average and record temperatures, comments on foliage changes, bird migration dates, farm and gardening cycles, and the rotation of the stars. The more I learned around Yellow Springs, the more I found applicable to the world beyond the village limits. The microclimate in which I immersed myself gradually became a key to the extended environment; the part unlocked the whole. My Yellow Springs gnomon that measured the movement of the Sun also measured my relationship to every other place on earth.

My occasional trips turned into exercises in the measurement of variations in the landscape. When I drove 500 miles northwest, I not only entered a different space, but often a separate season, and I could mark the differences in degrees of flowers, insects, trees, and the development of the field crops. The most exciting trips were taken south in March; I could travel from Early Spring into Middle Spring and finally into Late Spring and summer along the Gulf Coast.

My engagement with the natural world, which began as an escape from academia, finally turned into a way of getting private bearings and of finding what I loved and believed. It was a process of spiritual as well as physical reorientation. In that way, all the historical statements in this collection of notes are the fruit of a strong desire to define where I am and what happens around me.

The Daybook Format

The format of my notes in this daybook owes more than a little to the almanacs I wrote for the *Yellow Springs News* between 1984 and 2023. The quotations, daily statistics, the weather outlooks, the seasonal calendar, and the daybook entries were and still are part of my regular routine of collecting and organizing impressions about the place in which I live.

Setting: The principal habitat described here is that of Glen Helen, a preserve of woods and glades that lies on the eastern border of the village of Yellow Springs in southwestern Ohio. At its northern edge, the Glen joins with John Bryan State Park to form a corridor about ten miles long, and half a mile wide, along the Little Miami River. The north section of the Glen Helen /John Bryan complex is hilly and heavily wooded, and is the best location for spring wildflowers. The southern portion, "South Glen" as it is usually called, is a combination of open fields, wetlands, and wooded flatlands. Here I found many flowers and grasses of summer and fall. Together, the two Glens and John Bryan Park provide a remarkable cross section of the fauna and flora of the eastern United States.

Other habitats in the daybook include my yard with its several small gardens; the village of Yellow Springs itself, a town of 4,000 at the far eastern border of the Dayton suburbs; the Caesar Creek Reservoir, twenty miles south of Yellow Springs and created by the Corps of Engineers in 1976. My trips away from that environment were principally northeast to Chicago, Madison, Wisconsin and northern Minnesota, east to Washington and New York, southeast to the Carolinas and Florida, southwest to Arkansas, Louisiana, and Texas, and occasionally through the Southwest to California and the Northwest, two excursions to Belize in Central America, several to Italy.

Quotations: The passages from ancient and modern writers (and sometimes from my alter egos) which accompany each day's notations are lessons from my readings, as well as from distant seminary and university training, here put to work in service of the reconstruction of my sense of time and space. They are a collection of reminders, hopes, and promises for me that I find implicit in the seasons. They have also become a kind of a cosmological scrapbook for me, as well as the philosophical underpinning of this narrative.

Astronomical Data: The *Daybook* includes approximate dates for astronomical events, such as star positions, meteor showers, solstice, equinox, perihelion (the Sun's position closest to earth), and aphelion (the Sun's position farthest from Earth).

I have included the sunrise and sunset for Yellow Springs as a general guide to the progression of the year in this location, but those statistics also reflect trends that are world wide, if more rapid in some places and slower in others.

Even though the day's length is almost never exactly the same from one town to the next, a minute gained or lost in Yellow Springs is often a minute lost or gained elsewhere, and the Yellow Springs numbers can be used as a simple way of watching the lengthening or shortening of the days, and, therefore, of watching the turn of the planet. For those who wish to keep track of the Sun themselves in their own location, abundant sources are now available for this information in local and national media.

Average Temperatures: Average temperatures in Yellow Springs are also part of each day's entry. Since the rise and fall of temperatures in other parts of the North America, even though they may start from colder or warmer readings, keep pace with the temperatures here, the highs and lows in Yellow Springs are, like solar statistics, helpful indicators of the steady progress of the year throughout most of the states along the 40th Parallel (except in the mountains). The daybook entries can be cross-referenced with the list of monthly average temperatures between 1981 and 2017 in order to compare the daily inventories with the month's weather in a given year.

Weather: My daily, weekly and monthly weather summaries have been distilled from over thirty years of observations. They are descriptions of the local weather history I have kept in order to track the gradual change in temperatures, precipitation and cloud cover through the year I have also used them in order to try to identify particular characteristics of each day. They are not meant to be predictions.

Although my interest in the Yellow Springs microclimate at first seemed too narrow to be of use to those who lived outside the area, I began to modify it to meet the needs of a number of regional and national farm publications for which I started writing in the mid 1980s. And so, while the summaries are based on my records in southwestern Ohio, they can be and have been used, with interpretation and interpolation, throughout the Lower Midwest , the Middle Atlantic States and the East.

The Natural Calendar: In this section, I note the progress of foliage and floral changes, farm and garden practices, migration times for common birds, and peak periods of insect activity. Some of these notes are second hand; I'm a sky watcher, but not an astronomer, and I rely on the government's astronomical data and a few other references for much of my information about the stars and the sun. I am also a complete amateur at bird

5

watching, and most of the migration dates used in the seasonal calendar come from published sources. And even though I keep close track of the farm year, the percentages listed for planting and harvesting are interpretations of averages supplied by the state's weekly crop reports.

Daybook Entries: The entries in the daybook section provide the raw material from which I wrote the Natural Calendar digests. The daybook section is a collection of observations made from the window of my car and from my walks in Glen Helen, in parks and wildlife areas within a few miles of my home, and on occasional trips. It is a record that anyone with a few guidebooks could make, and it includes just a small number of the natural markers that anyone might discover.

When I began to take notes about the world around me, I found that there were few descriptions of actual events in nature available for southwestern Ohio. There was no roadmap for the course of the year. My daily observations, as narrow and incomplete as they were, were especially significant to me since I had found no other narrative of the days, no other depiction of what was actually occurring around me. In time, the world came into focus with each particle I named. I saw concretely that time and space were the sum of their parts.

As my notes for each day accumulated, I could see the wide variation of events that occurred from year to year; at the same time, I saw a unity in this syncopation from which I could identify numerous sub-seasons and with which I could understand better the kind of habitat in which I was living and, consequently, myself.

When I paged through the entries for each day, I was drawn back to the space in which they were made. I browsed and imagined, returned to the journey.

Journal Essays: At the end of many of the daybook entries, I have included brief essays from my almanac column in the *Yellow Springs News.*

Companions: Many friends, acquaintances and family members have contributed their observations to the daybook, and their participation has taught me that my private seasons are also community seasons, and that all of our experiences together help to lay the foundation for a rich, local consciousness of natural history.

March Average Temperatures from 1981 through 2023
Normal Average Temperature: 40.4

Year	Average
1981	39.3
1982	40.0
1983	42.0
1984	30.9
1985	43.6
1986	42.4
1987	43.3
1988	40.3
1989	42.2
1990	44.9
1991	42.9
1992	41.0
1993	37.7
1994	39.3
1995	43.0
1996	34.0
1997	41.8
1998	41.7
1999	35.6
2000	45.5
2001	37.2
2002	39.4
2003	42.1
2004	42.9
2005	35.9
2006	39.3
2007	46.2
2008	37.2
2009	44.7
2010	42.8
2011	40.8
2012	53.6
2013	35.3
2014	35.5
2015	38.7
2016	47.4
2017	50.3
2018	36.7
2019	38.1
2020	46.5
2021	46.6
2022	45.0
2023	42.3

March 1st
The 60th Day of the Year

In our hearts those of us who know anything worth knowing know that in March a new year begins, and if we plan any new leaves it will be when the rest of Nature is planning them, too.

Joseph Wood Krutch

Sunrise/set: 7:09/6:27
Day's Length: 11 hours 16 minutes
Average High/Low: 42/25
Average Temperature: 34
Record High: 66 – 1976, 75 – 2023
Record Low: 0 – 1980

Weather

There is a ten percent chance of a high in the 60s today, 30 percent for an afternoon in the 50s, the same for highs in the 40s, twenty percent of 30s, ten percent for 20s or teens. Skies are cloudy with rain 25 percent of the days, snow 20 percent. No below-zero temperatures have been recorded on this date.

The Week Ahead

Although the first cold front of March arrives on the 3rd, bringing a 60 percent chance of highs in the 40s or below, the first quarter of the month also brings a steady five-to-ten-percent chance of an afternoon in the 70s for the first time since early November. In fact, 70s occur more often on the 2nd and 3rd than on any days in the first three weeks of March. And 50s or 60s occur about 30 percent of the time through the week, similar to what happened during February's third week. This time, however, the percentage never drops below that level until late autumn.

Also this week, the percentage of afternoon highs in the teens and 20s drops to between five and ten percent per day, the first time that has happened since early December. The skies continue to brighten, with the 3rd bringing a 70 percent chance of sun, and the 7th an 80 percent chance. The wettest day of the week is usually the 4th; it has a 70 percent chance of showers or flurries.

The 5th and 6th aren't far behind: 50 percent chance of precipitation those days. Storms are likely around the 3rd, especially in the South.

The March Outlook

Throughout March, average temperatures climb almost a dozen degrees, the world warming twice as fast as it did in February. Starting in the lower 30s on the first of the month, normal averages rise one degree every 50 hours, reaching the middle 40s by the beginning of April. Typical lows swell from the 20s to well above freezing, and highs climb from the lower 40s up to near 55.

A typical temperature distribution for Yellow Springs and the surrounding area includes up to two days in the 70s, five days in the 60s, six days in the 50s, nine days in the 40s, eight days in the 30s, and one day in the 20s. Frost occurs on about a dozen of the 31 mornings in March. The last hard freeze of the season frequently takes place prior to the first of April.

Although March is the most unpredictable month of spring, certain weather patterns are visible in the majority of years: the first ten days of the period are usually the coldest; and a second major cool spell is often experienced between the 15th and the 22nd. Milder south winds normally prevail during the second and especially the fourth week. The coldest days of March, those with at least a 35 percent chance of highs in the 30s or below, are the 3rd, 5th, 6th, 7th, 11th, 12th, 13th, and 21st. The warmest days, those having a 35 percent chance of highs in the 60s or 70s, are the 22nd, 23rd, 25th, 26th, 28th, 29th, and 30th.

Precipitation increases with the coming of Early Spring in the middle of February. The normal water equivalent for March is around three inches, almost an inch more than in February. The days with better than a 50 percent chance of precipitation are the 3rd, 4th, 5th, 10th, 20th, 24th, 29th, and 30th. The driest days in March, with less than a 30 percent chance of precipitation, are the 8th, 14th and 21st.

The average amount of snowfall for March in Yellow Springs is about five and a half inches, usually coming in three major installments. The 6th of the month has a higher chance of snow (35 percent chance) than any other day. The typical March day is sunny to partly cloudy between 50 and 60 percent of the time. The brightest days, those with better than a 75 percent chance of sun, are the 7th, 15th, 21st and 26th. The darkest days, with better than a 55 percent chance of cloud cover, are the 5th, 19th and 29th. The average percentage of possible sunshine is 49 percent, up four percent from February.

Springcount

Approximately 23 major spring cold fronts cross the nation between the middle of February and the last week of May. The first three passed through in February. March brings the last seven weather systems of the subseason, Early Spring.

March 3: As the last front of February moves towards New England, mild temperatures occur more often than any time during the first three weeks of March. Chances of highs above 60 surge along the 40th Parallel. Skies often clear with the passage of the March 3rd high, but then they darken quickly as low pressure anticipates the March 5th front with showers or snow.

March 5: The day before this front arrives is typically the wettest day of the month, with rain or snow likely 70 percent of all the years. Across the South and Border States, this high can be accompanied by thunderstorms or tornadoes. Once the March 5th front moves through, expect steady winds and brisk temperatures followed by sun.

March 14: The March 14th front is comparatively uneventful, compared to the equinox front to come. It is often accompanied by brighter skies for a day or so before it moves toward the Atlantic to make way for the much stronger and more disruptive weather system of March 19th.

March 19: The cold front that arrives within a day or two of equinox is one of the last wintry fronts in the South; even in the central portion of the country, it marks the end of the worst of the weather systems of the first half of the year.

March 24: This front, like the March 14th system, is often mild, and it is followed by some of the driest and brightest days so far in the year. In the low-pressure trough that precedes the March 29th cold front, the 28th is typically one of the warmest days in March, with highs above 60 degrees occurring five days in ten at the 40th Parallel and below.

March 29: This last front of Early Spring introduces tornado season to the nation's midsection, and the likelihood of a thunderstorm is six times greater this week than it was last week. As this front moves east, a significant chance of a high in the 80s occurs for the first time this year in the Lower Midwest.

Key to the Nation's March Weather

The typical March temperature at average elevations along the 40th Parallel, the average of the high of 48 and the low of 29, is 39 degrees. Using the following chart based on weather statistics from around the country, one can calculate approximate temperatures in other locations close to the cities listed.

For example, with the base of 39 you can estimate normal temperatures in Minneapolis by subtracting 11 degrees from the base average. Or add 13 degrees to find out the likely conditions in Atlanta during the month.

Fairbanks	-25
Minneapolis	-11
Cheyenne	-6
Portland	-6
Des Moines	-3
Chicago	-3
AVERAGE ALONG THE 40th PARALLEL: 39	
New York	+2
St. Louis	+4
Washington DC	+6
Atlanta	+13
New Orleans	+22
Miami	+32

A Floating Sequence for the Blooming of Shrubs, Trees, Wildflowers and Perennials

The following list is based on my personal observations in southwestern Ohio over a period of 30 years. The dates are approximate, but I have tried to show a relatively true sequence of first blossoming times during an average spring. Although the dates on all flower calendars are somewhat arbitrary (and may vary by up to 60 days between the Canadian border and the South), a "floating calendar" can be used throughout the country by adjusting the sequence to fit the climate and the particular year.

Many of the events mentioned in this March daybook occur up to a month earlier in the South and up to a month later in the North. For example, if snowdrops bloom in your yard on March 20th instead of February 20th (see below), subsequent blooming dates will follow more or less in the order given, but on later dates. Since precipitation, temperature, soil quality and the day's length determine blooming times, personal records can refine and reorder sequences to reflect local conditions.

Day	Flower
February 2:	Skunk Cabbage (*Symplocarpus foetidus*)
February 18:	Snowdrop (*Galanthus nivalis*)
	Aconite *(Eranthis)*
February 22:	Snow Crocus (*Crocus chrysanthus*)
February 23:	*Iris Reticulata*
February 25	Silver Maple (*Acer saccharinum*)
March 3:	Baby Blue Eyes or Green Field Speedwell (*Veronica agrestis*)
March 4:	Common Chickweed (*Stellaria media*)
March 5:	Small-Flowered Bittercress, "Baby Blue Eyes" (*Cardamine hirsuta*)
March 8:	Snow Trillium (*Trillium nivale*)
March 9:	Purple Deadnettle (*Lamium purpureum*)
March 10:	Mid-Season Crocus
March 11:	Dandelion (*Taraxacum*)
March 15:	Early Daffodils *(Narcissus)*
March 18:	Dutch Hyacinths (*Hiacinthus orientalis*)
March 20:	Glory-of-the-Snow (*Chionodoxa forbesli*)
March 23:	Hepatica (*Hepatica Americana*)
	Dutchman's Britches (*Dicentra cucullaria*)
March 24:	Periwinkle (*Vinca major*)
	Cornus mas
	Scilla (*Scilla sibirica*)
March 25:	Violet Cress (*Cochlearia acaulis*)
	Lesser Celandine (*Ranunculus ficaria*)
March 26:	Lungwort (*Pulmonaria*)

March 28:	Bloodroot (*Sanguinaria canadensis*)
	Spicebush (*Lindera benzoin*)
March 29:	Spring Beauty (*Claytonia*)
March 30:	Twinleaf (*Jeffersonia diphylla*)
March 31:	Virginia Bluebell (*Mertensia Virginica*)
April 1:	Grape Hyacinth (*Muscari armeniacum*)
	Purple deadnettle (*Lamium purpureum*)
	Taxus
	Field Peppergrass (*Lepidium campestre*)
April 2:	Ground Ivy (*Glechoma hederacea*)
	Forsythia (*Forsythia*)
	Box Elder (*Acer negundo*)
April 3:	Small-Flowered Buttercup (*Ranunculus abortivus*)
	Creeping Phlox (*Phlox subulata*)
April 4:	Swamp Buttercup (*Ranunculus septentrionalis*)
	Serviceberry (*Amelanchier*)
	Shepherd's Purse (*Capsella pursa-pastoris*)
April 5:	Wood Hyacinth (*Hyacinthoides hispanica*)
	Puschkinia (*Puschkinia libanotica*)
April 6:	Dwarf Plum (*Prunus domestica*)robi
	Wind Flower (*Anemone nemorosa*)
	Rue Anemone (*Thalictrum thalictroides*)
April 7:	Purple Violet (*Viola papilionacea*)
	Toad Trillium (*Trillium sessile*)
	Star Magnolia (*Magnolia stella*ta)

March Phenology

When pussy willows emerge all the way, that is a sign that maple syrup time is just about over for the year and that red-winged blackbirds have started to stake out their territories.

When maples flower and woodchucks dig up the hillsides, then ducks are scouting for nesting sites and onion sets can be tucked into the garden soil.

When coltsfoot buds in the hills of Pennsylvania and West Virginia, azaleas are past their prime in Georgia.

When aspens bloom in the Rocky Mountains, grizzly bears emerge from hibernation.

When bleeding hearts are an inch tall, then purple cress is

blooming in the bottomlands.

When bumblebees and carpenter bees work in the flowers, then it is time for termites to swarm.

Cabbage butterflies in the cabbage sets announce that bass and sunfish are moving to spawn in shallow waters.

When forsythia flowers, then Middle Spring has arrived, and that the first major wave of wildflowers – the trilliums and bloodroots and Dutchman's britches and more – bloom throughout the woods.

When ponds and troughs turn green with algae, then leaves appear on honeysuckle bushes.

When the rhubarb is up a few inches, then daffodils are blooming and maples are coming in.

When raspberry and rose bushes are developing fresh leaves and wild onions are getting lanky, then bald eagle chicks are hatching and peregrine falcons lay their eggs.

When box elders bloom and pussy willow catkins get their pollen, the first mosquitoes bite.

When magnolias are blooming in the Ohio valley, then sandhill cranes are migrating in the Rocky Mountains.

When the mourning cloaks, the question marks, the tortoise shells and the cabbage butterflies come out, catfish are feeding and goldfinches are turning gold.

When the first monarch butterflies appear and the iris start to bud, then armyworms, slugs, corn borers, flea beetles and leafhoppers reach the fields.

When the annual robin chorus begins an hour or so before dawn, then green-bottle flies hatch and garter snakes emerge and earthworms migrate up from their winter locations toward the surface – to feed the robins and snakes.

First Forsythia Bloom An Unofficial Record for Yellow Springs, 1979 - 2023

February 15: 2002
February 22: 2017
February 25:1998
March 4, 2023
March 6: 1983
March 7: 2020

March 8: 1992
March 12: 2006
March 21: 1987
March 22: 2021, 2022
March 23: 2007, 2011
March 25: 1989, 2003
March 26: 1986, 1991
March 27:1985
March 29: 1979, 1981, 2005, 2019
March 31: 2018
April 1: 1982, 1984, 2019
April 3: 2001
April 5: 2015
April 6: 1980
April 8: 2013

Borders of the Arrival of Daffodil Season
in Yellow Springs, Ohio
1981 – 2023
First Bloom Summary:

January 20, 2013: After an unusually warm early winter, two daffodils were halfway open before I cut them and brought them in.

February 21, 2023: First daffodil opens by the peach tree, and robin sing-song chorus getting underway at 7:00 a.m.

February 24, 2017: First daffodil unravels by the peach tree.

March 6, 1983: First forsythia opened today. First daffodils bloomed. Honeysuckles leafing out. One hepatica found open in North Glen.

March 6, 1992: Daffodils open on Wright Street.

March 6, 2000: Mild temperatures over the past weeks have brought the first daffodils into bloom today. The library downtown has a small clump open.

March 6, 2018: The first daffodil opened so slowly, and as the wind turned and came from the north in the night, that daffodil opened all the way, just before snow and cold in the 20s.

March 8, 2012: First daffodil unfolds slowly in the north garden, fully open by the middle of the afternoon

March 9, 2016: Likely date of the first daffodil at Peggy's and here by the old peach tree. (I was in Rochester until the 11th – and highs were in the 60s and 70s in Yellow Springs much of the week of March 6 – 10.)

March 14, 1987: Cardinal sang at 6:29 a.m. First daffodil seen.

March 14, 2020: First daffodils seen at the corner of High and Limestone Streets.

March 17, 2009: Our first daffodil opened up all the way this afternoon, one squill is showing blue, and bittercress with its white flowers is open.

March 17, 2011: First daffodil unraveled in the yard.

March 17, 2021: First daffodil opened in the north garden. Squills show some blue. Bittercress budded.

March 17, 2022: First four daffodils opened in the sun today.

March 18, 1991: First daffodil seen on Dayton Street.

March 18, 1995: Along the streets, forsythia is just starting, the first daffodils and squills are blooming, a few tulips are budding.

March 18, 2010: First daffodil open in the yard this morning.

March 20, 1998: Crow seen with nesting material in its mouth. First daffodils are opening in town.

March 23, 2004: Peonies are between one and two inches. I saw the first daffodil in bloom at Evadine's this afternoon.

March 24, 1981: First daffodil seen today in town.

March 26, 2015: Rick reported the first daffodil opened overnight in the south corner of his neighbor's yard.

March 29. 2019: First daffodil

March 30, 1982: Dutchman's britches are budding. The first bluebell, star of Holland and scilla blooming in town, first daffodil in bloom.

March 31: 1994: In the south garden, the first daffodil is half open, and snowdrop season is over.

April 1, 2014: Squills gathering momentum in southwest garden and an entire bed of daffodils in full bloom along Dayton Street.

April 3, 1996: The first day in the 70s since October brings out the first daffodil in the yard (only a day behind the other first daffodils seen in town yesterday).

April 9, 1984: First daffodils seen on Elm Street near St. Paul's Church.

First Tulip Bloom: An Unofficial Record
for Yellow Springs, 1979 - 2023

March 14,1983: The first tulip opened today.

March 22: 2012: More tulips opened: the old orange and white ones by the south wall, and the new ones by the pond.

March 25, 1995: Termites are out, and the first cabbage butterfly. Peony leaves unravel from their ten-inch stalks. Crocus full bloom now, first tulip seen.

March 26, 2007: First tulip blooms.

March 26, 2016:. A couple of red tulips seen opening in front of a house on the way to Jill's.

March 27, 2016: Two new red tulips bloomed in the north garden.

March 30, 1986: First tulip seen. Very first pussy willow pollen forms.

March 31, 1982: First tulip seen in town.

April 4, 2023: First tulip opening in the yard

April 5, 2018: First tulip bud seen at Jill's

April 6, 2020: One of the last tulips, a white one, from decades ago, has braved the bamboo to open by the pond.

April 6, 2021: Today, the first red tulip opened in the north garden, and the first and only white tulip in the south garden (planted in 1978). Jill's first tulip (a red one) opened, too.

April 7, 1980: First tulip blooms.

April 10, 1979: First tulips open today in the south garden.

April 10, 2015: The early yellow tulips by the south wall, the first tulips Jeanie and I planted in the fall of 1978, opened in the night. Other tulips in the yard have buds.

April 11, 1992: First tulip blooming. Pears full bloom downtown.

April 11, 2013: The first tulip, a red one, has come out.

April 12, 1984: At home, the first tulip blossomed.

April 12, 2019: First tulips, red, seen along Winter Street.

April 12, 2022: First tulip reported by Maddie.

Natural Calendar

Before we break unfathomed ground,
Let us care to learn the winds and the moods of the sky,
the nature and ways of the land.
Virgil (bf)

This is the earliest date for planting most hardy vegetables directly in the garden along the 40th Parallel. Farmers also put in oats, spring wheat, and ryegrass for quick vegetative cover. Only eleven weeks remain before the most delicate flowers and vegetables can be planted outside, four weeks until most hardy varieties can be set out. Fertilizer spread on lawn and field will have a month to dissolve in the ground before April or May planting.

Daybook

1982: First tulip shoots seen.

1983: Just below the Covered Bridge, water striders were out in a clear, backwater pool. Above them, I found lavender bittercress in full bloom, bees moving through the flowers. At the swamp, skunk cabbage was blossoming. Cinquefoil was pushing out a little further down river. Up the hill, a groundhog had been digging a new den, mounds of black dirt beside his hole. Daffodils are budding at the bookstore downtown.

1986: Juncos and song sparrows still feeding.

1987: A flock of starlings walking the yard. Daffodils budding. Garlic mustard has new leaves. Maple buds swelling. Pussy willows almost fully out. In the greenhouse, mother-of-millions are done blooming for the year.

1990: Pussy willows almost fully emerged. I found the first bluebells up at South Glen, one clump above the first swamp, the earliest I've seen them. Honeysuckles were leafing out close to the ground. Some geese were paired off, setting territories, honking along the river. Snowdrops and aconite still bloomed under the peach tree in the south yard. Garlic mustard seeds from last summer were sprouting, will bloom in 14 months.

1991: South Glen, 4:45 p.m., soft 58 degrees, overcast, cardinals, red-winged blackbirds, doves, a whip-poor-will, a flicker all singing. Leafcup foliage new and deep green, tips of the rose bushes flushed red. Near midnight, two tan moths came to the front porch light.

1992: Peonies up an inch.

1993: The increased bird activity along Wilberforce-Clifton Road has stopped now, the juncos, cardinals, and sparrows having passed through. Robins have been absent since the arrival of several flocks a few weeks ago.

1998: The first thunderstorm of the year yesterday afternoon. And today the late crocuses came into bloom, first the gold and then the purple.

1999: First resurrection lily starts to emerge along the south edge of the yard.

2001: Snow crocuses, snowdrops and aconites in full bloom throughout town

2004: The first mosquito of the year attacked me as I was working at the computer this afternoon (I had left the back door open for a while this morning). By the pond, much of the bamboo foliage has turned brown and has started to fall. The change came suddenly at the end of February, even without unusually cold weather.

2005: Snow and ice all across the Lower Midwest today, but the cardinals still sing before dawn. Large flock of starlings seen feeding by the freeway on the way home from Washington Court House. One small flock of robins surprised on Cedarville-Yellow Springs Road this afternoon at 2:00 p.m., the first flock I've seen this year.

2006: Robins peeping in the morning when the cardinals and doves are singing, but no robin chorus in the dark yet.

2008: The cold remains, snow still on the ground, but some daffodils are up under the garden arbor.

2009: Big Bend National Park in southwestern Texas: Hiking along the path to the Rio Grande with afternoon temperatures in the high 70s. Yesterday's hard wind has calmed down, and the sky is perfect robin's-egg blue. Several deciduous trees leafing out around the campground. Creosote bush sports dark berries and bright yellow flowers. All around the camp, tall, rough narrowleaf globemallows with pink-violet flowers, and tall mustard with divided leaves like wild lettuce with clusters of tiny yellow flowers. Large patches of bluebonnets, *Lupinus texensis*, or possibly Big Bend Lupines seen along a spur path. Other flowers were common, among them purple wood sorrel, *Oxalis drummondii*; one clump of Heller's Plantain, *Plantago helleri*; wild grape vines with small leaves and small buds; *Carrizo* (a tall, bamboo grass – *Arundo donax*); tree tobacco with golden trumpet flowers; several clumps of what appeared to be desert marigolds; ocotillo bare but with red flower bud heads just starting to form – about an inch long. All the flowers adding to the grand palette of spring.

2011: Snow crocus continuing to come in around the yard, red-winged blackbirds seen setting territories on the way to Beavercreek. Two flocks of blackbirds or starlings noticed along Dayton-Yellow Springs Road.

2012: Jekyll Island, Georgia: Mild and mostly cloudy: creeping bluets seen at the south end of the island, along with common wood sorrel. A blue toadflax kind of plant found. The shrub by the bookstore: a sweet bay? Some kind of magnolia with pink flowers? Searched to identify a striking white flower with five or more white petals, yellow center, leaves divided in threes, toothed, opposite, red stems, petals with toothed edges; a five-petal yellow flower, sprawling with leaves long and thin in clusters of three, probably alternate; and yellow daisy-like flower with more than seven petals, leave slightly toothed, hairy stems. None of those in Newcomb's wildflower book.

23

2013: Portland, Oregon: I feel like I am on the cutting edge of Portland spring: A soft and partly sunny afternoon in the 60s, patches of blue sky for the first time in days. First periwinkles seen open today, first grape hyacinth, a few small sow thistles in bloom, holly budded, and the very first forsythia blossom on Jeni's forsythia. In Vermont, John Ordway says he is getting ready to tap his maple trees. Back in Yellow Springs, Kit saw sandhill cranes: "It was around five o'clock, I think, and there were about four or five of them. They seemed like geese as I saw them flying, looked like they were coming in toward the river at the edge of a farm just near our bike path. I walked on for about ten seconds after I no longer could see them, and realized what sounds I had heard them making! That garbelley-garbelley sound!"

2014: Mild this morning: Cardinals at 6:41; doves at 6:51; crows at 6:53; song sparrow at 6:58. But the state is bracing for yet another winter storm in a day or two.

2015: More snow in Yellow Springs, more snow throughout the East. At least six inches on the ground here, and more storms to come. In the middle of all of that, John Blakelock called to report a near-albino cardinal at his feeder this morning.

2017: Tornado watch before dawn this morning, hard wind and rain. Blusters of wind through the day, temperature in the 50s. Red quince buds fat, maple flowers blown apart by the storm. Jeff called to say he and Kit had their first open daffodils, and Jill and I saw a large clump blooming on Wright Street.

2018: Influenced by full moon and perigee, March comes in like a lion with heavy rain, flooding and snow.

2020: A few daffodils have budded, and Jill reports fat, purple crocuses blooming near Winter Street.

2022: Jill's aconites are in full bloom now as the high reaches 62 degrees, the highest so far this year. Some daffodils in the north garden climb quickly to three or four inches. The white buds of the dooryard snowdrops are starting to nod. The purple buds of the red-flowered hellebores have suddenly spread out in the center of their basal leaves. In the neighbor's lawn this afternoon, a small flock of robins. In the wider world, Russia's invasion of Ukraine has unsettled everyone, the possibility of nuclear weapons being used is increasing rapidly. At the same time, a new report by scientists states that the effects of global climate change are now irreversible.

2023: After the second-warmest February in my records (2017 being the warmest), March comes in like a lamb, hazy cirrus sky, 17 daffodils in bloom, pussy willows all emerged, aconites almost gone behind the Danielsons' house, snowdrops still full flower with petals spread wide, maples flowering and just beginning to fall on Stafford Street, robin chorus underway, GDDs between 40 and 50. This evening, Jill sends a photo of her daffodils open by the street. The first cabbage white butterfly flew by me in the alley. And today's high, another record for the year, 75 degrees.

Journal
A Note on Buzzards for the *Yellow Springs News* in 2017:

It used to be that turkey vultures (*Cathartes aura* – the ones with red heads) left Yellow Springs at the end of October and returned in the second week of March, about the same time they came back to Hinkley, Ohio up near Lake Erie.

When I moved to the village in 1978, the first vulture sighting of the year, usually several days before equinox, would coincide with the emergence of pussy willow catkins and the blooming of snowdrops and aconites. When I saw vultures circling the Glen, I felt that the clock of the world was working the way it should: the great birds were on schedule.

Then on the sunny afternoon of January 28, 2002, I noticed a turkey vulture as I walked downtown. I had seen no vultures and had received no reports so early before that, so I am fairly confident that, at least prior to this century, no vultures spent the winter in this area.

As the years passed, I saw more buzzards, and so did village residents. Phil spotted the first one of 2003 on February 11. Then on February 4 of 2004, Ed had a sighting a little north of

Yellow Springs, and I saw one here on February 12 that year. On February 22, Bob stated that he had seen them all winter near his place on the south side of town, and Casey watched a great flock fly in on February 27.

Since 2004, the turkey vultures have stayed close to Yellow Springs throughout the year. Not only that: in 2010, Casey called around 2:00 in the afternoon to say he had seen *black* buzzards (*Coragyps atatus* – all black, including the head):

"Get in your pickup," he said, "and drive down Grinnell Road by the spring. There's a deer carcass there and about fifteen black buzzards." I did what he said to do, and indeed there were fifteen *black* buzzards, tame as could be, feeding by the side of the road.

So not only had turkey vultures become year-round residents, but now the black buzzards, which normally wintered well below the Ohio River, had moved north during the past decade and were feasting, along with their red-headed relatives, on winter road kill. And so it has continued to this day, *Cathartes* and *Coragyps* informing Yellow Springs about changing weather patterns and the likelihood of milder winters to come.

Place is dynamic, equal parts geography and imagination; it is a complex intermingling and, ultimately, fusion of mind and landscape, so that neither is finally separable or meaningful without the other.

Kent C. Ryden

March 2nd
The 61st Day of the Year

Say, what impels, amidst surrounding snow
Congeal'd, the crocus' flamy bud to glow?
Say, what retards, amidst the summer's blaze,
The'autumnal bulb, till pale, declining days?
The GOD OF SEASONS; whose pervading power
Controls the sun, or sheds the fleecy shower:
He bids each flower his quickening word obey;
Or to each lingering bloom enjoins delay.

Gilbert White

Sunrise/set: 7:07/6:28
Day's Length: 11 hours 21 minutes
Average High/Low: 43/25
Average Temperature: 34
Record High: 73 – 1992
Record Low: - 7 – 1980

Weather

Despite the likely arrival of a high-pressure system, this is another pivotal date in the progress of spring: from now on there is at least a five percent chance of warm 70s each day. Expect 60s ten percent of the time; highs in the 50s come 20 percent of all the years, and 65 percent of the time temperatures are brisk in the 30s or 40s. Once in a decade or two, the thermometer goes below zero and then never even comes up to 20. The sun shines 55 percent of the time; snow is rare; rain comes one year in four.

Natural Calendar

All that I had dreamed was true, is true.
The earth is fair, more fair
Than I had known or imagined.

Harlan Hubbard

In the Early Spring of the Ohio Valley, islands of new life

emerge from the waves of warmth and cold that move across the landscape. Within these islands, often separated from each other by broad expanses of chilling winds, weeks of gray skies, sometimes only narrowly divided by a night of frost, the season reveals its stunning topography.

Early Spring is an archipelago of forms rising out of February's great sea, and like ephemeral atolls, the events of this temporal, mottled continent multiply, swell, and recede to alter the face of our habitat with an inexorable beauty. The geography of Early Spring is fixed in shape and order but not in time. The archipelago of winter's end is fluid, what chronologists call a "floating sequence," a sequence the dates of which are relatively well known in relation to one another but not in relation to when exactly they will occur on the brittle Gregorian calendar.

Observation and memory, however, easily decipher the secret code of the floating sequence, uncover the fluid terrain from which fauna and flora materialize, and spread a map of promise across the seemingly uncharted expanse of winter. In Yellow Springs, Early Spring fills the six weeks between the middle of February and the end March. This month and a half links the deep cold with the lushness of April, and it is made up of constellations of color, motion and sound, and musterings of new sprouts and leaves, birds, insects, mammals and fishes. In the South, this season can arrive in the middle of the year's first weeks; along the Canadian border, it comes in May. Wherever the floating sequence begins, it follows something of the order below; no matter where it takes place, the following landmarks are only fragments of a far greater ferment.

Starting with the major thaw of February's third week, the first cluster of spring's appearance takes the form of snowdrops and aconites flowering together in the warmest microclimates beside the prophetic hellebores and Chinese witchhazels of late January. Within a few days, snow crocus and *iris reticulata* complete this island of time at the chilliest edge of spring.

A parallel cluster rises from the swamps: the skunk cabbage blossoms at Jacoby. In alleyways and lawns, common chickweed, dandelions and henbit complement the cabbage. Above them all, red-winged blackbirds stake out different limits.

After Snowdrop Winter (between February 23rd and 27th),

ducks and geese follow the lead of the blackbirds, marking ownership of the more favorable river sites for nesting. Migrant robins join the sizable flocks that overwintered in the Glen.

Past the seasons of the snowdrops and aconites, midseason crocuses initiate more complex configurations that lead to fat pussy willows, bright blue squills, delicate yellow jonquils, then to the full-size daffodils, then to purple grape hyacinths, then to pale wood hyacinths and pushkinias. Towering on the horizon, silver maples and the red maples and box elders prepare to fruit.

To these outcroppings come the pollen seekers: the honeybees and carpenter bees. Other creatures follow. Mosquitoes and newborn wolf spiders look for prey. The mounds of ants rise from winter's prairie. In rivers and ponds, water striders mate. Earthworms come out of hiding, lie together in the mild night rains. It is salamander season in the slime and snake basking season in the sun. Spring peepers peep.

Then the root and insect eaters become active, joining the beavers that have been cutting trees and eating bark since January. Groundhogs dig up the hillsides. Opossums, skunks, raccoons come seek their mates and sustenance. Turkey vultures circle the roads looking for road kill. Wild turkeys start to call. The first woodcocks spiral in the woods. In the village, the tufted titmouse spirals, too.

When pussy willows are at their peak, new configurations take shape, adding multiple pathways to all the recent temporal spaces. Into the world of pussy willows come the white star magnolias in town, snow trillium along the Little Miami, spring beauties on the college green. Across the bottomland, soft touch-me-nots sprout, coveted ramps push up their medicinal foliage to pace the stalks of day lilies, rhubarb and precocious bleeding hearts.

The Sun

In the southeastern states, the morning gains half an hour this month, the sun coming up around a quarter past six by April Fool's Day. Sunset slowly moves later in the day, adding another 15 minutes to the 15 it gained in February.

In the Pacific Northwest, the day now lengthens more than twice as quickly as it does near the Gulf of Mexico: the morning increases by a full hour during March, and sunset becomes up to three-quarters of an hour later. In the Midwest and the Northeast, the gains are similar.

And even though the day lengthens at different rates at different locations throughout the country, equinox is still equinox on March 20, 21 or 22 and brings equal day and night to Bangor, Maine as well as to Seattle, Washington, and Miami, Florida.

Daybook

1983: Cardinals chasing each other in the honeysuckles.

1986: Flock of bluebirds seen at the mill, 4:30 p.m.

1991: Cardinal sings 6:45 a.m. Robin in the maple tree, loud at 10:00 a.m. Crocus blooming in the round south garden, four purple, one gold budding, one aconite open, a full clump of snowdrops. Some daffodils six inches. Lupine foliage beginning. Tan moth in the greenhouse.

1992: Bees and flies are out in the new record high of 73 degrees. Six golden crocuses in full bloom, aconites and snowdrops full, pussy willows completely emerged. First robin seen in front of the house.

1993: The sun sparkles on the snow this morning, reminding me of how often I saw that in my Wisconsin winters forty years ago. This afternoon by the side of the street, sparrows washing and preening in the snowmelt.

1999: Crow at 7:34 this morning, clear skies, moon setting behind my apple tree. Geese came over at 7:45. First robin seen in the yard at 8:45.

2000: Blue scilla, opening on Whiteman Street today. Flickers calling.

2001: Titmouse loud and clear this morning. David Cassenheiser called tonight: two buzzards circling over Susi's house this morning. He said he saw one buzzard on the 28th, but he thought "it might be the tame one."

2004: Starlings fighting over a nesting spot under the eaves at 7:50 a.m. Along the road to Washington Court House this morning just after sunrise, the winter wheat was showing an undercoat of golden green. All the ponds were completely open, bright blue. The air was soft, and the cirrus, alto cumulus; altostratus clouds were broken and benign.

When I drove along Stafford Street this afternoon, I saw banks of yellow aconite and white snowdrops. Judy wrote from Goshen, Indiana: "A short bulletin: the red-wing blackbirds came through last Wednesday, and yesterday the robins arrived. Isn't that just a tad early? Anyway, the anemones are waving bravely in the stiff breeze we have today and the moth mulleins are coming up in encouraging style."

2005: The low was in the teens this morning, light snow covering the yard. Judy reports her anemones and crocus leaves are barely up.

2006: Casey called me from the Antioch golf course around noon yesterday to say that in all his years he had never seen so many robins in one location. "They're all over the place," he told me. "There must be hundreds of them just hanging out." He noted now it was relatively common to see flocks of 30 or 40 robins in the late winter moving through honeysuckles in the Glen to eat the last of the berries, but this flock indeed was unusual. It could be, in fact, that this was the flock that brought the amount of Yellow Springs robins to critical mass, to just the right number of robins to begin the spring chorus. That ritual of mating song begins in early March and follows a schedule all its own.

The timetable below lists the approximate time of the morning for robins to begin singing in Yellow Springs. When I get up early in the dark and listen closely, I hear them in the distance, their steady, blended calls filling the high trees. One could use this table with any sunrise time, subtracting the proportional number of minutes for robinsong time.

Day	Sunrise	Robin Chorus Begins (EST)
March 10:	6:55	6:00

March 21:	6:37	5:40
March 25:	6:31	5:30
April 1:	6:20	5:10
April 7:	6:10	4:50
April 10:	6:05	4:25
April 15:	5:58	4:00
May 1:	5:36	3:45
June 1:	5:09	3:40
July 1:	5:10	4:00

July 8: Robins continue to communicate with one another throughout the remainder of the summer and fall with chirps, peeps, whinnies, and long, full-throated songs; however, their early morning mating chorus ends as sunrise begins to occur later than at solstice.

2008: The weather has been breaking for a couple of days now, snow melting, revealing snowdrops ready to open, daffodils three inches tall, the red tips of peonies, the first foliage of daylilies, stonecrop and hyacinths, buds on the Lenten roses. Casey called this afternoon, said that he saw three buzzards heading north from Xenia along the river, riding on the south wind. This is the first multiple vulture sighting of the year around Yellow Springs.

2009: Big Bend National Park to Van Horn, Texas: After a side trip up into the Chisos basin, we drove north and west up to the Interstate. One pie cherry seen in bloom in Alpine, and a pear or pie cherry in bloom here at the campsite. Occasional yuccas flowering along the increasingly dry and flat roadsides, but no wildflowers seen at all.

2011: Robin chorus full at 6:40 this morning.

2012: Jekyll Island, Georgia, through the mountains to Knoxville, Tennessee: the landscape seeming much further along than it was five days ago when we went south, many more fruit trees budded and blooming, mostly white flowers, all the way through the Appalachians.

2013: Portland, Oregon: The very first daffodils, mostly the diminutive jonquils, seen opening today. In Jeni's backyard, the maple has flowered, along with another tree with gray bark. Tonight in the distance, frogs chanting.

2014: The first spring opossum road kill noticed on Dayton-Yellow Springs Road this afternoon.

2015: Clear skies today, a little melting, but another storm is due in the morning. The moon is almost full, ringed closely by a dusky rainbow.

2016: Below-normal temperatures keep the snowdrops and crocus in suspension. From Goshen, Indiana, Judy writes that the red-winged blackbirds arrived today, and that more geese are gathering at her pond.

2018: Yesterday's storm moved east today, our rain turning to snow across the Northeast. Here, the day is cold and sunny and windy.

2019: A new storm is dropping down from Canada. Robins in the neighborhood, but no morning chorus yet. Leslie reports a goldfinch beginning to turn gold.

2020: A mild, rainy morning, cardinals and doves strong at 7:30 this morning. No robin chorus yet, but one singsong robin call heard as I returned from a walk with Ranger.

2021: Full cardinal song this morning at 6:36, and a pair of Canadian geese (the second pair I've seen together this spring) flew over at 6:48. No robin chorus yet, but robins are here, calling occasionally. A flock of maybe two dozen turkey vultures was circling Greene Street when Jill and I walked there late in the afternoon. Red-winged blackbirds reported in southern Wisconsin today.

2022: The first two grackles seen at the back feeders this morning. Jeni reports the first daffodils seen in Portland.

2023: This morning's daffodil count is 37 after yesterday's record high of 75. This number is about the same as last year's around March 21.

But these your winter bunches, jealously
Picked on a February morning, they
Are dearer than the plenteous summer. See,
One colored primrose growing from a clump,
One Lenten rose, one golden aconite....

Vita Sackville-West, *The Garden*

March 3rd
The 62nd Day of the Year

Early spring: frost melts down
The furrow in the west wind,
Plowshares glisten in the sun,
The sleek, black land shines, open.

Virgil (bf)

Sunrise/set: 7:06/6:29
Day's Length: 11 hours 23 minutes
Average High/Low: 43/26
Average Temperature: 34
Record High: 77 – 1976
Record Low: - 3 – 1943

Weather
Seventies or 60s occur 10 percent of the days, 50s ten percent, 40s thirty-five percent, 30s thirty percent, 20s fifteen percent of the time. Rain: 25 percent of the days, snow 15 percent. A morning below zero happens only once or so in a century.

Natural Calendar
Bluebell Growing Season begins as the first bluebell foliage emerges from the hillsides. Daffodil, Chickweed, Purple deadnettle, and Dandelion Blooming Seasons unfold slowly as Clover Season spreads through the waysides. Red-Winged Blackbird Migration Season peaks as pussy willows come out all the way. Indoors in flats under lights, it is Tomato Seeding Season, Green Pepper Seeding Season, Eggplant Seeding Season and Annual Flower Seeding Season. As water temperatures rise to the upper 30s in March and early April, the Season of the Walleye Run begins in Lake Erie. That season reaches its climax in northern Ohio on the Sandusky and Maumee rivers when the water reaches 44 degrees, then activity declines slowly through early May.

The Stars

Early in the month, Deep Winter's Orion has moved off to the west by 10:00 p.m., and Corvus, May's corn and soybean planting constellation, appears on the horizon. Spica, which will be centered in the southern sky as peak planting ends this spring, emerges from the east. June's Corona Borealis follows it.

Before dawn, all the constellations that ride the Milky Way into summer lie in the east. To the far north, Cassiopeia zigzags towards Cepheus, the house-like constellation just east of the North Star. Following the Milky Way to the south, Cygnus, the Northern Cross, shines overhead. Below Cygnus, is Aquila, with its bright star Altair. Below that, summer's Sagittarius.

Daybook

1983: Rhubarb is barely emerging in the mild days – this was the first afternoon in the 70s this year.

1986: Four robins seen at the south end of town, 4:45 p.m.

1987: Cardinal singing at 6:33 a.m., a little more than a half an hour before sunup.

1988: In a steady rain, I counted 50 robins hunting worms on the soggy grass near Antioch, 4:00 p.m. Jeni called later from Florida, said the azaleas were blooming in Jacksonville.

1990: The season is shifting. The first spring changes came a month ago, ground covers starting early, pussy willows coming out, first bulbs up. It's been a month since Mrs. Hurie's crocus bloomed. Almost all of the snowdrops are gone, aconites old. In the greenhouse, the last impatiens plant saved from fall is still flowering, struggling with spider mites.

1992: Purple crocus bloomed today. Crocus are supposed to bloom seven weeks before the last spring frost, making this year's last frost date about the end of April, first of May.

1993: The snow melted away from the snowdrops today, revealing them fully developed and ready to open. Before they were covered with snow, their buds were barely visible. From February 16th through today, ground temperatures at or below freezing, the plants continued their spring progression and were prepared for the thaw.

2000: Squills opening today.

2002: Cardinal close to the house, singing at 6:44 a.m. Then a robin-like singsong joins in from the back trees.

2004: At 6:20 this morning, I went outside and listened: The spring robin chorus was faintly underway. A cardinal sang outside the bathroom window at 6:38. At 7:00, the yard was alive with song. In the south garden, the red peony tips are finally starting to push up. Mrs. Lawson's early tulip foliage is about three inches high now, started coming up a little after the daffodil shoots. Brian Sterns sent me this note this afternoon from Xenia: "The silver maples in our neighborhood started to bloom yesterday and I saw the bees gathering in some of that pollen. That is the first pollen that they collected this year."

2006: Clear and cold. A cardinal sang outside the bedroom window at 6:41 this morning.

2008: High above 60 today as a cold front approaches with rain and sleet. Doves, cardinals and titmice singing throughout the village, the snow completely gone. Peggy was out looking to see what was up around her house. People at the bank and credit union told me to enjoy the windy day. In the east garden, the first snow crocus has a bud. Several snowdrops have pushed out of their sheathes. At 4:45 this afternoon, a large flock of grackles arrived on High Street from the northwest, rested in the trees near the corner of Limestone, all facing west.

2009: Van Horn, Texas to Las Cruces, New Mexico: Vast, brown expanses of land with no signs of life in the vegetation. Near record high in the middle 80s. Cirrus clouds gathering. Along the highway north of Las Cruces, many fields green from recent planting and irrigation. Willow trees greening in urban areas, and more cherry trees and redbuds seen in bloom. In spite of the drought, flowering trees place Las Cruces at about the same point as southern Louisiana and Alabama were a week ago, about six weeks ahead of Yellow Springs, Ohio. The tow-truck driver that brought us back from Truth or Consequences for repairs said that white bass were running in the nearby reservoir.

2010: Cardinals were singing at 6:40 this morning. At 9:30, Casey reported 25 black buzzards on both sides of Grinnell Road up by the spring, pretty much clinching the fact that flock has been here throughout the winter. Judy writes from northern Indiana: "Just a short note to let you know that yesterday, on the way back through the yard from our walk, Angel and I saw our anemones blooming! And the buds are starting to show on the forsythia; magnolia buds look to be two inches at least."

2011: When I went outside this morning at 6:38, cardinals were singing (but no robins I could hear). This afternoon, I saw one very young skunk and three small opossums by the road, recently hit. Then at about 4:30, coming into Yellow Springs from the south, I saw dozens and dozens of vultures circling the south end of town.

2012: Knoxville to Yellow Springs: Tornadoes struck all around us last night. This morning, more signs that spring had moved further north during our absence: daffodils blooming in Cincinnati - had not been open when we came through on February 27.

At home in the yard, the standard crocus had opened, gold and purple. Under the mock orange, the bright blue of a half-opened squill, and the pink of the first lungwort blossom of the year. From Goshen, Indiana, my sister Judy says that the red-winged blackbirds are back, less than a week later than their arrival here in Yellow Springs, two hundred miles to the southeast of Goshen.

2013: Portland, Oregon: Willows greening, blackberry brambles leafing, frogs croaking in the sunny afternoon.

2017: In spite of the chilly last few days, the pussy willows have continued to fluff, have become almost ready for pollen. The snowdrop and snow crocus patches are in decline, flowers disappearing, and the aconites are gone by the pond. The forsythia that opened in last week's thaw, however, is holding well, and I am nostalgic for the Aprils of the early 1980s when the forsythia came in around the first of that month, signaling the start of Middle Spring.

2018: Tat reports sighting sandhill cranes flying overhead in Madison, Wisconsin. Along the East Coast, a major Northeaster is disrupting travel, several people dead.

2019: Light snow all day here, heavy snow in the Northeast. Tornadoes in the South, 23 people killed in Alabama.

2020: Robins very present, whinnying and chirping, but no mating singsong calls at 6:40. Sylvia called to report bicolor crocuses in full flower near the college. In the dooryard, snowdrops and hellebores are completely open. A few aconites and snow crocus have flowered in the yard near the pond. Leslie reports Baby Blue Eyes (*Veronica agrestis)* in flower. More than 20 people killed in overnight tornado in Memphis, Tennessee.

2021: Sun and chilly: Loud cardinals, doves, titmice, chickadees, house sparrows and a grackle at 6:45 this morning, but only chatter from the robins. Snowdrops all emerged, trying to open. From his farm, Chris Walker reports: "Woodcocks and wood ducks! And our nesting doves are back. So happy around here!" (His first woodcocks appeared on the 5th last year.)

Casey just saw me at the post office and said he'd been having red-winged blackbirds at his feeders for the past week, and from Goshen, Indiana, Judy writes: "Looking out the window a while ago, I saw three geese and a couple of pairs of mallards on the pond. A red-winged blackbird lighted on our neighbor's deck, and the doves have been back since Sunday. A friend said that she had redwings at her bird feeder last Sunday (February 28), so maybe they were here a tad earlier."

On the way to the post office this morning, I noticed the first purple snow crocus opening in the dooryard. And when I walked Ranger in the alley after lunch, I rediscovered the huge patch of aconites, complete with honeybees, in full bloom behind the Danielsons' old property. Then more purple crocuses in front of Don's house and the first grackle at the bird feeder. And back home, the snowdrops were opening all the way and the pussy willows were all emerged. I saw the first red peony sprout and the first leaves on the stonecrop. Later in the day at the Glass Farm wetlands, temperature 61, Jill and I heard red-winged blackbirds singing for the first time.

2023: A hard rainstorm, the first major one of the year, flooded the yard and brought the river so high that Libby was worried that the road to her house would be flooded.

Journal

The field of spring, like the field of gravity or the electromagnetic field, can seem fluid and elusive, but spring's *quanta*, its miniscule particles smaller even than atoms, sometimes become most apparent at dawn, sometimes through the mist of dew or the first sun on the new leaves of the undergrowth, becomes most audible in the rhythmic chorus of the birds.

To experience that confluence of events and conditions is to be aware of an enveloping force, like a fog or cloud of power and beauty.

That field romances the particles of the spring, blurring their edges, creating an ether that may nurture mood and meaning. It is a tidal force that swells and recedes, its apparent forward motion deceptive because it brings back the past with each pace toward summer.

In the fog of spring, I cannot or choose not to see outside its temporal limits. I am blinded by an enclosing energy that takes hold like a passion or lust, its haze obscuring or channeling my vision and good sense.

Sometimes memories rise and fall in the shape of emotions, and nostalgia filters their source and content, allowing them in and out of the porous self like the elusive residue of dreams, plot and actors forgotten.

The field of spring flows among those and so many other slippery and untouchable quanta, veiling and transforming and referring each marker to somewhere else, to all that might have been and still might be.

A light exists in Spring
Not present in the Year
At any other period –
When March is scarcely here
A Color stands abroad
on Solitary Fields
That Science cannot overtake
But Human Nature feels.

Emily Dickinson

March 4th
The 63rd Day of the Year

Forth from its sunny nook of shelter'd grass -- innocent, golden,
and calm as the dawn
The spring's first dandelion shows its trustful face.

Walt Whitman

Sunrise/set: 7:04/6:30
Day's Length: 11 hours 26 minutes
Average High/Low: 44/26
Average Temperature: 35
Record High: 77 – 1976
Record Low: 0 – 1943

Weather

Today is typically the wettest day of March, with rain recorded 50 percent of the years in my record, and snow another 20 percent. Along with the precipitation, however, comes a fair likelihood of mild weather: a 20 percent chance of highs in the 70s, and a 15 percent chance of a high in the 60s, the best odds for warmth during the first two weeks of March. When the weather isn't temperate, it's cool: 40 percent chance of highs in the 50s or 40s, twenty-five percent of 30s. Highs in the twenties and teens are almost never recorded on this date. Today, the 19th, the 29th and the 30th are the cloudiest March days (only a 40 percent chance to see the sun).

Natural Calendar

An inventory in the third week of Early Spring (often the first week of March in the Lower Midwest) adds several new dimensions to the scope of the first or second weeks. Daffodils have often put on several inches since Valentine's Day, are now three to nine inches high, many of them budded. Tulips, daylilies and resurrection lilies pace the daffodils, only an inch or so behind them. Red peony stalks, barely visible a few weeks ago, have push above the mulch.

Snowdrops, aconites and snow crocuses approach the peak

of their seasons in milder years; the end of their bloom cycle usually marks the end of maple sugaring. The first deadnettle and ground ivy flowers have opened in the sunniest microclimates.

Lupine leaves push out of the ground beside the crocus, snowdrops, and aconites. The earliest blue squills open. Woodchucks dig up the hillsides, making new dens. Ducks scout the rivers for nesting sites. Daylily spears are strong. The rivers are often high, and carp mate in the shallows. Flocks of robins continue to move north, even in the coldest springs. Red-winged blackbirds sing in the swamps. Red-tailed hawks, the horned grebe, the common snipe, black ducks and all types of gulls migrate across the Midwest.

Daybook

1982: First robin seen in town. Daffodils starting to emerge.

1985: Chickweed blooms at Wilberforce. At the Covered Bridge, violet cress is budding. New garlic mustard foliage everywhere.

1986: A cardinal sang at 6:49 a.m., the sky cloudy, windy, cold, snow on the ground. Juncos still coming to the feeder.

1987: The first red-winged blackbird and meadowlark seen along Wilberforce-Clifton Road this morning. The first crocus bloomed downtown. More chickweed flowered along the south brick walls. At Sycamore Hole, river chubs bit at 5:45 p.m. Four caught.

1989: River high, temperature near 70, crows and cardinals were loud at the Covered Bridge. Leaves were coming out on some multiflora roses. The first two bluebells had come up on Bloodroot Ridge. A lot of skunk cabbage was blooming, bees around it. Also moths and flies were out, and wolf spiders in the field past Sycamore Hole. Geese flew over at sundown. In the yard at home, snowdrops blooming, rhubarb up.

1991: Doves making a nest in a back locust tree. Starlings nesting in holes in the limbs of the same tree. Small-flowered bittercress found blooming at Wilberforce.

1992: Some golden crocus fading now, daffodils ready to open after three days in the 70s. Red-winged blackbirds have returned to Wilberforce-Clifton Road fences, the first seen this morning. Robins chanting, long mating calls (the robin chorus). Rhubarb finally coming along. Grape hyacinths about three inches, tulips three inches. Yarrow up, lupines, phlox, strong new dandelions, horseradish leaves, fresh mint. Garlic mustard seeds have sprouted. Blue eyes (*Veronica)* blooming (having opened with the first crocus). First purple anemone and scilla emerged at the south wall. First pink hyacinth opened. Lady bugs hatching under logs. First groundhog road kill along Grinnell.

1993: Long rains melting the snow. Tulips have grown to three inches in parts of the south garden. Daffodils up the same. But this spring is slow, more like 1984's so far.

1999: Crows in the wind and raw cold at 6:41 this morning.

2000: Robin chorus singsong at 6:30 this morning, dawn just starting to light the eastern sky, crows in the distance. When I left for work at 6:50, cardinals were calling on High Street. The flocks of crows were still absent from Springfield. When I got home at five this afternoon, Casey called: buzzards sighted, one yesterday and three more arriving from the west heading to South Glen at maybe 5:20 p.m.

2001: Touch-me-nots have sprouted at Jacoby Swamp. First buds swelling on the daffodils.

2003: In spite of weeks below freezing and six inches of snow remaining on the ground, the spring movement of small animals becomes apparent. Three skunks and two groundhogs killed so far on the roads between here and Washington Court House.

2004: Pussy willows have come out almost all the way.

2007: Back in January, Cathy sent this vision of sugaring in Vermont:: "The end of March there is a state-wide maple open house where you can visit any/all the sugarhouses. Last year

Charles and I were delivering the paper on that day, way into the evening. I don't think anyone could imagine how many people are sugaring in Vermont. I wish I could describe how it looked.

"At dusk, when the sky is that medium electric blue, the yellow light shown out of the sugarhouses and the grey smoke and white steam poured up against the woods and darkening sky. And you could look at the hills all around you and see these places spotted one here and one there. Some are by the road and some are up long driveways. Some are big, and lots are tiny and small.

"At each stop people offer you a free taste, and you can get pretty sugared out. Inside are always old women in old jackets, and their husbands, sons, kids, and neighbors. And the steam smells so sweet. The driveways are muddy. And everyone is welcoming and pleased to get the paper.

"What an experience! You can't get it from visiting one sugarhouse. It's the discovery of this whole civilization you didn't ever really see, that blooms only once a year. Like Brigadoon. I wish you could see it."

2008: Heavy rains have filled the yard with water. At the Antioch School, the west-side play yard is flooded, and Chris was concerned that it might reach her classroom – but it didn't. The rivers are swollen and brown, up over their banks. At dusk in Wilmington, I saw two robins hunting worms in the college lawn.

2009: A little driving in and around Las Cruces, New Mexico. A long planting of daffodils blooming in Mesilla (just like in Yellow Springs), a crab apple in full flower, another greening willow tree and rows of greening cottonwoods, increasing the sense of middle April here. At Rock Hound State Park, one bright yellow bladderwort with fuzzy, thin leaves (like lamb's ears) and a purple locoweed. Called Catalina State Park near Tucson, and they said the poppies were in bloom.

Cathy writes from Vermont: "Spring seems here even though it's snowing and cold: 0 degrees. Crows are cawing and the squirrels are hopping around. No sign of spring birds, but I'm trapped inside so maybe some are here. Anyway, the sun is higher and it's light really early, and I feel the burden of winter lifted. Hope you do too."

Rebecca, at home in Yellow Springs: "Not much is happening in the yard yet. A few snowdrops near the front corner of the fence and the daffodils are showing a bit of foliage poking through the ground." That means there hasn't been much progress since we left on February 20th.

2010: Woke up to a clear moon setting into the dark blue sky. Even though the temperature was in the teens before daylight, the next few days are supposed to bring the first big thaw since Groundhog Day! Cardinals and doves sang early. In the yard, snowdrops were budded through the snow, one hellebore stalk had fat buds, a few pussy willow tips were showing, foliage of motherwort, wild strawberry, deadnettle, ground ivy, primrose were stretching a little into the daylight. Wild onions were unraveling after having been pushed down by the snow. Tulips were up an inch, the leaves tight and red, some daffodils at the west edge of the yard were up full three inches, and many were budded. The snow has retreated away from the sidewalk on both sides, sometimes leaving a remnant of the straight banks that had been cut in when I was shoveling. The driveway is still icy, but some of the gravel is showing through. From Vermont, Cathy writes: "My brother in Fresno said the trees bloomed there a couple weeks ago and that the air is perfumed.

2012: The tornadoes and storms have moved east, light snow is falling here and all across the Midwest. In the alley, the aconite season has ended, blossoms starting to turn brown (even though the snow crocus and the snowdrops are still full). A robin pair seen on the sidewalk in front of Don's house on Dayton Street. In the garden and around the neighborhood, the tiny bittercress flowers pay no attention to the cold. Along the stone fence, one daffodil bud is showing yellow, will open this week when the weather warms. When I walked with Bella, our border collie, at 7:00 this evening in the twilight, robins were peeping in the undergrowth. In spite of the cold and the wind, the birds were on the move.

2013: Portland, Oregon to Meridian, Idaho: The sun appears in a blaze of fog and mist, then disappears behind Mount Hood as I enter the Colombia River gorge. Immediately, I am struck by the vast scale of everything around me, unapproachable cliffs and mountains. (I think about the immensity too of memories and longings, a desire for a more manageable scale. I have never known what to do with this grand a scale. I think about the myopia of painting zinnias when I get home). Hundreds of windmills on the bluffs across the river. Crows solitary and in pairs scavenging up and down the road. Western jays courting. All the advances of spring in Portland totally lost. And I keep checking in my rear-view mirror and see Mt. Hood still there after 100, 150, 200 miles as though the world were flat, only disappearing behind other mountains near Pendleton where the land is brown and pocked with great stacks of hay bales. Mountain after snow-covered mountain and down into Meridian where I will meet with Barbara.

2018: The snowdrops, earliest crocus and aconites holding at February levels in clear, cold days, midseason crocus keeping tight in their long buds. From Madison, Wisconsin, Tat called and left a message: "I was heading home… and I wanted you to know that there was a small flock of sandhill cranes in the oak savanna right by the water. Gosh, they were beautiful, maybe six or seven of them doing their beautiful slapping wing dance so gorgeous flying in couples and making that beautiful nose. They are here, on the way north to Horicon marsh, I am guessing."

2019: I see more geese flying in pairs these days.

2020: I went outside this morning at 6:20, and I immediately heard robins in full mating singsong chants, mixed with whinnies. The full chorus has begun. Cardinals and doves joined in at 6:30. Jill reports her tulips have started to come up. Only a handful of Canadian geese at the pond today. Chris Walker sent a note that he had heard sandhill cranes above his land this evening.

2021: Sun and frost: Cardinals and robins loud at 6:30 this morning, one mating robin singsong heard, but not a full chorus yet.

2022: Snowdrops still early, only a few nodding and open. Aconites full flower for several days. From Madison, Wisconsin, Tat reports sandhill cranes flying overhead.

2023: Mock orange leafing ahead of the honeysuckles by the back shed. At the entry to the front walk, the first forsythia blossoms. In the dooryard, almost all the snowdrops have suddenly disappeared. In the alley, all of the Danielsons' aconites are gone, retreating into the brush piles around them, Through the garden, I counted 61 daffodils open and many more coming on, and many more blooming in the village. In the North Glen, no wildflowers seen, almost no new foliage, but the river was rushing from yesterday's deluge. Chris reports: "First dandelion here today, and tonight I heard our first woodcock. I could hear the whistling twittering sound of its dance."

Now husbandmen in March prepare
And order take against the teeming year.

Buckminster Almanack, 1675

March 5th
The 64th Day of the Year

The stormy March is come at last
With wind, and cloud, and changing skies.

William Cullen Bryant

Sunrise/set: 7:03/6:31
Day's Length: 11 hours 28 minutes
Average High/Low: 44/26
Average Temperature: 35
Record High: 77 – 1983
Record Low: - 1 – 1978

Weather
Five to ten percent chance of highs in the 70s today, five to ten of 60s, twenty percent of 50s, twenty-five of 40s, forty-five percent of 30s. Skies are completely cloudy more than half the years, with rain 40 percent of the time, snow ten percent.

Natural Calendar
Leaves of the April primroses and tansy ragwort have started to unfold. Dock leaves unravel, blushed from the frost and snow. The buds of the quince have become deep red. The buds of the lilac are losing their beige winter coats. Forsythia buds are becoming brighter, and once in fifteen years, forsythia blooms by this day in March along the 40th Parallel.

Daybook
1983: Record high of 77 degrees today: robins in the yard, lilac buds flushed and tender. First wasp seen. First red maple flowering. More strawberry leaves in the garden. Purple deadnettle is blooming along High Street. Three people called with reports of crocus opening. Celandine coming back. Pussy willows completely emerged.

1985: Cardinal sings at 6:39 a.m. A flock of red-winged blackbirds crossed Wilberforce-Clifton Road in front of my car this afternoon.

1986: First red-winged blackbird seen on a barbed wire fence on Wilberforce-Clifton Road, 8:45 a.m. First silver maple flowering. Flocks of starlings along the road. One bedraggled dandelion bloomed at Wilberforce.

1987: More red-winged blackbirds seen today. The first star magnolia opened at my southeast wall. Cardinal sang at 6:41 a.m. One more robin seen.

1988: South Glen: 35 degrees, trees covered with ice after the storm. River as high as I've ever seen it. Two geese flew south along the water at 2:20 p.m. Four mallards followed an hour later. I walked southwest into the ice shining in the sun, the woods bright, steaming from the melting water. When I returned northeast with the sun at my back, the wet Osage branches were golden and spring-like. As I moved, the ice fell around me, pieces like cocoons or cicada shells, fossils of the branches, the winter's hulls shattered in the March sun. It was like walking in rain and hail, the sky pure blue. At one point, I turned around and saw the biggest red fox I've ever seen jogging after me. He stopped when I stopped, put his ears back, sniffed my tracks, then turned and climbed up into the woods. At home in the greenhouse, the first leaf of a violet, the plant brought in last fall, had grown out. In the yard, one snowdrop, two aconites blooming, grass getting long.

1989: Juncos still come to the bird feeder. Yesterday a meadowlark seen. Today, the arrival of red-winged blackbirds along Grinnell Road. Sprouting of honeysuckles. The first fly.

1990: Robin song is common now these mornings. Cardinal sang at 6:35 a.m., one seen building its nest at dawn. Jeni says Jacksonville is all green now, azaleas in bloom, people setting out their bedding plants.

1991: First calf seen in the fields today. At the Covered Bridge, the river was low and clear. Up the ridge, I found the first bluebells coming up; they hadn't been out long, maybe their tips had shown at the end of February. Moss growing, red. Spring beauty and violet cress foliage visible. Touch-me-nots had sprouted in the rocky high swamp area, protected by the watercress and the moving water. The first honeysuckle was leafing, as were the love vines.

1993: Cold March continues, the third snowstorm of Early Spring peaks this morning. Flooding began yesterday in parts of South Glen. Hawthorn berries thinning noticeably now, probably to the robins.

1998: Blue-eyes *(Veronica)* seen in bloom along the sidewalk this morning.

1999: Crows at 6:38 this morning, the sky clearing as the moon was setting. Cardinal at 6:41, loud, piercing. Then suddenly the hard and insistent sound of the spring day, almost no space between bird calls at all.

2000: Screech owl this morning at 4:15 in the soft darkness, temperature maybe 50 degrees, stars out. Flickers strong all day. They have become much more prominent throughout the past weeks, at first distant and occasional in the middle of February, now insistent and steady.

2001: A ladybug walked across my desk just before my anatomy exam.

2002: Flock of robins seen at the dairy north of town at 9:30 a.m.

2004: A high of 73 today, the koi frolicking in the pond, snowdrops, aconites, snow crocus all full bloom. Hyacinths, tulips, and daylilies are two-inches tall, daffodil three to five inches. The first sprouts – probably garlic mustard – have emerged. The first ramps are up about an inch. The west row of daffodils has started to produce buds.

2005: We had an inch of snow, large wet flakes, this morning, but now everything's melting in the sun. In the east garden, Jeanie and I found primrose foliage pushing through the mulch. All around us, starlings cackled and cardinals sang.

2006: Judy reports from Goshen: "When Angel and I went out to pick up the paper this morning, what did we hear as a counterpoint to the cardinals but a Red-Winged Blackbird!!!! I was so excited-- spring is really coming despite the snow that just covered the tips of the iris and daffodils that are peeking out. Thought you should know just about as soon as it happened. When we went for our walk later everyone had quieted down. The cardinals are mating. At least they're chasing each other around."

2007: Grackles seen at the bird feeder and in the alley for the first time this year.

2008: Yesterday's rain turned to snow late last night, about half an inch on the ground this morning. Water droplets hang from the tree branches, tiny frozen waves. Cardinals and doves and titmice singing throughout my morning walk, and Jeanie saw a buzzard along President Street. This afternoon, two grackles were clucking in the back trees. I received a letter from Margaret Lacey in Richmond, who said that she had heard her first dove on March 1st.

2010: Cardinal heard at 6:35 this morning. The thaw continued today, larger islands of brown and green appearing in the backyard, especially against the south wall and the southern exposure of the stone fence. Now there are continents of thaw, the great glacier of February ceding to the first sunny week since January. Foliage that had been pushed down by the storms stands up and even seems to put on growth. Snow crocus sprouts, still flattened by the snow yesterday, pushed through today and stand a full inch tall, their four leaves spreading to leave room for the flower bud to come. Bamboo, bent over and held fast by the weight of the snow, is regaining its balance in spasms.

2011: Two days of heavy rain, temperatures in the 50s. Daffodils to three inches now, lawn green and flooded, grape hyacinths and wood hyacinths pacing the daffodils. Grackles common now throughout the neighborhood.

2012: Cardinal sang at 6:30 sharp, light snow and low in the low 20s.

2013: Meridian, Idaho to Rawlins, Wyoming: Starting in the dark across the high plains desert, towns and lone farm houses shining like constellations across the black land, trucks on the highway far to the horizon. The dawn so bright and gold in my eyes. Violet horizon, sun rising through rows and rows of white, spinning windmills. Hard east wind, tumbleweed crashing into the car. Pairs of crows, constant companions throughout the trip, one crow all puffed out in mating ritual, magpies, a small flock of starlings. Deep snow in the mountains of Utah, then I pass through down into the red cliffs of Wyoming.

2014: Cindy reports the first sighting of a red-winged blackbird, the first actual sighting so far in the year.

2017: Forsythia is in full bloom around the village now, crab apple leaves starting, mid-season crocus and *iris reticulata* full, squills and daffodils coming on strong, pear tree buds ready to burst, blue eyes and one dandelion in the grass along the bike path south, dusky bluebell foliage up an inch by the mock orange and the studio. One periwinkle found in Jeanie's old planting of the late '70s at the south edge of the dooryard garden. And Rick Walkey reported a clump of white violets in full bloom.

2018: Two daffodil buds are showing yellow, the sun is bright but the air is cold. Squills gathering momentum, more sky-blue in the southwest garden. Dusky blue-gray bluebells have emerged by the studio, are up about two inches.

2020: I was outside at 6:00 this morning. The robins were quiet until 6:15, and then they started all at once, full mating chorus. A cardinal heard through the robin chanting around 6:25. Chris Walker sent a note: "This morning as I walked out for Lauds around 6:00 a.m., two woodcocks were peenting to each other in the upper field. And as I stepped out of the woodshed with a cart of firewood, a bald eagle flew over. All that, and sun and blue sky too! A rich morning." Around town, it is full snow crocus season in lawns and gardens. And Jill sent a photo of a honeybee in a violet snow crocus in the sun.

2021: Clear and 25 degrees. Once again, I walked the neighborhood at 6:00 a.m. No robins seen or calls heard, but one cardinal sang at 6:19, and more cardinals came in at 6:24. Then geese became restless at the north edge of town. A small flock of grackles flew into the yard at 8:30.

2023: Daffodil count: 57. Maggie sends a photo from Madison, Wisconsin, showing the first aconite and the first pussy willow emerged.

The natural world itself is the primary economic reality, the primary educator, the primary governance, the primary healer, the primary presence of the sacred, the primary moral value.

Thomas Berry

March 6th
The 65th Day of the Year

Up from the sea the wild north wind is blowing
Under the sky's gray arch;
Smiling, I watch the shaken elm-boughs, knowing
It is the wind of March.

John Greenleaf Whittier

Sunrise/set: 7:01/6:32
Day's Length: 11 hours 31 minutes
Average High/Low: 44/27
Average Temperature: 35
Record High: 74 – 1910 and 2023
Record Low: 0 – 1901

Weather
Snow falls 35 percent of all years on this date, making it the snowiest day in my March record. It is also one of three of the windiest days of the month and one of the three days most likely to see a thunderstorm. Highs remain in the 20s one year in ten, reach only to the 30s four in ten, climb into the 40s ten percent of the years, to the 50s twenty percent, 60s fifteen percent, and 70s five percent.

Natural Calendar
Even in the coldest years, pussy willows squeeze out by the first week of March. They open well before the weedy henbit, partial to around a dozen thaw days, maybe five or six afternoons in the upper 40s, one or two near 60, and about three warm rains. The catkins generally reach their prime when crocuses bloom, and woolly bear caterpillars come out from winter hibernation.

Pussy willow time is the time that clover and wild violet leaves start to grow; horseradish stretches out to an inch or two, and red rhubarb unfolds in the sun. Honeysuckle buds are unraveling on the lowest branches. Bleeding hearts are pushing their heads from the ground as daylilies reach to the top of your boots, and white snow trillium blossoms appear in the bottomlands.

Earliest spring is over when the sleek pussy willow nubs flush with pollen, almost always a week or ten days after equinox, just after forsythia and box elders, spring beauties, violet cress, bloodroot, hepatica and twinleaf come into flower. Horseradish and comfrey shoots are two inches long then, raspberry leaves the size of honeybees.

The catkins start to drop the first week in April, falling for a week and a half until redbuds and cherry trees blossom. Then come bright blue squills, delicate yellow jonquils, then the full-size daffodils, then purple grape hyacinths, then pale wood hyacinths.

Pussy willow branches finally leaf out when daisies and bleeding hearts have buds, when tulips are in early full bloom, between the first asparagus and the first rhubarb pie.

Daybook

1983: First forsythia opened today. First daffodils bloomed. Honeysuckles leafing out. One hepatica found open, fresh foliage around it. New leaves too on some garlic mustard, waterleaf, Dutchman's britches, and celandine. Chickweed and lavender cress flowering.

1985: Crows and starlings restless at dawn, their activity continuing to increase as the days lengthen.

1988: Garlic in the garden pushes up the mulch, making its height equal to that of the crocus and daffodils, about two inches now.

1989: The village shut down: sleet, snow, wind and cold.

1991: Worms cross the sidewalk in the rain, temperature about 50 degrees. Daffodils nearest the house are budding. More aconites in bloom today, and the small, scraggly anemones.

1992: Daffodils open on Wright Street. New garlic mustard and beggartick sprouts seen. A goose honking on the Little Miami. One *Cornus mas* is in full bloom in Xenia. Doves nesting in my ginkgo. Bleeding hearts up half an inch.

1993: Peonies up a half inch today. The snow most all melted, rhubarb underneath unhurt, pale green. Male cardinal chasing a female this morning. Tonight, a skunk was out right in the middle of the area's largest commercial development. Scent of spring.

1998: Chives grow back inside in the greenhouse at the same rate as outside in the garden.

2000: Mild temperatures over the past weeks have brought the first daffodils into bloom today. The library downtown has a small clump open. Around the yard, crocus and snowdrops are in full bloom, the hyacinths show their squat buds close to the ground. Peonies are three to four inches. The bleeding heart foliage is just barely visible. Robins are common in the yard now, and flicker calls fill the morning and the afternoon.

2002: Crows at 6:33 a.m., cardinals two minutes later.

2003: South Garden: In one patch of bare ground surrounded by snow and ice: a small clump of snow crocus just starting to bud. Along the west wall of the house, daffodil foliage two inches high. No sooner does the snow move away than the spring foliage takes its place.

2004: At 6:05 this morning, the robin chorus was underway. By 6:30, everyone was singing.

2005: Cardinals and titmice at 6:30, but no robins heard. By the shed, no waterleaf emerged yet, leaves stubby and pale under the mulch. Roly-polies found under a rock in the garden.

2008: Pussy willows have come out about half way so far, unchecked by the below-normal temperatures for the past months. In the south garden, one gold and one purple snow crocus are half open in the intermittent afternoon sun by the bamboo.

2009: Chiricahua National Monument, western New Mexico: Manzanita bush in full bloom (the only shrub flowering in this environment now), Emory oaks identified, their leaves with sharp points), alligator juniper with new buds, Arizona white oaks common around the campground, sycamore bark and fruits lying about the paths, mullein leaves, dwarfed by drought and cold. The ocotillo here has green leaves and many flower spikes – some open and reddish, some already done, full-blooming creosote bush.

2010: A third day of sun in a row, and the thaw continues with the temperature close to 40 degrees. Doves and cardinals at 6:34 this morning. In the east garden, the snow crocci show buds tight within their cluster of leaves, and the snowdrops tall enough to lean over, getting set to open. In the south garden near the pond, the regular crocus show tall purple buds. The pussy willows are edging out, more white against the pure blue sky. In the woods, the unevenness of the land seems to have favored the thaw, the white now intermittent, in full retreat, the fallen logs, the rocks, and the tall trees above them attracting the sun. A pileated woodpecker calling at the college. A tiny fly seen on the leaves of the primrose under the redbud tree.

2011: Ramps, thin and pale, are up under the mock orange bush. Peonies are slow, just an inch high. Many daffodils have buds, tulips are two to three inches, daylilies the same.

2012: Small flocks of grackles grackling in the high trees around the neighborhood. The very first periwinkle flower seen along High Street. Robin chorus not heard this morning. Rose bushes with small red leaves about half an inch long. Mid-season crocus, blue eyes and bittercress in full bloom all over town. Hydrangeas and viburnums budding.

2013: Rawlins, Wyoming to beyond Kearney, Nebraska: Another start at daybreak, altostratus clouds building at first, sometimes softening, sometimes filtering or hiding the rising sun. Snowcapped mountains, frozen rivers and lakes, snowy hills, and past Cheyenne, the mountains recede, vast pastures with dark soil spreading out on either side of the road. All along, more white windmills spinning in the hard wind. I sailed along the great prairies to the music of Bach, past more bales of hay and lone black bulls. The hide of the land became softer and browner with grasses, and suddenly there was a hint of green, and then fields of stubble added a touch of gold. And hints of gold and green all across Nebraska. The sun was out so that I drove across the vast layout, the panoply of Early Spring, all the rivers now running free and open, deep blue green in sloughs and ponds. And then more and more trees appearing, lining the river as I worked my way toward the sandhill cranes.

A little past Kearney, I took a room in an old motel, went to the Audubon center nearby where a group was going out along the river to a blind, with hopes to see the cranes come in for the night. At 5:00 p.m., the sky was deep blue, gigantic plumed cirrus up above us, the wind steady east, the river, maybe 200 yards wide, moving west, swirling above and around the sandbars below us. And the cranes came and came and came, always east to west as if guiding on the red setting sun. And there was constant trilling chatter, alternating sometimes with the moaning whistle of a train off near Kearney, accompanying the wave after wave of the cranes in undulating formations of from a few dozen to many dozen birds, that slid from "vees" to horseshoes to ragged lines and back again, cranes often changing groups, but never flying alone, their formations making me think of clever, determined phalanxes, moving on to some known destination in gangly discipline and order, held in place by their constant, guiding conversation.

The closer the sun to the horizon, the more flocks appeared, formations in tandem sometimes stretching all the way across the sky from east to west, and as the sun went down, a great number of the birds gathered together and swirled and swarmed down, spinning onto the river flats to spend the night, and I could just make out their nighttime posture, standing together, close ranked, constantly conversing.

2014: Walked Bella at 6:25 this evening. Robins all around in the neighborhood, constant peeping. They are getting set for the morning chorus. And on Stafford Street, two large beds of aconites budded, the first flowers of the year.

2016: Today began a marked warm-up throughout the East Coast. Here in Danville, Pennsylvania, a large flock of grackles settled in the trees early this afternoon near the farmhouse where we stayed overnight. Large-flowered snowdrops were fully open there. In Corning, New York, pussy willows were about a third open.

2017: A barometric trough at the approach of a strong high-pressure system, mild temperatures, light rain, several daffodils opening on the circle garden.

2018: sun and 54 degrees: Two daffodils by the peach tree almost starting to unfold. One bee seen in the mid-season crocus. Casey reports the first red-winged blackbird sighting. A few more honeysuckles leafing. John Blakelock called to say that his ant lion larvae were active for the first time this year.

2019: The last morning in the single digits, maybe for the year? The pond is almost completely frozen over, and the ground is hard, covered with about an inch of snow. Cardinals were setting territories every few hundred yards as I walked with Ranger before dawn this morning, the first cardinal song at 6:34. I saw a sandpiper as I drove to Springfield this afternoon. From Cadiz in Spain, Lois sends photos of bird-of-paradise plants and bougainvillea in early bloom.

2022: The milder weather of the past week brought more landmarks of Early Spring: more reports of red-winged blackbirds (Casey calling to say he had seen them at his feeder, "picking through the peanuts). Grackles have arrived to mate and raise their fledglings in Yellow Springs. Mosquitoes have started to bite. Jill photographed a speedy woolly bear caterpillar that emerged from hibernation. On March 2, Audrey and Grant saw a rare Mourning Cloak butterfly along Pleasant Street, possibly the earliest butterfly of 2022 (the earliest previously recorded sighting of a Mourning Cloak being on March 23, 2000). Throughout town, many white and pink hellebores have opened wide, snowdrops have come all the way out, yellow aconites are wide open, purple and golden crocuses are blooming by the fish pond, and daffodils are three or four inches high in the north garden some of them budded.

2023: Daffodil count this morning: 70. Grackles visiting the feeders. Ad red-shouldered hawk visited the yard early in the afternoon, perched in one of the high locust trees and ate what it had captured, making its sharp calls from time to time. After a day in the 70s, there are 85 daffodils in bloom, with six of those coming in the circle garden (its first). And Aida wrote: "The blue herons are back. About 12:15 today, I was riding south on the bike path: first sightings of two great blue herons sitting on nests at the rookery near Highway 68."

Journal

"On this side of the hedge," writes the French author, Jacques Dulieu "in our everyday garden, grow the rosemary, juniper, ferns and plane trees, perfectly tangible and visible.... On the other side of the hedge, however, reality is ours. If we find them intact in our memories, the same as when we saw them before, it is because we have invested them with the image that we have of them, with the opaque skin of our own confirmation."

In Dulieu's ruminations, there are two gardens or two realities: One is the visible-tangible garden with prickly weeds and sweet vegetables; the other is the garden of images.

Every March, I cultivate both spaces. I count the steps to Ohio Valley spring, taking care to note specific times and places, watching for the pieces of the month to gather momentum, wondering about the here and now.

In the back of my mind, however, I am always going back to the harsh Wisconsin springs in which I grew up, Lents of snow and the most bitter cold, Lents of fragile thaws in which water only ran on ice. Always peering out at me is this primal season, the indelible imprint of the season of childhood.

And so Ohio spring is always astonishing to me, and every fierce thaw before April is a miracle. When I lived in North Carolina, I was amazed by its February daffodils. When I worked in Puerto Rico, I and my friends swam in disbelief in a tepid pool on a hot Christmas Day.

The disbelief continues, always against the backdrop of the white childhood landscape on the far side of the hedge, persists like rebellion against ancient, infused dogma. I bask in the sun of this radical warming here in the Ohio Valley, I see behind my back the cold springs of childhood, and I seize the annual surprise of this early season, the surprise of this unexpected gift to my boyhood longing to be free.

Dulieu asserts that memories are choices; I find that's not always so. The hedge of time has many sides, and in the maze of spring, I stumble down temporal passageways in search of synthesis and direction, always coming out on something new, always returning to the place from which I started.

The earth lies out now like a leopard, drying her lichen and moss spotted skin in the sun, her sleek and variegated hide.

Henry David Thoreau

Lord and gentle Maker,
Move the Axis of the Season
From the troubled Winter.
Wake the fertile Beauty
Of the tawny Flowers,
And restore your Pleasure
To the Pastures of the Spring.

Vespers Hymn, Tuesday before Ash Wednesday

(bf)

Sunrise/set: 7:00/6:33
Day's Length: 11 hours 33 minutes
Average High/Low: 45/27
Average Temperature: 35
Record High: 76 – 2000
Record Low: - 2 – 1943

Weather

Today is usually one of the two sunniest days in March. Storms bring rain or snow four years in ten, but clouds typically give way not long after precipitation ends. Colder temperatures often accompany blue skies: a 25 percent chance of a high only in the 20s, and a 30 percent chance of 30s. On the other hand, highs reach the 40s ten percent of the afternoons, the 50s twenty-five percent, the 60s five percent and even the 70s five percent of the time.

Natural Calendar

Azaleas and camellias are blooming in the South. In the Mid-Atlantic States, celandine has sprouted. When the rivers are high and the water temperature is warm enough, carp begin to mate in the shallows. Red-winged blackbirds sing in the swamps. Buds lengthen and brighten on multiflora roses, mock orange and lilac bushes. In the pasture, nettle tops may be ready to pick for greens.

Daybook

1981: Found Virginia bluebells coming out of the ground past the Covered Bridge today. Pussy willows are in full bloom at home. Garlic, planted in November, paces the emerging daffodils.

1983: Bleeding heart stems came out today. The first crocus bloomed in the yard. Red-winged blackbirds on the fence posts outside of town, whistling in the wind. Wolf spiders in the field grass at the Covered Bridge. Saw two pairs of ducks scouting the river near sundown.

1985: Bleeding heart stems are up today. Weeping willows on the way to Cincinnati are bright yellow green.

1988: Rivers very high. Mrs. Bletzinger reports carp "frolicking" in her pond, the first time this year.

1992: Daylilies are about three inches tall now, waterleaf two inches. Willows are yellow green. The flickers and blue jays give their mating calls all day. Mock orange is leafing. Violet foliage is up. Bradford pears bud.

1993: Cardinal wakes me up at 6:33 a.m. Bird song loud, constant throughout the day convincing me that it's really March and that the cold will really end.

1994: Despite the mean March weather and the stagnation in wildflower foliage throughout South Glen, the golden snow crocus in the east garden opened just a little today. The south garden snowdrops bloomed yesterday, and more snow crocus are coming up there, will blossom soon. Pussy willows are about half out. Weeping willows along the freeway are bright yellow.

1998: Blue jay outside the back door, calling with his bell tone call this morning, over and over.

1999: Crows at 6:39, bright and clear morning.

2000: Young craneflies spinning in the early afternoon. The first daffodils open in the east garden, a day behind the first of the year, which bloomed in front of the library. By late afternoon, the first forsythia flowers came undone, and I saw the first mosquito in Fairborn an hour or so after sundown. Honeysuckles are leafing, and Japanese honeysuckles, barberry bushes, wild roses, and raspberries. Star magnolia open at Springfield, along with periwinkles, purple deadnettle, blue eyes, shepherd's purse.

2001: A flock of crows calling in the dark of early morning, 6:33.

2004: Maples are in bloom in Yellow Springs and throughout Dayton. There was something like a week gap between the first flowering of snowdrops and snow crocus and the opening of the first trees.

2005: An inventory at the end of March's first week, adds several new dimensions to the scope of middle-February spring. Daffodils have put on an inch or two, are now three to four inches high, many of them budded. Tulips and Resurrection lilies pace the daffodils, only an inch or so behind them. Red peony stalks, barely visible on Valentine's Day, have pushed up above the mulch. Snowdrops, aconites and snow crocuses have reached the peak of their seasons all about town; their time will be over in just a few days. Pussy willows, slow to respond in the cold start of 2005, are now completely emerged. The first purple deadnettle and henbit have opened in the sunniest microclimates. Among the most recent events, leaves of the April primroses and cressleaf groundsel have started to unfold. Dock is beginning to unravel, blushed from the frost and snow. The buds of the quince have become deep red. Forsythia buds are becoming brighter, anticipating their flowers, which will be out two weeks from today.

2006: Faint twittering in the dark at 6:00 in the morning, robins warming up. Screech owl calling in the back trees at that time, too – relatively common these mornings. Cardinals and doves are singing now near 6:30 a.m. Grackles are here, and the small flock of starlings no longer sits on the tree at the end of the alley. Pussy willows are a third to half emerged. Coral berries darken; some are black. Sweet gum and bittersweet still keep many of their fruits.

On the way to Dayton this afternoon, I saw a groundhog running in the brown grass.

2008: Yesterday, the first robin on High Street and robins chirping in Wilmington when I drove over there in the evening. Lorie, who cuts hair downtown, said her neighbor's yard was full of blooming crocus and that she even saw a bumblebee.

Then today, a regular northern blizzard, high winds swirling the snow from the rooftops. The birds fed heavily in the storm, the rose-breasted nuthatch even coming by. By midmorning, a small flock of red-winged blackbirds, males and females descended on the back feeder. The first grackles and cowbirds of the year came, too, and even a crow.

For several hours, the starlings, house sparrows, song sparrows, titmice, chickadees and cardinals vied for positions on the seed bell, the suet and the tube feeder. Under the arbor a small flock of gold finches clung to the sack thistle feeders, the wind swinging them back and forth and around in circles. Juncos cleaned up after them below.

The blizzard continued throughout the day, snow blowing and spinning so hard that it was sometimes hard to see even the blackbirds fifty feet away. When I went out to get wood about five o'clock this afternoon, the blackbirds had moved over to Greg's yard a few hundred yards away and were cackling and whistling.

So in the middle of the worst storm in recent memory, the signs of spring continued to appear. The blizzard was not a sign of the return of winter so much as it was a part of this changeable season, coming within the traditional March storm window, covering but preserving the hesitant progress made in the first days of the month, the first blooming crocus and snowdrops, the spears of daffodil foliage. The cardinal, titmouse and dove calls that continued to mark the progress of Early Spring through the last weeks of February and the arrival of robins to High Street a few days ago were affirmed by the advent of the blackbirds, grackles and cowbirds. In the frigid mornings, the birds sang on schedule, telling that the cold was ephemeral.

2009: Saguaro East and Catalina State Park near Tucson, Arizona: We have finally come fully into spring with orange globe mallow, poppies, fleabane, a magenta penstemon-like plant. The ground at Catalina is literally solid green with foliage, enhanced with tiny white, yellow and violet flowers. The grass is lush in the mesquite glades, the moon three-quarters full, rising over the mountains.

2010: Cardinals and doves started to sing at 6:27 this morning, and the bird chorus was strong for hours. In the alley, I heard cardinals, doves, red-bellied woodpeckers, starlings and nuthatches. Geese flew over near 7:30. The first grackles of the year arrived at the birdfeeder about 8:00, and I saw more along the alley later in the morning. Two male cardinals seen chasing each other, jockeying for territory. In the forsythia bushes, sparrows chirping and mating.

At the covered bridge, skunk cabbage red, most plants closed but a few in bloom. The ground muddy, patches of chickweed, garlic mustard, sedum. No bluebells or violet cress foliage seen. The hillsides alternated between full snow and full brown, depending on the curve of the riverbed.

Ellis Pond was still completely frozen, but DeWine's Pond was a little more than half open. When we checked the crocus along the south wall at about 2:00 this afternoon, we found three of them partially in bloom. The thin grape hyacinth stalks are flushed red, three inches high. Later, we saw six doves in the backyard – the first time so many this year. Two of them were courting under the honeysuckles, chasing back and forth. At the back porch, the icemelt falls in a complex rhythm into flooded flowerpots and onto the bricks and the green plastic watering can. Clouds in the evening, the first rain shower of spring after dark.

2011: Robins peeping and twittering at about 6:40 this morning. Full birdsong with doves, grackles, cardinals, sparrows, red-bellied woodpecker after sunrise. Along Dayton Street, lilac buds are green, and Japanese honeysuckle vines are just beginning to leaf. Along High Street, the orange bittersweet berries decay into the soggy ground.

2012: I went out a little after six this morning to see if I could hear the first of the robin chorus. I had heard nothing yesterday, and so today was sort of the "point vierge" of the year for robins. The moon was round and golden, setting between the dark trees due south, and the air was mild, maybe in the 40s (and 60s due by the afternoon). At 6:15, the sky still quite dark, geese flew over to the north of Dayton Street. At 6:20, I heard a faint twittering of birds, and then a few minutes later, it became clear that this was indeed the robin chorus of 2012 just starting. From a distant chirping, the sound became louder and louder as the High Street flock came into song right in the yard. At 6:35, I heard the first cardinal - in spite of the road noise from the street and the boisterous robins. Then crows a few minutes later. The very first squill opened by the mock orange this morning, but the daffodils are holding out, fully budded and yellow petals visible but tightly bundled. Early Japanese honeysuckle leaves, half an inch or so. Very similar progress to last year.

2013: Near Kearney, Nebraska to Springfield, Illinois: I listened for cranes at 6:00 in the morning, but I heard nothing. Then at 6:30, their cries began, and I looked up east and saw line after line of cranes advancing along high above the river. By the time I left the motel, the sky was pale, the waning moon up in the southeast, and the cranes kept on coming, swirling their sinuous, evolving phalanxes north to south and sometimes landing in a clockwise spiral, so dense they hid the fields beyond them as they dropped down to the river or to feed in an open areas. And they kept coming as I drove into the sunrise, their mutating formations moving into the west, reaching from north to south and filling the sky. The sun rose deep red, filtered through the altostratus, so I could watch the black lines of cranes against it, and I drove on toward Grand Island, below thirty miles of continuous waves of cranes arriving to feed along the Platte River.

I went east to Lincoln then to St. Joe, then across Missouri, by woods and small farms, most of the land snow covered until I crossed the Mississippi. And then near Winchester, Illinois (where my wife Jeanie spent the best years of her childhood), 500 miles from where I had left the Nebraska cranes, suddenly to my left in a corn field, another congregation of cranes, several giant flocks spinning down to feed, and above them and around them, more and more cranes moving west, line after line on the way to join the thousands already assembled at the Platte.

2014: At 6:30 this morning, cardinals, crows, doves, even geese calling, and a few robins peeping. On Stafford Street after sunup: two aconites were blooming among hundreds budded, and a few of Liz's snowdrops were ready to open.

2016: Corning, New York: The first real warm spell of spring covers the Middle Atlantic and East. One clump of snowdrops and three bees sighted in one yard, but no other blossoms.

2017: After a night of warm rain, five daffodils have opened in the circle garden, the first pink lungworts near the studio, the pachysandra along the west property line, momentum growing in the middle of uneven temperatures. The forsythia hedge, fleshing out and in full bloom, looks almost the way it used to look here in the yard in April of the early 1980s. South on High Street, two plum trees are covered with white blossoms.

2018: Yesterday the first daffodil opened so slowly, and as the wind turned and came from the north in the night, that daffodil opened all the way, just before snow and cold in the 20s. From Billings, Missouri, Jeffery Goss reports white bass have begun to spawn.

2019: Cardinals and doves in full, steady song at 6:30 this morning, crows late at 6:50. In the early afternoon, I saw and heard sandpipers in the field near Ellis Pond.

2020: Leslie reports her first honeybee, a leafhopper, her first forsythia and periwinkle flower.

2021: A few grackle clucks in the bamboo as I walked with Ranger about 6:30 this morning, cardinals singing, robins occasionally peeping. Audrey told me she saw a mockingbird (as did I a week or so ago). They overwinter here, but do they just come to town for nesting?

2023: The warm February slowly merges with a cool March. But the daffodils keep coming: 92 this morning. In the afternoon, John Blakelock called to say he had found a green frog in his grotto pool.

Journal

Waiting for spring can be like trying to go to sleep when I have insomnia. Sometimes the best thing to do is to count. Counting is a simple measure of time. Counting limits time to individual pieces, takes away some of its mystery and emptiness. Counting is an act of will, forces focus, works against discouragement, places the counter in opposition to the psychology and physiology of sleeplessness.

Numbers are infinite, and so are the pieces of winter. Counting in sequence creates apparent progress and finite limits. Even though awareness of winter's events seems to produce few results and seems to have no sum or substance, observations can be like digits in a sprawling but promising nighttime equation, the fruit of persistence and dogged hope.

Like counting sheep or breaths or numerals, counting dimensions of the interval between winter and April requires no rules or ethics, is not competitive, does not require special study or skill. Like counting sheep or breaths or numerals, the choice of things to be counted is arbitrary, has no necessary socially redeeming value, does not end poverty or bring peace, has no theology. This is the anarchy, the freedom of mindfulness that looses the mind's eye to rhythm or accumulation or listing or repetition or the emptiness of any single object until something new suddenly occurs without our creating it, and we fall asleep and dream or discover spring.

Winter will lash back again out of the north, bringing snow and freezing weather...But spring will advance nonetheless, silently and unnoticed. The rearguard actions of winter will be repulsed in the end; the higher sun will assert its dominance through the longer days, and the winds will dry the fallow land wherein a million shoots from the seeds of least year's growth are slowly stirring.

Eliot Porter

Sunrise/set: 6:58/6:34
Day's Length: 11 hours 36 minutes
Average High/Low: 46/27
Average Temperature: 36
Record High: 77 – 1974
Record Low: - 4 – 1943

Weather

There is a five percent chance of highs in the 70s today, 15 percent of 60s, thirty percent of 50s, twenty-five percent of 40s, twenty percent of 30s, five percent for 20s. Rain or snow comes just 15 percent of the time; the skies are completely overcast four days in ten.

The Week Ahead

March's second quarter brings one more major pivot in the year's weather patterns. The rate of spring's advance quickens, and odds for milder weather increasing with every sunrise. Chances of an afternoon above 50 degrees rise to 40 percent by the end of the week. The third cold wave of the month arrives on the 9th or 10th, but it is typically one of the mildest so far in the year. Frost strikes the early garden 60 percent of all the nights, however, and there is still a five to ten percent chance each day this week for a high only in the 20s. Odds for rain or snow are about one in three most days of the period; the 10th is the wettest day with a 50 percent chance of precipitation. But the sun typically shines a little more than it did last week, with the 14th and the 17th often producing fewer clouds than any time since January 26th through 28th.

Natural Calendar

When lilac and mock orange buds are glowing defiantly against the gray sky, Virginia bluebells always push out from their hillsides. Raspberry and rose bushes are developing fresh leaves. Wild onions are getting lanky. Everything is growing back: Jacob's ladder, ragwort, leafcup, spring beauties, wood mint, ground ivy, catchweed, moneywort, waterleaf, sweet rockets, leafcup, hemlock, parsnip and garlic mustard. Skunk cabbage is red, fat, and blooming in the swamp flats. Chickweed and dandelions flower in the woods. Earliest henbit blossoms in the gardens. Lamb's quarter sprouts in the waysides. The pods of last summer's dogbane open in the fields. Ducks arrive in their mating plumage.

White tundra swans reach Lake Erie as wolf spiders hatch in the gray fields of the Miami Valley. Starlings and crows continue to pair off and select nesting sites. Bobwhites call, and the male titmouse spirals in its mating frenzy. The first mosquitoes may be ready to bite, as cherry trees get ready to bloom in the nation's capital. The most dramatic change of all occurs when enough robins have assembled to make their mating chorus heard in the early morning darkness.

The Stars

By ten o'clock tonight, the spring stars are taking over the sky. The fertile planting constellation of Cancer is almost overhead, between Pollux and Regulus. Hydra follows at its heels. May's Virgo approaches along the southeast horizon. The Big Dipper swings deeper into the southern sky.

Before dawn, all the constellations that ride the Milky Way into summer lie in the east. To the far north, Cassiopeia zigzags towards Cepheus, the house-like constellation just east of the North Star. Following the Milky Way to the south is Cygnus, the Northern Cross. Below Cygnus is Aquila, with its bright star Altair. Below Altair: July's Sagittarius.

1982: Sparrows seen building a nest under the eaves.

1983: Clover, parsnips, leafcup, mint, winter cress, bedstraw, chickweed, sedum, and corn salad are growing new leaves. Nettle is coming back: it even stings this early in the year! First cabbage butterfly seen along High Street. Two tan moths in the woods at South Glen. First spring beauty found along the river, paired ducks on the water. First snow trillium. First harbinger of spring. First toothwort. Tulip buds are prominent in the yard.

1984: Record six-inch snowfall, high winds, temperatures in the 20s.

1985: Like love, it seems to me, spring can depend on the slightest movement of an object, the faintest scent, a glimpse of what might happen, an oblique suggestion of fulfillment. And so the sight of one daffodil or the first robin in the yard can create sudden spring, spring-at-first-sight. It can also grow and accumulate year after year like long, true love until each corner of its nature and each crevice of its devices are part of us.

1986: Cardinal sings at 6:46 a.m. despite the temperature at 5 degrees. Geese fly over the house at 8:23 a.m.

1987: First groundhog of the year seen along Grinnell. Pussy willows fully out. After two warm days, peonies send up red stalks. Daffodils six inches. Fishing at the river this morning, I caught two chubs and two shiners. The fish had moved out of their hole, were biting in the shallower upstream water.

1988: Pussy willows three-fourths out. First calves seen in the fields. First red-winged blackbirds on the fence posts along Wilberforce-Clifton Road.

1990: North to Niagara Falls. Pruning being done in the northern Ohio and New York vineyards.

1991: Red maple full bloom in Yellow Springs and in Switzerland

County along the Ohio River. New shepherd's purse and bittercress flowering throughout.

1992: First forsythia flowers. Astilbe is two inches high, about eight daffodils full bloom in the south garden.

1993: Despite the cold and snow, the first golden snow crocus has formed a bud in the east garden.

1994: The red-winged blackbirds are back on the fences at the junction of Wilberforce-Clifton Road and Tarbox Cemetery Road, three seen this afternoon when I came home from work.

1995: Yesterday, heavy rains and winds, and temperatures in the middle 50s brought the first worms of the year onto the sidewalks at Wilberforce. Today on the way to work, there were robins in the new snow along Corry Street, robins all along Grinnell. They must have flown in on yesterday's storm. Another sign of spring: the first spiders emerge in the bathroom!

1998: The first miniature jonquils have opened on the west side of the house today. Mock orange is leafing. First comfrey has appeared. In the pond, the loosestrife has started to grow under the water. Lilac buds bulging.

1999: Crows at 6:33 a.m., clear skies, temperature in the teens.

2000: At the Cascades this afternoon, I found the first purple cress and the very first hepatica. Maples were blooming everywhere, and there were hulls on the ground from the bloom of the high trees overhead. Tonight as I came home from church, I heard the first toad calling from the pond. I went out into the backyard and stood listening to him. In the west, the new moon was setting, most of its globe veiled in the earth's shadow. Above it, bright Jupiter, above and to the south of Jupiter, Saturn, and then the stars arched west and south, up into the red eye of Taurus, to Orion, to Sirius and then to rising Leo. About 9:00 p.m., Dave Cassenheiser called with a buzzard update; he'd counted almost 50 vultures, a record number for this date, sailing above the village and the Glen, playing in the wind: "It was a sight to see," he said.

2003: South Glen: Clear frosty morning, snow and ice thick on the forest floor. But the birds know it's spring: cardinals from 6:30 on this morning. Pileated woodpeckers, titmice, blue jays calling. In the south garden, one golden snow crocus opening in the afternoon sun. A high of 62 degrees for the first time this year! Cold and more snow forecast for tomorrow.

2006: The koi have begun to move around in the pond.

2007: Most of the daffodil spears are only an inch or two high except for those along the back near the redbud trees. Those bulbs are up four or five inches but are not budded.

2008: The blizzard continued throughout most of the day, the sun only coming out late in the afternoon. Birds fed less intensely today, maybe even full from yesterday's binge. The total amount of snow was ten to fifteen inches at various points in the yard, the second-greatest amount on record. Columbus, fifty miles away, received twenty inches, the most in its history. The streets are packed with snow, but driving out of the snow banks around the car was easy, the snow so fine and dry that it simply gave way under the tires.

2009: Catalina State Park just north of Tucson, Arizona: Walked several paths in the morning and afternoon, wind steady, clouds moving in through the afternoon. Flowers found (only shoddily identified): yellow four-petaled bladderpod (*Lasquerella arizonica* or *gordonii*), a variety of locoweed, a low lupine with narrow leaves (*Lupinus bicolor* or *sparsiflorus*?), Mexican poppy (four petals) in colonies across the hillsides, a blue stargrass (purplehead: *Dichelostemina*), a white chicory-like plant (*Rafinesquia neomexicana*), a dominant, common five-petaled small yellow flower with a red center prickly stem and leaves, alternate leaves with a single rib, maybe a mountain gromwell (*Lithospermum*), a smooth-leaved dock just heading up – desert rhubarb (*Rumex hymenosepalus*), several Texas thistles ready to bloom, fairydusters in full bloom, yellow four-petaled *Sisymbrium* (like a cross between London rocket and hedge mustard, a six-petaled white globe-like flower, a dominant five-petaled white-flowered ground cover, yellow center, alternate leaves, one rib, hairy leaves and stem, maybe a stickseed (*Lappula*), a five-petaled violet flower growing from blue-green finely divided basal leaves (also found north in Arizona).

2010: A soft rain overnight, and the day is a mix of hazy clouds and sun, the snow continuing to retreat. The high reached into the 50s this afternoon, several snowdrops and the purple crocus near the pond opened up all the way. Pussy willows continue to push out slowly, but no catkin has emerged completely. Jeanie and I worked outside for a while after lunch, and when we came in, there was a message from Naida Sutch, who said that two of the geese she had been watching for several years returned to the Friends' Care pond, the earliest she'd seen them come back.

2011: Robin chorus underway when I went outside at 6:30 this morning. Crows heard at 6:45.

2012: Warm winds and rain, opening up the very first daffodil. Robins in the storm at 6:25, then singing through the dawn into morning. A bluebird flew in front of the car as we drove along Dayton-Yellow Springs Road this afternoon.

2013: Springfield, Illinois to Yellow Springs: Once again, a sunny day, as another storm follows behind me in the west. I have ridden this space between storms all the way from Oregon, remaining under the auspices of the south and east wind, in mild temperatures of near 40 degrees. At home, still plenty of snow cover, only one pale snow crocus trying to bloom, all the snowdrops standing up, a few open.

2014: Walking Bella this morning before sunrise: The first cardinal sang on Stafford Street at 6:18. Silence until 6:22 when more cardinals started singing. Then the robins started cheeping at 6:24, but no generalized robin chorus. Thad reports two yellow crocuses at her office. At home, a couple of snowdrops are barely opening. First aconite foliage seen in the circle garden.

2015: I have been waiting for the weather to break. It finally looks like the vast Arctic high-pressure systems that have plunged the barometer down and thrust it up so high are finally abating. All across the Midwest, the temperatures are warming. Here today into the 50s, snow stubbornly holding but will surely cede in the week ahead. A few snowdrop buds struggle out from the crusty remnants of the last storm. The pussy willows along High Street are showing a little white, but still remain scraggly and timid. This afternoon, I saw two black buzzards and many crows working the road kills from last night. Three red-tailed hawks seen on the way out of town, and one chased away the buzzards from a dead raccoon. Tonight, John Blakelock called as dusk was ending, 6:55 p.m. He had just seen five waves of sandhill cranes circling to land in a field near the freeway.

2016: Ithaca, New York: The ground showing little promise until we rounded a corner and I saw a great patch of yellow aconites in bloom.

2017: Grackles courting outside the back door on the bird feeder. Near the pond, a second group of aconites is in full bloom, the first generation already darkened and gray. Along the bike path, one violet cress and two spring beauties found. And I saw a small flock of blackbirds, probably rusty blackbirds, conversing in the trees as I walked by.

2019: More killdeer at Ellis Pond, and the number of geese at fewer than 100. Tom Lemaire called from Dayton Street to say he saw an Eastern bluebird at his feeder this morning, "a good sign for their recovery in this area." The temperature finally got close to 40 today, the end of the extremely strong recent Snowdrop Winter. In Washington D.C. the Park Service gives April 3 – 6 as the estimated dates for cherry blossom time.

2020: Three pairs of geese flew over me as I walked with Ranger this morning at 7:00. Yesterday, the great winter flock of geese was virtually gone. Looking out the east window of the studio at the mock orange bush, I noticed that the buds that had greened in middle February and had started to unravel just a little a the end of the month were now tiny leaves. Below them, the Virginia bluebells were just barely visible, deep purple. (Jill said that a person's identity is tied up with what they notice. That is how all these notes are memoirs.) Leslie reports the first mating trill of the junco, as well as anthills in the woods. And also crow courtship with bobbing and upward "whoop" ("Community Spring" continuing to become part of my memoir). After sunset: robin whinnying vespers, and two tiny moths seen fluttering in the last light.

2021: Yesterday only about 50 geese on the pond, and another small flock in the field across the road. This morning, cardinals vociferous at 6:25, but only a few robin peeps. Some strange clicking-peeping calls at Stafford Street and Limestone, possibly mating sounds from a screech owl. Not a descending sound, actually rising slightly after several seconds. At the pond this afternoon, only a couple dozen geese floating on the water, looking abandoned. From Madison, Wisconsin, Tat reports hearing sandhill cranes at 10:06 a.m. She said Maggie heard them yesterday. John Blakelock reports a pair of marsh hawks looking to take up residence on his property.

2022: Geese gone from Ellis Pond, robins now common in the yard, the first tiny, red quince leaves and new basal stonecrop leaves have emerged. From Goshen, Indiana, Judy reports that her doves have come to her back porch where they nested last year.

2023: Daffodil count: 100. A short trip to the southern Dayton suburbs. Some star magnolias and forsythia in bloom, one pink magnolia opening.

Journal

"An inevitable dualism bisects nature," states Ralph Waldo Emerson in his essay, 'Compensation,' "so that each thing is a half, and suggests another thing to make it whole."

These days pull time and nature one way and then another. It is spring but winter. Signs of change accumulate, but they are still often overwhelmed by the cold fields of their nemesis.

I am compulsive about ignoring the dominant brown and gray of late February. I only watch the movement not the stasis. I see what I choose, the suggestive blush of color or the swelling of one bud or another.

The real dualism of which Emerson writes is still a month or so away. In April, I can look both ways; the sides are almost even: bright hepaticas, twinleaf, bloodroot on the one hand – bare branches and dead grass on the other. But now, I have to compensate by collecting fragments and by blowing them all out of proportion.

John Burroughs makes a drama of this annual process: "We are eager for Winter to be gone," he writes, "but he will not abdicate without a struggle. Day after day he rallies his scattered forces, and night after night pitches his white tents on the hills, and would fain regain his lost ground; but the young prince in every encounter prevails. Slowly and reluctantly the gray old hero retreats up the mountain, until finally the south rain comes in earnest, and in a night he is dead."

In the skirmishes of early March, I unfairly watch for the isolated standards of resurrection: white tips of the snowdrops, the first crocus leaves, daffodils an inch high. If I were to judge by the appearance of the land around them, I would have little hope. But I remember that "each thing is a half." I cheat, knowing the code of half: Everything is also whole.

March 9th
The 68th Day of the Year

The Exact Description of things, however small and seemingly contemptible, and faithful Accounts of what is observable in them, will always be of Use to those who study Nature, to what End soever that be;...I have spared no Pains, or cost to make (this book) as compleat as I could; I have visited almost every Quarry, Wood, Spring; and, to be short, every Thing that I coud think, merited Remark and Observation.

John Morton, *Northamptonshire* (1712)

Sunrise/set: 6:57/6:35
Day's Length: 11 hours 37 minutes
Average High/Low: 47/28
Average Temperature: 36
Record High 72 – 1974
Record Low: - 4 – 1984

Weather
Today is one of three March days on which the chances of a high of 70 degrees are near five percent. An afternoon in the 60s comes 20 percent of all the years. Highs in the 50s occur 20 percent of the time, the 40s thirty percent, 30s twenty percent, 20s five percent of the years. Precipitation occurs one day in three. After today, chances of a morning below zero fall to almost nothing for the first time since December 5.

Natural Calendar
Buckeye buds are swelling along the 40th Parallel as white tundra swans land at Lake Erie. Asian ladybeetles mate after they emerge from hibernation.

Daybook
1983 Comfrey, horseradish, and even the mock orange are sending out leaves.

1984: Record cold this morning: four below zero.

1985: Bleeding heart emerges below the mulch. Mock orange budding.

1986: First chipmunk of the year runs in front of the car.

1988: First violets send out leaves at Grinnell Pond. They emerged four days earlier in the greenhouse; so their appearance apparently isn't related to the air or ground temperature, but to the plant's own internal clock synchronized to trigger growth when the day's length reaches eleven and a half hours.

1989: First red-winged blackbirds seen along Wilberforce-Clifton.

1990: First daffodil unraveling in Cedarville.

1991: On the way to southern Indiana: Small flocks of robins seen throughout the trip.

1992: First star magnolias crack. Hedge lines pale green. Red maples flowering.

1993: Cardinal sings at 6:30 a.m. Golden crocus ready to bloom. \

1994: Golden snow crocus opens slightly in the east garden. Other crocus are up in the south garden, not ready to bloom yet. This season is pacing March of 1984 and 1993. All the flowers will be late.

2000: This morning, the daffodils and squills are in full bloom; the crocus and snowdrops and aconites are getting old. The forsythia is coming out all at once. Resurrection lilies as tall as daffodils. Mock orange and privet are leafing. More dry sweet gum tree seed balls fall to the ground. There are grape hyacinths open in the yard, and baby blue eyes. I saw the first willow bright April green in Springfield.

2002: Blackbird/grackle flock in the backyard this morning. Greg calls: he's got them, too.

2005: The space between seasons in early March sometimes allows me a certain disconnection, a feeling similar to what I experience when I am completely free of obligations, or when everything is suddenly beyond my control.

The fact that the advance of external spring is outside of my power gives me an excuse to imagine that I do not have influence in matters of internal spring. Allowing myself to be caught at the crossroads of interseasonal ambivalence, I willingly give up my autonomy for a neutral sanctuary.

My anticipation about the approach of equinox and regret at the end of my winter hibernation clash like the frontal dichotomies of late winter weather, and a resultant stalemate spins me into a temporal and spatial slough, an eye of the storm.

Or it is as if the end of the road were still a ways off, as though I were safely between home and my destination, as though there were still plenty of time, as though the moment of truth had been delayed indefinitely.

My clear January orientation has been shunted away by the split personality of the current landscape, its signals and signs mixed, pointing one way and then another. Caught between the first warm snowdrops and the daffodil snows, I lose control over which way I am going, and I take on the ambivalence of nature, pretending to imitate it, riding that excuse at this peak of freedom in which the past hides and the future is unimagined, in which I, for a moment, live suspended above concern and judgment.

2007: Cardinal sang at 6:32 a.m., a screech owl calling in the backyard then. In the front garden, snow crocus foliage has pushed up overnight, two plants budded. Yesterday, I found two golden buds by the fishpond. I haven't noticed aconites in the alley yet. This year is so far behind 2006.

2008: At 6:31, a cardinal sang in the backyard, no matter the foot of snow and temperature in the teens. The sun is in and out today. The thaw is underway. Few birds at the feeders. This evening as I walked Bella after supper, just before sundown, I heard doves calling steadily, a spring and summer sundown sound.

2009: Catalina State Park near Tucson, Arizona north to Flagstaff and then east to Holbrook, Arizona: One pale yellow four-petaled primrose had blossomed in the rain over night at the Catalina campground. All along the highway north of Tucson, past Picacho, tufts of large yellow roadside flowers, clumps about a foot or two tall, centers darker than the petals, leaves seeming pale and large, some orange globe mallow as well. In Phoenix, lush flowering of roadside bushes, almost tropical. Then north up beyond 3,000 feet, a whole different world, snow in drifts along the road, hard wind from the northwest, no green vegetation.

2010: At 6:15 this morning, the robin chorus was already underway, the crescent moon rising, temperature just below freezing. (This is the earliest I've heard robin chorus this year.) At daybreak, grackles were clucking in the walnut trees, the sky streaked pink and blue and gold, cardinals and doves singing. Walking downtown, Jeanie and I saw crocus ready to open and the bright globes of new aconites. In the alley, grackles in the high maples. A little before 9:00, four turkey vultures circled the yard then moved west.

By the middle of the morning, the first yellow snow crocus opened in the east garden. At noon, Greg called with the news he had seen the first groundhog of the year behind his house. He had seen the first chipmunk out and around the snow two days ago. Then Judy wrote from Goshen, 200 miles northwest of here: "The first redwing blackbird song of the season! Heard this morning about 9:00 a.m. on Angel's walk."

And Casey called about 3:00 to say he was watching about three dozen vultures, some black vultures, some turkey vultures circling along Corey Street, the first mixed flock he had seen. Working in the garden later in the afternoon, I saw that the rhubarb had pushed through the mulch just a little and the peony stalks were barely visible in the places the snow had gone. By the end of the day, snowdrops were in full bloom, the last ground snow in full retreat, rain moving in.

2012: Maples flowering, daffodils now common about town, a large patch in the Phillips Street alley, mid-season crocus time winding down. The robins were awake and calling when I went out at 6:05 this morning - the earliest I've heard them. Grackles and starlings have dominated the bird feeders so far this month, sharing with sparrows, chickadees, cardinals and the red-bellied woodpecker. And grackles have been flocking around the neighborhood when I walk Bella after breakfast. When we came back from our walk, a Cooper's hawk flew south from our peach tree.

2013: Frost on the cars this morning. At 6:00 and 6:15, no bird sound. I went out again at 6:30, and the air was full of crows and cardinals, a few robins whinnying. When I came back from Cincinnati this afternoon, four light violet snow crocus plants were in bloom. Against the south wall in the backyard, twelve violet crocuses. In the pond, algae is taking over, the koi nestled in its soft green folds

2014: First cardinal at 6:14 this morning, more joining in at 6:20. No robins until they started cheeping at 6:33, no chorus yet.

2015: Cardinals at 6:16 this morning along Stafford Street, doves at 6:23. No robins heard. No grackles heard or seen so far this year. Temperature of 32 degrees, sky clear, frost on the car windows, moon fat gibbous in the high southwest. Snow still inhibits all the bulbs (even most of their foliage) except the snowdrops. I ate the last of the greenhouse tomatoes with salad today.

2016: Rochester, New York: Silver maples just starting to blossom here – in 70-degree weather. From Yellow Springs, Katie Egert sent a photo of a white hepatica. She says it's the earliest she's ever found one, and her records go back to 1981. In my daybook, I have the first open on February 15, 1999; March 6 in 1983; March 8 in 2000. Katie's has to be right up there with the earliest. Based on what I found when I returned to Yellow Springs on March 11, the first daffodil opened at Peggy's house and here near the peach tree on March 9.

2017: Another violet cress plant and a scrawny white hepatica in bloom along the Rim Trail in Bryan Park. I saw one star magnolia half open on the way to the mall.

2018: A blustery day barely reach 40 degrees, but now two daffodils are open by the peach tree, and two more are trying to come out. Pussy willows all open, snowdrop blossoms beginning to thin.

2019: Rain all afternoon and evening. Cardinals at 6:22, doves at 6:32 this morning. From Hamtramck, Michigan, Kristin Rose reports that she has been hearing robin morning songs for about a week. And grackles are there but no red-wings.

2020: Robins were chirping at 6:00 this morning, singsonging by 6:15, cardinal calls by then. Several dozen geese at the college pond at the west end of town, nesting there, I am guessing. Today John Blakelock wrote to say that his cattails have begun to break apart. "Mine started unwinding, and spilling their fluff to the breezes, on Monday, the 2nd of March. This can't be biological, because all the tissue is brown, and dead. It must be mechanical." Leslie reports the first goldfinch with patches of gold.

2021: The first morning above 35 degrees, and the robin chorus began for the year, the singsonging calls underway at 6:15, competing with strong cardinal songs and doves, too. Geese and a black-capped chickadee by 6:30. From Madison, Wisconsin, Maggie sends photos of the first snowdrops and aconites blooming there. This afternoon at home, only paired geese in the pond area.

2022: Emily reports the first phoebes at Agraria, a farm right outside of town. Walking at the Glass Farm wetland, Jill and I watched and listened to many red-winged blackbirds singing as the flew back and forth. In the north garden, two daffodils showed yellow buds.

In early March, after a good rain, and then the sun came out, and you'd go out the next morning, and you could find mushrooms. We'd roll them in flour and fry them in butter.

Mrs. Lena Shaw, on mushroom hunting about 1916

March 10th
The 69th Day of the Year

Daffodils are up, my God! What beauty
concerted down on us last night. And if
I sleep again, I'll wake to a louder
blossoming, the symphony smashing down
hothouse walls, and into the world: music.
Something like the birds' return, each morning's
crescendo rising toward its brightest pitch,
colors unfurling, petals alluring.
The song, the color, the rising ecstasy
of spring. My God. This beauty. This, this
is what I've hoped for. All my life is here
in the unnamed core — dogwood, daffodil,
tulip poplar, crab apple, crepe myrtle —
only now, in spring, can the place be named.

Camille T. Dungy

From the poem "What To Eat, And What To Drink, And What To Leave for Poison"

Sunrise/set: 6:55/6:36
Day's Length: 11 hours 41 minutes
Average High/Low: 46/28
Average Temperature: 37
Record High: 75 – 1973
Record Low: 10 – 1884

Weather
Skies are clear to partly cloudy 65 percent of the time on this date, but a thunderstorm or snow-shower occurs 50 percent of the years. Today's temperature distribution: like the 9th, the 10th brings very little hope of 70s, but highs in the 60s come 25 percent of the afternoons; 50s occur 20 percent of the time; 40s come 25 percent, and 30s thirty percent. Frost strikes three nights in four.

Natural Calendar

Purple martins migrate to the Lower Midwest. Peregrine falcons lay their eggs. Bald eagle chicks hatch. Lawn growth is usually perceptible now three weeks before grass is ready to cut. This is an early date for cherry trees to be in bloom in Washington D.C., and the average date for flower and garden shows throughout the East.

Daybook

1986: Sudden burst of sparrow chatter wakes me up at 6:49 a.m. In the yard, fresh dock leaves two inches long and Japanese honeysuckles one inch. Rhubarb is up about three inches, bright red and green. After two warm days, pussy willows are breaking out all at once.

1991: Snow this morning on the wide-open crocus, snowdrops and aconite.

1993: Continued gray and in the 30s and 40s, but the bulbs keep on pushing out, the daffodils extending an inch or so this week, snowdrops hanging with their buds to the earth, ready to open when the temperatures warm, hyacinths inching up, snow crocus budded and waiting.

1995: First meadowlark of the year seen as I was coming home from work this afternoon along Wilberforce-Clifton Road.

1998: Baby camel cricket on the bathroom floor this morning.

2003: Spring road kills: One groundhog yesterday, one raccoon (the first of the year so far) this morning. The cold remains intense.

2004: The first purple deadnettle flowered this afternoon, but most of the purple deadnettle plants are still stunted by cold, with only small, tight buds.

2006: A thin robin chorus this morning at 6:30 (only faint twittering at 6:25). The aconites in the alley have passed their best; they look damaged from frost, but the mornings have been relatively mild. Starlings no longer seen in flocks – grackles in pairs have replaced them. Growth is accelerating around the yard, pussy willows becoming more prominent. Mike reported: "The redwings finally showed up a week ago on Tuesday (February 28th). I heard a killdeer for the first time Sunday (March 6), and I believe the mockingbirds might be back. Bluebirds were singing today." In the woods, the first leaves of a few honeysuckle buds have started to unravel.

2008: The air is soft this morning, the snow melting, birds singing. Juncos still seen in the alley.

2009: Holbrook, Arizona to Gallup, New Mexico, the sky perfect blue against the reds and blues and grays of the exotic Painted Desert landscape. Some trees just starting. Saltbush identified at the Petrified Forest National Park, its leaves soft, evergreen.

2010: The robins were singing near 6:25 – along with doves and cardinals. On my walk at 9:00, grackles, robins, cardinals were loud. Behind Mrs. Timberlake's house, the yard was yellow with aconites. More snow crocus bloomed today in the east garden, yellows and purples. Almost all the pussy willow catkins have emerged now. Waverly writes: "It's so good to hear spring has arrived in Ohio. It's been early all year here in Seattle. The cherry blossoms which started falling at the end of April last year and are already falling this year."

2011: This morning, Jeanie and I, along with our border collie, Bella, set out in the rain to look for Middle Spring. We left behind the first weeks of Early Spring, the full blooming yellow aconites, the white snowdrops, the gold and purple snow crocus, the pussy willows that were almost all the way out, the budded daffodils, the raucous morning birdsong, and went south down the corridor highway of I-75 through Kentucky to Knoxville, Tennessee, east on I-40 to Ashville and then down to the low country of South Carolina, then further south to Jekyll Island off the coast of Georgia.

    Like we always do, we looked for signs of spring all the way. Our practice is a kind of elementary botanizing which finds landmarks, glimpses that suggest larger vistas, signs that reveal the deeper transformations underway. It is a kind of plant identification that leaves most of its significance to the imagination. We were off to imagine spring as much as see it, to fill in the blank spaces around us with what we knew or remembered from other times and places.

The first hours of the trip were gray and slow, traffic and wind and rain slowing us sometimes to a crawl. The land around us was brown and gray, only recently emerged from winter. The first sign of a change of season was a brightening of the roadside grass and fields through the rain near Lexington, a hundred miles or so south of the Ohio River.

That sign seemed to open the window to Middle Spring. An hour later, we saw a willow trees glowing pale yellow green. In another hour, bright yellow forsythia bushes. A half an hour later, daffodils in flower on a hillside. Hills turned to mountains as we approached Tennessee. The tree line became flushed with buds and early flowers.

By the Knoxville valley, five hours south of the Ohio River, plum trees and pear trees were in bloom, their white flowers marking southern Ohio April, and Minnesota May. More signs at a rest stop buttercup leaves, the first dandelion, curly dock six inches long.

Then as we headed up toward Asheville and the Carolina continental divide, snow still visible on some of the mountains, we drove by great patches of daffodils and cascades of rainwater from the all-day spring rain. We camped in the mountains, still in the rain. And in the morning fog and mist, we made the descent into the south and the coastal plain. At one rest stop: ground ivy, black medic and countless dandelions, lanky wild onions. An azalea was budded.

Then at Columbia, pear and plum trees were leafing, pushing aside their April flowers, redbuds were blossoming, and yellow Jessamine hung from the fencerows. And the tree line was red and orange and yellow and glowing pale green, the spring flush overtaking us the closer we drove toward the sea. When we turned south on I-95, red clovers early, the giant yellow thistles with heads as big as my fist. Red-flowered "cross vine" seen open on several trees.

On Jekyll Island, sea rockets open on the beach, yellow sorrel, sow thistle, purple sorrel, violets and pale "Innocence" bluets, toadflax, wild grape, spiderwort, sprawling wild blackberries flowering beside the inland waterway, pear trees all leafed out here, redbuds getting old, dogwoods and wisteria coming in. New bamboo sprouts just emerging. Blackbirds mating, darners mating, cedar waxwings and kinglets migrating, black skimmers, willets and sanderlings feeding in the surf, webworms hatching, sulphur butterflies looking for flowers.

2012: At 6:10 this morning, full moon setting in the southwest, air chilly, I went inside after waiting for the robins to sing: no birds at that time. I went out five minutes later: the full robin chorus. First honeysuckle leaves reported in the area. Throughout the garden, daylily foliage is two to five inches tall, the foliage forming low drifts, coloring the ground with green.

2013: Waiting again this year for robins, I heard them clearly at 6:17, cardinals at 6:25, sparrows at 6:30, crows at 6:35. The full morning chorus is underway on schedule. Snowdrops all nodding and most of them open, seventeen violet snow crocus in bloom in the east garden, along the very first yellow crocus. In the backyard, around a dozen violet crocuses and one precocious blue squill all by itself. Quite a few grackles all around the house today, and the silver maple at Ellis Pond was just starting to flower.

2014: Chris sent a photo of Rosemary's aconites in bloom. Our snowdrops are opening, and three pale violet snow crocuses blossomed along the south wall, the crocus planted so many years ago before the bamboo took over that part of the garden. When I saw Vic at the store, he told me he had a squill in bloom.

2015: Mild in the 40s this morning, snow continuing to melt, light rain: the cardinals slept late to 6:35; the crows and doves held off until almost 7:00. Snowdrops wait, buds tight and straight up. Scott reports red-winged blackbirds arrived at the Glass Farm today. He said a huge flock of blackbirds passed over and the redwings "just dropped down out of the flock." He added that spiders had started to make webs and beavers were starting to work on the trees.

2016: The news reports that this past winter (2015-2016) was the warmest – worldwide – in recorded history, 4.6 degrees above 20th century levels.

2017: A deep cold wave settles in across the region, lows in the teens expected for several days, most likely freezing the daffodils and maybe even the forsythia.

2018: Frost this morning and sun with 40s through the day. At St. Clare, the *Cornus mas* was in early bloom, the honeysuckle undergrowth showing a little green. On the drive home, I noticed several weeping willow trees with yellow-green auras. In the southwest garden, lungwort is budding. Jill's lilac buds were opening just a little.

2019: Jeff called to say he was finding plenty of earthworms near his compost pile and around the edges of his lawn – no reason to worry, he reassured me, about a *Lumbricus* Armageddon just yet.

From Talus Drive, Leslie and Bruce continue to watch Yellow Springs born again from signs of March's second week: more large flocks of grackles and red-winged blackbirds; more pairing and cooing of mourning doves; more pairing and calling of tufted titmice; sightings of song sparrows in pairs, white-throated sparrows in pairs, male and female downy woodpeckers together; the sudden early departure of pine siskins and red-breasted nuthatches; squirrels chasing each other more frequently and with greater acrobatics.

2020: The first blue petals of the first squill seen by the shed.

2021: Jeff mentioned that he had seen a bald eagle in Xenia yesterday, and that a friend had seen one near Fairborn a week ago.

2022: Ditch lily foliage pushed up in the night. The first tulips planted last fall have appeared in the sunniest corners of the north garden. In the circle garden, hyacinth and tulip foliage bristles in clumps an inch to four inches high.

A redwing singing almost furiously from a marshy site, meadowlarks calling from swamp grass, the orange sunlit swamp grass around the edge of a small pond. A toad or two send up their trill – water bugs are out -- a cold wind blows out of the North....

Charles Burchfield, *Journal*

March 11th
The 70th Day of the Year

In gardens you may note amid the dearth
The crocus breaking earth;
And near the snowdrop's tender white and green,
The violet in its screen.

Henry Timrod

Sunrise/set: 6:54/6:37
Day's Length: 11 hours 43 minutes
Average High/Low: 46/29
Average Temperature: 37
Record High: 76 – 1990
Record Low: 5 – 1948

Weather

Chances of precipitation are 30 percent, and the sun shines a little more than 50 percent of the time. As for temperatures, today and the following seven days all offer a five to ten percent chance of summer-like 70s. Highs in the 60s occur 15 percent of the afternoons, 50s come another 15 percent, 40s twenty percent of the time, 30s thirty-five percent, and 20s ten to 15 percent of the time.

Natural Calendar

Bittercress and dandelions, some of the first wildflowers of the year, are often open by today. Gardeners often set out flats of pansies on milder days to harden them for late March planting. Onions seeds and sets, potatoes, radishes, beets, carrots, and turnips can be sown directly in the ground as soon as the soil is ready. Parsnip, horseradish, dock, and dandelion root are dug at this time, when foliage just begins to emerge; root quality is usually at its best before the soil begins to warm, and leaves are more tender for salads.

Daybook

1986: Cardinal heard at 6:39 a.m. At the Cascades, buds found on violet cress. Daylilies two to four inches high along the hillside at Wilberforce.

1987: Autumn's small-flowered asters growing back. Cardinals sing at 6:36 a.m.

1989: Flies are common now. An Eastern box elder bug, which had overwintered in the woodpile, crawled out this afternoon when I was sorting logs. Aconites and blue eyes bloomed in the sun and 70 degree temperatures. Snowdrops and crocus were open downtown.

1990: Return from Toronto. There the snows have just melted. Water is standing in the fields, ice underneath in places. Ponds still frozen. All the roadside and field grass is brown, mottled with patches of old snow. Near Toledo, a slight greening. By Lima, it's more noticeable, and winter wheat has some color. Then home to spring. Bleeding hearts are up, thyme is showing, and waterleaf and bluebells have emerged. The crocus is open, wild rose and raspberry buds opening, grass growing, sweet rockets lush, more rhubarb, tulips all up, quince buds are red, leaves of the common violet emerging, first columbine pushing through, Japanese honeysuckle leafing – all from the warm January and February, and today a record high at 76.

1993: Snow and 36 degrees, but between dawn and this afternoon, four more golden crocus buds pushed out in the east garden.

1994: To Jacoby with Buttercup, the family bulldog, approaching the swamp from the river's side, the ground still snow covered and firm in places, I was able to come right up to the skunk cabbage. It seems to be in full bloom, colonies bold and spreading now, no longer tentative and thin like they were in February. The sky perfect blue, the brooks full and sparkling in the valley towards High Prairie. Pussy willow hulls on the snow this morning, spring falling on top of the winter.

1995: Robins common now, whinnying throughout the village. Cardinals and doves calling, too. A few of the new spring iris, planted last fall under the cherry tree, bloomed for the first time this morning, three golden, two purple. In the east garden, the snow crocus are in full bloom, probably a hundred in the six by six space: yellow, violet, purple, white, gold. Bees all over them.

1996: Casey called today: he saw buzzards this evening flying so low, he said, he could see their feathers, see them cock their heads to look down. That sighting makes the earliest the turkey vultures have returned to Yellow Springs - and in the middle of a tremendous high pressure system: did they ride it into town?

2000: Crows at 6:32 a.m.

2003: One buzzard seen on the way back from Washington Court House. Casey told Jeanie he saw five. In the backyard, six golden snow crocus flowers opened this afternoon in the south garden. One purple snow crocus budding. Crocus foliage has pushed out in the east garden. Another raccoon noticed by the side of the road. Red-winged blackbirds sitting on the wire fences today.

2004: On the way home from Washington Court House, I had to slow down in order to allow a turkey vulture to fly off the highway away from its lunch, a young raccoon that had been killed overnight.

2006: In Cincinnati, purple deadnettle and cress open, many honeysuckles in the first stage of leafing. At home, the first mosquito was flying inside the car as Jeanie and I drove to Dayton (mosquitoes appearing on schedule with the turkey vultures).

2007: Covington, Kentucky: High in the 60s, banks of snowdrops in full bloom, daffodils budded.

2009: Gallup, New Mexico to Tucumcari, New Mexico along I-40: Many cottonwood trees budded in eastern New Mexico. At the edges of the campground in Tucumcari, the violet five-petaled (pointed petals) flower that I saw also at Catalina State Park in

Arizona; I also found the tansy-leafed mustard. In Santa Rosa, a cherry tree was blooming.

2010: A mild 50 at daybreak, clouds, robinsong at 6:10. Grackles all over throughout the morning. We cleaned out the east garden today, transplanted some stonecrop (about an inch tall), cut away the old stalks and vines. The grape hyacinth stalks are gradually losing their flush, turning greener. From Goshen, Judy writes: "Heron has started his early morning trips upriver to fish."

2012: The robin chorus began at 5:53 this morning, the earliest and loudest ever, making it almost impossible to distinguish cardinal calls until later. Today: the first in a projected week-long mild spell in the 60s, daffodils early bloom, mid-season crocus late bloom, snowdrops holding but flower petals becoming more translucent in the morning - by midday suddenly wilting, their season finished. Inventory this afternoon: butterfly bushes with plenty of new leaves; peony stems three inches and starting to unravel; ramps three inches; bluebells out of the ground in just the last day or two; one red primrose fully open, yellow ones starting; waterleaf one to two inches; first grape hyacinth and puschkinia in bloom; first honeysuckle leaves emerged in the north hedge; pussy willow completely out and fat, ready for pollen to form. Peach buds just starting to show color; viburnum buds cracked. Tat reports that red-winged blackbirds arrived in Madison, Wisconsin last week, maybe around the 6th. She has one crocus budding there. The first mosquito got in the house when Jeanie and I came in from the yard this evening.

2013: Grackles all about the neighborhood this morning, aconite flowers on Stafford Street all pale and weathered from the snow and cold. More golden crocus buds, but no flowers today in the heavy rain. This evening, cardinals sang, grackles continuing to fly back and forth among the trees.

2014: Cardinals began singing at 6:09 this morning, sang steadily throughout my half-hour walk with Bella. Robins started chirping at 6:15, but I didn't hear their constant singsong until 6:22, and then it faded after a few minutes. A screech owl heard at the south end of Stafford Street. Now eight violet snow crocuses are blooming along the south wall. Tulips and daylilies are up around the yard about two inches.

2015: Heavy fog this morning, 40s, after so much rain. Almost all the snow is gone. Cardinal call notes in the honeysuckles at 6:18, first mating call at 6:28, the fog darkening the advent of the cardinal's day. No crows heard, but the first song-sparrow song of the year came at 6:55. Still no grackles, no robins heard, but one lone robin later in the yard.. The temperature rose to the 60s. In the east garden, snowdrops surged up, along with the previously hidden spears of crocus and daffodils. In the afternoon, a clump of more than a dozen pale snow crocuses burst into bloom, the first flowers of the year.

2016: Returning from Rochester, New York to Yellow Springs: Gray-brown landscape throughout western New York, but several large flocks of geese seen flying quite high. Driving into Ohio, we found suddenly (it seemed) that we entered a zone of greening: pastures and winter wheat, especially about a hundred miles north of Columbus. One golf course was bright green, one field of wheat maybe three or four inches tall.

At home, a marked change since I left on March 5. After a week of weather in the 60s and 70s, snowdrops and snow crocus were done for the year (snowdrop flowers no longer fresh and firm, were ragged and torn); the pussy willows along the street had all come out; mid-season crocus were in full bloom; the small jonquils and five standard daffodils were open (and two at Peggy's); a handful of blue squills had bloomed; a few lungwort plants had pink flowers; the Lenten roses had burst into bloom – the white and the violet; henbit, bittercress and chickweed were blooming; my aconites – always late – had come up and opened; a few of Jeanie's periwinkles (that she planted against the odds of the clay soil thirty years ago) were showing through the tangle of the dooryard garden. Peony stalks were about six inches high, and the first snow-on-the-mountain was pacing the waterleaf. This evening, John Whitmore called to report he had seen a woodcock courting by the Pine Forest near his house.

2017: On a drive to Cincinnati: star magnolias, plums and probably pear trees in full bloom will be hurt by tonight's low in the teens.

2018: From Billings, Missouri, Jeffery Goss reports the first tick.

2019: Clear morning sky, light spreading with shades of gold and red, light frost, no wind. Doves were the earliest birds at 6:15, then cardinals at 6:20, and then, finally, a patch of robins chanting along Phillips Street about 6:25, and a song sparrow over by the school park. No crows by the time I went inside at 6:35. Emily reports that Violet saw the first chipmunk and the first red velvet mite (*Trombidiidae*).

2021: The first soft spring rain after a night of gusty winds, highs in the 60s. At the pond, all the geese seem to be gone or paired.

2022: Mild and sunny this morning, turning to snow and sleet this evening. Before the weather shifted, grackles were flocking and courting at the back feeders, strutting and fluffing.

2023: Daffodil count: 100. At the St. Clare monastery, *Cornus mas* is in full bloom, a hint of honeysuckle green in the undergrowth, and pear trees are in full bloom, many pink magnolias open between Dayton and Cincinnati.

Before a tip of green showed in any brushy place you could feel spring growing through the sky. The robins came early, cocking heads in the cold. The gray bodies of the goldfinches yellowed, for all the world like pussy buds blooming. And where no other sign held on wood or field, finger twigs of elder and willow and service swelled beneath their hull of bark.

James Still

March 12th
The 71st Day of the Year

*At dawn the chorus begins. I awake early, and from my bed listen
to the announcement of spring, and count the number of bird songs
I can hear.*
Eliot Porter

Day's Length: 11 hours 47 minutes
Sunrise/set: 6:52/6:39
Average High/Low: 47/29
Average Temperature: 37
Record High: 68 – 1929
Record Low: - 1 – 1948

Weather
Chances of a day in the 70s are five percent, of 60s five
percent, of 50s fifteen percent, of 40s forty percent, of 30s thirty
percent, of 20s five percent. Rain or snow comes a little better than
35 percent of the time, and the sun appears one day out of two.
Freezing temperatures occur this morning 65 percent of the time.

Natural Calendar
When one thing happens, then something else is
happening, too. That is the simplest rule of phenology. Deep in
Early Spring, the most dramatic one event is the start of the robins'
mating chorus in the early morning dark.

When the robin chorus begins before sunrise, then pollen
forms on pussy willow catkins, and the first mosquito bites. The
first spring beauty is budding, and the foliage of yarrow, mallow,
phlox, columbine, coneflower, waterleaf, goldenrod, buttercup,
snow-on-the mountain, New England aster and Queen Anne's lace
is coming up.

Robins have found their way to every yard, knowing that
worms will be waiting for them, at the same time that the tufted
titmouse courts in spirals, when flickers and purple martins are
migrating and willow trees glow yellow green and mock orange
leafs out, pacing the new privet foliage, the lilac, black raspberry,
multiflora rose, clematis and coralberry foliage.

When robins sing before dawn, the first violet lungwort flowers open and bleeding hearts get bushy. The early leaves of honeysuckle bushes green the countryside, and the tree line is tinged with red and orange from flowering maples. In the garden, pale snow-on-the-mountain parallels the waterleaf in wetlands to the mating songs of red-winged blackbirds in the swamps and the gobbles of turkeys in the deep woods.

Daybook

1983: The red quince at the northeast corner of the yard is budding. Lilac bushes, raspberries, peach tree leafing. Sparrows mating under the eaves.

1986: Cardinal heard at 6:36 a.m. A few bluebells up about an inch at the Covered Bridge. First rose leaves seen. Bobwhites calling, red-winged blackbirds whistling. New sprouts on the woodland ground. Variety of foliage increasing.

1988: Tulips six inches, poppy foliage four to five inches. Several buds on six-inch daffodils. New garlic mustard leaves are strong.

1990: A handful of daffodils has opened in Clifton. One box elder is flowering. First pussy willows have pollen. Flowering crab apples starting to leaf. First wasp seen. Hepatica is open along the Cascades walk. One white, star magnolia flower unraveling at Wilberforce. Blooming purple deadnettle is common now. Garlic mustard sprouts are up. Columbine is out. Peonies are four inches tall. Rhubarb: some stalks over my shoes. Bradford pears are budding downtown. Worms came out last night in the warm rain, were stranded at dawn in the sun. Mosquitoes out last night and today. Ants at work around their fresh mounds. Squirrels in the woods this afternoon were slow, seemed drugged with spring. Three deer stood unafraid watching me in the Cascades parking lot.

1991: The Early Spring flower season is still in full bloom, including red maples and pussy willows, blue eyes and shepherds purse. Some tulips up almost half a foot now.

1992: A flock of robins arrived in the ginkgo by my window in 20-degree cold.

1995: First carpenter bee zooms by me at the north garden wall.

1996: First silver maples in bloom at the triangle park in spite of the cold.

1998: Juncos at the feeder. In North Carolina, strawberries and peaches full bloom killed by deep cold. Crops lost throughout the South.

2003: Purple snow crocus coming out now this afternoon. Pussy willows all have emerged. Zelda and Emmett, the pond's two koi, have started to feed. All that after only a couple thaw days. At the Covered Bridge, one fly and two black wolf spiders. Beavers had been stripping bark not far from the skunk cabbage swamp.

2004: At 6:10 this morning, I didn't hear the robins, but cardinals and doves were calling in the yard when I went outside at 6:25. In South Glen, Mike and I saw four nuthatches probably involved in some kind of courtship rituals. The towhees were in their usual place, male and female markings clearly visible.

2006: After two days of hard rain and highs around 60 degrees, the koi in the pond began to feed. The first miniature jonquil opened. The first forsythia has come undone. Snow crocus and snowdrops are in full bloom. Blue eyes (*Veronica*) , purple deadnettle and small flowered cress are blossoming.

2007: Pale violet snow crocus are in full bloom in the front and backyards now, having started to come in on March 9th. Snowdrops are opening – maybe a third of them are completely out. Grape hyacinths pace the daffodils at about three inches. In the alley and across the street at the Danielson's yard, a large patch of aconites is in full flower. Robins, doves and cardinals singing when I went out at 7:45 to go to work in Wilmington (the first time I have heard morning robins this year). Driving south, I saw that the farm ponds were finally thawing, but ice still remained on parts of them.

2008: The blizzard arrived on the 7th, and the weather was cold for three days. Now, the purple and gold crocus are in full bloom by the back pond, completely unhurt by the weather of the past days. As I looked for the koi fingerlings (which did not appear), I saw a honeybee near the crocus at the edge of the pond. In the front garden, snowdrops are opening. Jeanie says that Chris has seen towhees this month. And Casey called this afternoon about 5:15. First he saw four buzzards sitting in their roost on President Street. Then about 5:30, he called again to say the buzzards were arriving as he spoke, that he had counted 18 already, and that they were sailing in from the east on "some thermal," hardly moving their wings at all.

2009: Tucumcari, New Mexico to Oklahoma City: We drove about 400 miles, leaving the high desert behind. About an inch of snow had fallen overnight, and this was the first time either of us had seen the desert other than beige and dry. Trees were greening in the Texas panhandle, maybe cottonwood seed clusters. At a rest stop, flaxweed or tansy mustard (*Descorainia)* was flowering; a dandelion had been blooming, and ground ivy. Into Oklahoma, redbuds and pear trees were open across the land.

2010: Continued mild, with lows only in the upper 40s, a high of 64 this afternoon (just a few degrees from the record). Mid-season crocus bloomed overnight, and the aconites at the Danielsons' (Katie's) yard are wide open. The grackles and cardinals are loud all around the neighborhood. Now the wild deadnettle is budding and the last traces of snow have disappeared at home. The tall ragwort is becoming bushy. The rhubarb pushes up a little more. The red peony shoots have grown a full inch. The golden crocuses have joined the purple crocus underneath the bamboo in the south garden. When I was splitting wood this afternoon, several black house flies were sitting on the logs, newly hatched – the first insects seen this year. When I walked over to the pond in order to remove the heater, a frog jumped into the water, the first seen so far this year.

2011: Riding the new spring, I feel nostalgia through daffodils and crocuses. In between the flowers, nostalgia is an ether that carries mood and meaning, an interstitial habitat that grows and dies, its apparent forward motion deceptive because it brings back the past with each pace toward summer.

Nostalgia lies between the details, between the items of the litany of events, loading each event, referring each marker to somewhere else, making zeitgebers of blossoms attached to things that might have been and to things that were.

My nostalgia confuses the individual particles of the spring, blurring their edges until they become subtle fog in the morning. Memories rise and fall, and nostalgia thins and filters them, allowing them in and out of the porous self, rushing in with tides of storms of crises and then ebbing away, the pendulum always evocative, a recollective presence like the residue of a dream, plot or actors forgotten.

2012: Rain and mild this morning. The robins were about 20 minutes later than yesterday, maybe put off by the showers. Euonymus vines are getting new growth now, beginning their new yearlong cycle. On my evening walk with Bella, the robins still sang.

2013: A cardinal heard at 6:25 this morning, but I missed the robins. Grackles still flying about the neighborhood in groups of fewer than a dozen.

2014: A note from Brad Roof: "I was digging in some dirt (mud) yesterday and managed to turn up a couple salamanders who were pretty frisky. I still have frozen ground six inches down! People other than nature people don't appreciate the invisible things going on. A week ago my dogs killed their first chipmunk of the year, so the chipmunks are out of hibernation, too."

2015: Frost, clear: At 6:17 this morning I heard a lone robin singsong call. Another followed, along with the start of cardinal mating songs, five minutes later. The aconites of Stafford Street are full of bright yellow buds, ready to open in the afternoon sun. Two of Liz's snowdrops have opened all the way, quite a bit ahead of mine.

2016: At 5:53 this morning, no robins. At 5:57, whinnies all around, and the chorus down the street. At the Monastery of St. Clair in Cincinnati, a good number of daffodils were in bloom, several days ahead of Yellow Springs, for sure; spring beauties blossomed in the lawn, and *Cornus mas* was bright yellow in full flower. I noticed resurrection lilies in the east and south gardens at home, not quite as tall as the daffodils.

2017: Yesterday's visit to St. Clare monastery: Daffodils and *Cornus mas* like last year, in spite of the varied weather. And today at the Covered Bridge, a high only of 33: two buttercup blossoms in the bottomland.

2019: To Columbus, cool and sunny: We saw the first pale green blush on a winter wheat field. At home, the grass around Ellis Pond was blushing, too. Leslie reports full robin chorus on Talus Drive and the first silver maples "full-flowering, with long ivory stamens protruding upward in graceful fluffy balls."

2020: Snowdrops and snow crocuses are at their peak, and mid-season crocuses are starting to flower by the back porch. The spread of algae is getting out of hand in the koi pond, the mild days and increased sun breaking the winter stability and water clarity.

2021: Exactly like last year on this day, snowdrops, snow crocuses, aconites full, and the dark purple mid-season crocuses are opening near the back porch. The pond, however, is still clear. Grackles haunt the honeysuckles around the birdfeeders; only the sparrows don't seem to care, the cardinals holding back. A pair of geese flew over, honking, around 7:00 a.m. In the countryside, a faint gray-green mood to the winter wheat. Jill's tulips have grown an inch just in a day or so, are three inches tall now. A mosquito attacked me in the greenhouse this afternoon.

2022: One of the rare days in the 20s, sun, wind, birds all over.

2023: Half an inch of snow this morning, one hundred daffodils drooping, paled by the snow.

The world we inhabit is not...a determinable set of objective processes. It is our larger flesh, a densely intertwined and improvisational tissue of experience. It is a sensitive sphere suspended in the solar wind, a round field of sentience sustained by the relationships between the myriad lives and the sensibilities that compose it

David Abram

March 13th
The 72nd Day of the Year

As if to yield ends one's life?
As if one is forever encased,
ice settled upon one's branches,
a rigid coating sealing all pores,
blocking all doors.

Are the trees afraid when spring startles?
They can't imagine leafing,
sunk in the comfort winter finally granted,
frost-clothed.

One has to fool them forward
Lure by light filtered oddly
and disguised in cold winds,
But then, don't even the trees
surrender?

Barbara Valdez

Sunrise/set: 6:50/6:40
Day's Length: 11 hours 50 minutes
Average High/Low: 47/29
Average Temperature: 38
Record High: 74 – 1925 and 2012
Record Low: 5 – 1960

Weather

March 13th is another pivot day in the progress of spring. Today, the chances of highs above 50 climb to 45 percent and they remain near that level until March 22nd, when they rise even higher. Seventies come five percent of the time, highs in the 60s fifteen percent, and 50s twenty-five percent. Cold weather still happens, of course: highs in the 40s come 25 percent of the afternoons, 30s another 25 percent, and 20s five percent. Rain falls 30 percent of the days, snow 15 percent.

Natural Calendar

A few days ago, not a bird, not a sound; everything rigid and severe; then in a day the barriers of winter give way, and spring comes like an inundation. In a twinkling all is changed.

John Burroughs

When I took inventory this past week, I saw everything had changed since my last accounting at the end of February:

Robins began their predawn chorus just after 6:00 a.m. Cardinals, doves, song sparrows, and chickadees joined them by 6:15, grackles, blue jays and house sparrows a little later. Honeybees, bumble bees and carpenter bees were looking for nectar. A snake was sunning. A mosquito followed me from the shade of evergreens.

Snow crocus and and aconites and hellebores and snowdrops were in full bloom. A whole row of daffodils were open at the corner of High and Limestone. My own daffodils were nodding and ready to follow suit, surrounded by bright blue squills, outriders of the daffodil gold.

Small flowered bittercress and the blue-eyed veronica had first flowers. Deep purple petals of mid-season crocus were open wide. Violet cress, antecedent to hepatica, spring beauty, toothwort and twinleaf, was budded along the river.

And all about, more prophets of the year ahead. The tulips of April were eight inches high, April's bleeding hearts three inches, April's red quince buds unraveling, the foliage of April's Virginia bluebells dusky purple and four inches, April' violets three inches, April's waterleaf two inches. The peonies of May were four inches tall and starting to unravel. May's rhubarb had pushed through the mulch, May's privets and mock orange and honeysuckles leafing.

The day lilies of June were six inches, June's touch-me-not sprouts new and soft. The ramps (wild onions) of July were seven inches high. The resurrection lilies of August were pacing the day lilies at eight inches. The small white asters, the zigzag goldenrod, the tall goldenrod of September had bold basal leaves. The leaf buds of October's witch hazel were swelling in the sun

Daybook

1983: First star magnolia about to bloom on Stafford Street. Box elders are flowering.

1984: A two-week cold spell with record snows and subnormal temperatures ended today.

1986: After a warm rain, worms are all over the roads and sidewalks. First buzzard of the year circling South Glen. First groundhog of the year out eating new grass along Corry Street. Hemlocks unraveling. More bleeding hearts push up the mulch. Blackberry leaves starting. Geese and ducks all along the river. The field at the Covered Bridge was full of small black hunting spiders, newborns.

1987: Cardinal sings 6:30 a.m. Chickweed seen blooming in the sun today.

1989: Purple deadnettle blooms along the garden wall. Peonies are two inches now, pussy willows three-fourths out, daffodil buds prominent.

1990: Flicker calls at 7:30 a.m. Spring beauties seen on Corry. Red tulips are open at the library. Pussy willow pollen full. Scilla blooms at the nursery. Bluebells in the yard are budding. The grass is getting longer and greener.

1992: Flock of brown finches seen in the back trees. Titmouse seen in mating spirals. But all the daffodils which were budding and blooming, forsythia flowers, and new tulips were destroyed by the cold last night.

1993: Heavy snows covered the South and the East: the worst blizzard of the century, according to some reports. Freezing temperatures expected all the way to Miami (according to Mrs. Bletzinger's cleaning woman). In Yellow Springs, hard north winds all day and blowing snow, accumulation to a couple of inches.

1994: In the south garden, peonies still not coming out, the latest they've been since I've kept records. At the Covered Bridge with Buttercup, the bulldog: We took the high path along the old fence looking for Virginia bluebells, searched closely but found none. The very first seeds of the year had sprouted, though, probably new garlic mustard. Down along the river, one violet cress plant with tiny leaves had its first cluster of flower buds. Coming out of the woods, I looked up, and there were three buzzards flying over the Mill Dam, first buzzards of the year.

1995: First mosquito of the season at the triangle park up the block, about 5:15 p.m. Silver maples (shaggy bark maples), with their yellow green flowers, are in full bloom throughout town. Jeanie says the sap won't run so well when the flowering has begun. The buds pull the sap to them, she says. The proof: her sap jugs fill slowly despite the warm weather.

1996: Coming home from work, I saw Casey's buzzards circling the Glen. Resurrection lilies are up in the south garden, pacing the daffodils.

1998: Third night in a row of deep cold kills peppers and tomatoes in northern Florida.

2003: First thunderstorm of the year this morning, then the wind shifted to the north, blew cold all day. Snowdrops pushed up, and more snow crocuses were budding in spite of the chill. Tulips, peonies, and daffodils are now an inch tall everywhere.

2004: Faint robin calls at 6:10 this morning, the very first cardinal at 6:16.

2006: Robins in full song this morning when I went out the back door at 6:10. Inventory in the yard, temperature 65, light overcast, steady breeze, barometer dropping: snow crocus and snowdrops full, two jonquils, purple deadnettle, small flowered cress, blue eyes all blooming, first flowers on several forsythia bushes. Mid-season crocus and the small red tulips budded. Daffodils eight to ten inches and well budded, hyacinths and daylilies five inches, tulips ten inches, ramps three inches, lungwort up with one-to-two-inch leaves, waterleaf with one-inch leaves, stonecrop two inches high, Canadian thistles three inches, peonies three inches and leafing, red quince leafing and buds cracking, rhubarb and hollyhock leaves to two inches, bleeding hearts up two inches, grape hyacinth seven inches, resurrection lilies six inches. Buds cracking on the serviceberry trees, buds cracking on the lilacs, privet and mock orange bushes leafing, pussy willows coming out all the way, buds reddening on the crab apple, new garlic mustard sprouts coming on. Koi are moving and feeding in the pond, the winter starlings have paired up and left their flocks; grackles and robins are everywhere in town.

2007: Robins not singing at 5:45 this morning, but full song by 6:15. They began their major calling one to two days ago. Cardinals had joined in by 6:25. Daffodils have started to show buds. Primrose leaves have appeared, small and gnarled. Poppy leaves are several inches long. First small bee fly and first mosquito seen.

2008: Cardinals and doves singing between 6:20 and 6:25 this morning. One robin whinny about 7:00, but no chorus heard. Grackles were flying back and forth in the neighborhood when I walked Bella around 9:00. Cardinals chasing each other in the trees. The silver maple appears to be flowering in Burl's yard. Pussy willows seem to be out much further than yesterday. Finches - still not gold - feed at the sack feeders, but the other feeders – even at the bank – have no birds.

2009: Oklahoma City east to Little Rock, Arkansas: Hilly, wooded landscape, not a little like southwestern Wisconsin: We drove across greening Middle Spring in light rain, past many redbuds, crab apple and pear trees in full bloom. Two blossoming forsythia bushes seen and many other white-flowered shrubs. Daffodils were flowering along the roads, clover foliage in clumps, wild onions getting lanky, and the roadside grass was bright, the tree line flushed with a little orange and dominant patches of pale green. At the campsite in Arkansas, redbuds were open and deep violet iris flowering. The sweet gum tree at our site was in full bloom, and small white bluet-type flowers, blue bluets and spring beauties were open in the grass.

2010: Heavy rain and some flooding in the yard punctuate the two-week thaw, completely erasing the cold power of this past February.

2012: I missed the first of the robins this morning, but they were singing by 6:00, and a cardinal was calling at 6:20, and crows in the distance. The weather has been warming these past days, and the whole week ahead is expected to be in the 70s. All sorts of things will happen early now, and I am getting restless and disoriented with the speed of spring's arrival - like the robin, so preoccupied with the rituals of mating, that I almost hit on the way to Xenia this morning. This afternoon, the Covered Bridge habitat with Jeanie: the ground green with chickweed, the undergrowth of honeysuckles and wild roses showing leaves, the first purple cress, the first cowslip (almost three weeks ahead of the average), the first spring beauties, and Dutchman's britches with buds. The very first touch-me-not sprouts in the rivulet by the skunk cabbages (which were getting tall). And one bright red mite crawling along the path.

2014: The day warming into the 40s, I took inventory around the yard: Daffodils four to five inches, several with buds, fifteen violet snow crocuses along the south wall, tulips, daylilies and hyacinths at least three inches, bittercress forming small clumps, celandine fattening, squill foliage up, stonecrop and rhubarb knuckles just barely showing, primrose leaves violet against the ground (I transplanted some.), spiderwort leaves just starting, my aconites just budded, two new Lenten rose leaves. No waterleaf seen at all. The red-bellied woodpecker has been calling off and on for over a week now.

2015: Midday: Very large high "V" of what looked and flew like sandhill cranes – but sounded like Canadian geese.

2016: Light rain and very mild: The first cardinal gave one wake-up call at 5:54 a.m., and robins began to whinny just a moment later. No chorus singsong heard, perhaps dampened by the rain. Steady, intense cardinal song in the backyard by 6:20. The weather has not stopped them. Or maybe they are announcing a break in the showers: Jeanie once surprised me one day forty years ago in Knoxville, Tennessee, by announcing that when the birds sang, the rain would stop, and it happened just like she said.

2019: Afternoon sun and clouds, temperature 64 degrees. Walking near Ellis, I was surrounded by the songs of red-winged blackbirds, song sparrow, white-throated sparrows. Robins worked the cornfields. The first snow crocus, pale violet and yellow, bloomed in Jill's side yard, and near my pond and among the snowdrops in the dooryard. I keep finding patches of aconites throughout the neighborhood, coming into bloom, continuing to bloom, spreading. Leslie reported Carolina wrens and downy woodpeckers courting.

2020: When I went out at 6:15 this morning, the robins were in full chorus, and I heard doves and cardinals over the din. Sun and mild this afternoon, some honeysuckle bushes are leafing around the yard – foliage growing at about the same time as the pond fills with algae. Now the first daffodils have yellow tips, mid-season crocus coming in, and blue squills are in early full bloom, aconites and snowdrops and snow crocus holding their seasons. And I found a termite crawling around on the kitchen floor. At Ellis Pond, hemlock is forming rounded clumps. In the alley and at my feeders, many grackles. Another mosquito at my window.

2021: Two pair of geese flew over calling before dawn, an early morning phenomenon now. Grackles, robins, cardinals, chickadees in garbled conversation as the sky lightened. The Lenten roses in the dooryard garden are in full flower now.

The localization of scientific knowledge should also include spaces outside the usual sites of knowledge: the pubic square, the field, the beach, or the rectory garden.

Vladimir Jankovic

March 14th
The 73rd Day of the Year

In the gardens, purple crocuses appeared – quite suddenly – and in the hills, small shoots of green rose among deadened stalks and branches. I sensed a rising feeling, a welling up, an expansiveness that filled up the dead spaces left by winter. If the universe expanded infinitely, as some said, this spring expressed that expansion.

Stephen Altschuler

Sunrise/set: 6:49/6:41
Day's Length: 11 hours 52 minutes
Average High/Low: 48/30
Average Temperature: 38
Record High: 77 – 2012
Record Low: 5 – 1993

Weather

Today is dry 65 percent of the years, with the sun appearing two days out of three. High temperatures for today: chances of 70s are five percent, of 60s twenty percent, of 50s twenty percent, of 40s thirty-five percent, of 30s ten percent, and for 20s ten percent. Chances of frost in the garden are one out of two.

Natural Calendar

Turkey vultures appeared in the sky of northern states by this time of March during the 20th century. In the 21st century, they stay throughout the year. In average springs, the tips of resurrection lilies have risen five inches above the ground, pacing the daffodils. Maples blossom, their flowers starting to fall to the streets and sidewalks, and star magnolias bloom.

Daybook

1981: First crocus blooms in the south garden.

1982: First bee seen.

1983: The first tulip opened today. First bluebells found blooming beyond the Covered Bridge. First frog of the year seen. First flower of the star magnolia by my south door unravels. The litany of firsts sets the outside limits of the seasons. The year takes on its character from those landmarks, finds its stride from the earliest measurements.

1985: Mill Habitat: The first new parsnip foliage is up. First waterleaf is sprouting. First new hepatica leaves. The very first buds unraveling on the lower branches of a honeysuckle bush.
  Grass becoming thicker. Daylilies up two inches. Saw the first spring chipmunk running though the oak leaves.

1987: Cardinal singing at 6:29 a.m. First daffodil seen in bloom.

1990: Fourth day in a row of warm temperatures. Crocus, scilla, and daffodils are in full bloom throughout the village. The first flock of turkey vultures was circling Glen Helen at 4:30 p.m. First red-winged blackbird seen.

1994: First lemon verbena seen growing back from the recent cold.

1995: First red-winged blackbird of the season seen this morning on the way to Xenia. All snow crocuses, snowdrops, and now the spring irises are in full bloom in the south garden.

1996: This morning, in the warm aftermath of the biggest high pressure wave in at least 18 years, I heard the first flicker call of the year. On the way to school, the first red-winged blackbirds had arrived at the corner of Tarbox Cemetery Road and Wilberforce-Clifton, the same day they took up residence there last year. In the parking lot at Wilberforce, robins were whinnying; the first time I'd heard their raucous spring calls, even though they've been around for weeks. By the afternoon when the temperature got up into the 60s, the first spring iris bloomed, and snow crocus, aconites, and snowdrops were in full flower. The pussy willows finally came out most of the way. Daffodil and garlic foliage pushed up another inch over night.

1998: Flicker calling this morning in the backyard. At Springfield, the huge flocks of crows still there.

2000: Now the peony stalks are up about six inches and starting to unfold. At the covered bridge, chickweed is taking over the woods floor. One early meadow rue unraveling, maybe three inches tall near the first swamp. One violet cress plant with buds seen, but no other flowers.

2003: One clump of snow crocus, the first of the year, in full bloom, maybe eight or nine golds, more than a dozen purples.

2007: A week ago, I couldn't find any tulip or peony sprouts to photograph. Now, after two days of highs in the middle 70s, the tulips are up three to five inches, the peonies two inches and fat. The rhubarb has just barely appeared. Grackles sang all around the yard yesterday afternoon and this afternoon. Yesterday evening, I watched a squirrel building a nest in the woods on the west side of the yard. Robins and cardinals and doves sang all day long. We saw the first yellow finch today, at least half turned.

2008: First cardinal heard at 6:25 this morning. I saw a flicker behind Eric's house along Limestone when I walked Bella, its call a hard "brrrrit, brrrrit." Ed Oxley called to report he had seen a question mark butterfly and a dozen honeybees yesterday. He has snowdrops and crocus and aconites in bloom. On tonight's walk at 6:00, I saw a small flock of grackles, all facing the setting sun, cackling in the trees. Flowers were emerging from one maple near the park. Doves and cardinals were calling, one robin whinnying. In the garden, thin ramps foliage has emerged, maybe an inch tall, pacing the peony spears. One daffodil is budded. At the mall parking lots, and in the wetlands on the way to Beavercreek, geese were looking for nesting sites. In our pond, the small koi have disappeared. They were active around the 5th, before the storm, but I haven't seen them since.

2009: Little Rock, Arkansas to Bowling Green, Kentucky – light rain and highs in the 50s. Through eastern Arkansas, middle April continues, the redbuds the surest sign. As we drove northeast to

Memphis and Nashville, the redbuds changed from full bloom to just an early deep purple. At Bowling Green, hollyhock foliage is a little more than a foot tall, daffodils and pears are full, but the season is early Middle Spring (early April) instead of Middle Spring. The whole trip along the 35th Parallel since Gallup, New Mexico has been a drive that lies between three and five weeks ahead of Yellow Springs, Ohio.

2010: A faint gilding to the finches now, and the ragwort is growing daily, up two inches already. Tat reports from Madison, Wisconsin that the robin chorus began there last week.

2011: At Jekyll Island in Georgia since the 10th, we were attacked yesterday and today by no-see-ums and ticks – the first time ever for ticks here. Loud pre-dawn chorus of cardinals, doves and blue jays every morning.

2012: Mild morning in the middle 50s, third quarter moon shining in the southeast, robins twittering at 6:00 a.m., in full song by 6:10, much earlier than I have heard them before. Highs in the upper 70s today, and record temperatures throughout the Plains and the East, 81 in Chicago, upper 70s in Madison. Cherry trees were in full bloom in Washington, D.C.

As I worked on refurbishing the pond, a cabbage butterfly and a carpenter bee flew by, the first of the year. I plucked a small dark frog from the water as I drained the pond. In front of the house and on the way to Fairborn, forsythia was opening, and a large patch of periwinkles was flowering along Dayton Street. Serviceberry buds cracking, Peggy's peach buds flushed. Maples are now flowering throughout, and at Ellis Pond this evening, robins whinnying and peeping, blackbirds yodeling, geese honking, ducks quacking.

2013: In spite of the continuing cold, a handful of mid-season crocus has opened in the east garden, and yesterday one daffodil started to break out just a little. Kit reports robins in Cedarville at 6:20, and I heard robins and cardinals here when I went outside at 6:25 (but no songs at 6:10), the sky clear, temperature in the low 20s. Grackles, robins and starlings continue to circle the neighborhood, pairing up and looking for nesting sites. The evening news reported that the monarch butterfly population is down by more than half since last year, a dramatic distant effect of human presence.

2014: Ed Oxley called this morning: "About 9:30, I saw probably 40 to 50 sandhill cranes flying north west, probably more north than west above the Great Miami River. They were just beautiful, maybe a quarter of a mile up, way up, and they were silent, not chortling. They were the first ones I've seen this season."

The first of my aconites started to unravel today, and now the snow crocuses are up to almost twenty. I saw the first bees gathering their pollen.

2015: High in the upper 50s, record highs forecast for the Dakotas and the West tomorrow. In the yard, multiple snow crocuses along the south wall: large violet clumps in full bloom. Some of my snowdrops have opened all the way and a handful of violet crocuses have opened in the east garden. No grackles in the yard, no grackle calls in the neighborhood. Of course the Stafford Street aconites fill their two beds with dense yellow blossoms. At the Monastery of St. Clare in Cincinnati, many earthworms stranded on the sidewalk because of the all-night rain.

2016: Mild and quiet in the 50s this morning, light mist: First robins heard when I went out at 5:53, a cardinal at 5:59, song sparrows at 6:09, doves by 6:20. Now the leafing of the shrubs and trees and vines has begun, led by the Japanese honeysuckles, peaches, roses, viburnums, privets, lilacs and honeysuckle bushes. And the first forsythia has opened in the old front hedge (probably overnight) – the same moment as in the recent record-setting March of 2012). Jill's aconites are completely spent, all to foliage like the snowdrops. The bluebells have emerged in the southwest garden by the old mock orange. Lemon verbena, primrose, small-flowered aster and goldenrod leaves are an inch or two long. The deep red peony stems have suddenly started to produce foliage. Even the ancient, overgrown rhubarb is emerging. Through the day, the red-bellied woodpecker called. Mosquitoes were pesky in the house when I left the back doors open. Jill's maple was shedding all over her driveway this evening.

2017: Snow overnight, a dusting here, all the daffodils bending low, forsythia dull and dyed by the frost, and the East is shut down with a blizzard.

2019: A "bomb cyclone" roars across the Plains. Here, mild, gusts of rain, clouds and sun, birds everywhere. From a little north of town, Chris Walker: "This should come as no surprise, given today's warm temps, but the spring peepers are singing their opening tune tonight. First time I have heard them this season." Jeffery Goss reports forsythia in bloom throughout Billings, Missouri.

2020: I saw the first daffodils were open in front of the house at the corner of High and Limestone Streets this morning. Throughout the afternoon, wet snow covered everything. Grackles still common in the back yard.

2022: First fly in the sun, high of 62. Phlox basil leaves have barely started.

2023: A deluge from a rain river in California as a nor'easter covers the Northeast. Only flurries in the Ohio Valley. Daffodils still upright (still 100 of them open) in the cold and wind.

There is no foliage on the trees yet; only here and there the red bloom of the soft maple, illuminated by the declining sun, shows vividly against the tender green of a slope beyond, or a willow, like a thin veil, stands out against a leafless wood.

John Burroughs

March 15th
The 74th Day of the Year

The human body is not a closed or static object but an open, unfinished entity utterly entwined with the soils, waters, and winds that move through it – a wild creature whose life is contingent upon the multiple other lives that surround it, and the shifting flows that surge through it.

David Abram

Sunrise/set: 6:47/6:42
Day's Length: 11 hours 55 minutes
Average High/Low: 48/30
Average Temperature: 38
Record High: 79 – 1977
Record Low: 8 – 1891

Weather
Highs in the 70s come five percent of the time, 60s twenty percent, 50s thirty percent, 40s another 30 percent, and 30s fifteen percent. Precipitation occurs three years in a decade, with snowfall relatively rare. Today is the second-brightest day in the first half of March, carrying a 75 percent chance of sun.

The Week Ahead
With equinox, the chances of highs in the 20s fall below five percent for the first time since the middle of December, but the 18th brings the greatest chance of frost in the entire month - a full 90 percent chance. March 20th is typically the wettest day of the week, with a 60 percent chance of precipitation and the most thunderstorms since autumn. The 21st is the driest, with just a 25 percent chance. The 21st also brings the most sun of any day in the third week of March: 70 percent of those days are clear to partly cloudy. Only two other March days get so bright - the 7th and today, the 15th.

Natural Calendar
This is ordinarily the latest date for seeding tobacco along

the Ohio River. In the warmest years, the first head lettuce and sweet corn are planted in the Midwest for early harvest. In the Southeast, live oak trees shed their leave as new growth appears.

This week's ephemeris is often marked by blossoms of grape hyacinths and the earliest tulips, as well as by significant growth on rhubarb and skunk cabbage leaves. In warmer springs, snowdrops, aconites and snow crocus decline as peony stalks reach at least two inches above the mulch. The first ragweed and touch-me-not sprouts emerge. Pollen often forms on the pussy willows, and gold finches turn gold. Between now and about April 15, up to forty thousand snow geese visit the Fort Boise Wildlife Management Area near Parma, Idaho on their way north for mating.

Daybook

1982: First worms seen. First crocus bloomed today.

1983: Pussy willows have all their pollen, a radical difference from last year's tight catkins.

1984: Mill Habitat: River high. The Glen floor is covered with three inches of snow, but the air is 65 degrees. A few flies are out; one tried to bite my wrist. Crows restless. Past the mill, I found new sprouts on the southern side of a log. A small tan moth fluttered across the path. At the Covered Bridge, more new sprouts found under the mulch. On the way home, the first groundhog of the year ran across the road. Starlings are migrating north along the highway toward Springfield. At home, the bleeding heart is emerging in the east garden.

1986: Cardinal sings at 6:20 a.m. Mourning doves at 6:38 a.m. Star of Bethlehem, forget-me-nots, and grape hyacinth up two inches. Forsythia flushed and ready. Water striders active in sloughs below the Covered Bridge. One honeysuckle bush getting leaves. First snow trillium seen, first small violet leaves.

1987: Cardinal sings at 6:26 a.m. First purple deadnettle found blooming. Mock orange and Japanese honeysuckle are sending out leaves. Grass is growing.

1989: Purple deadnettle blooming in the cold.

1990: Young crane flies, half the size of the winter adults, swarm outside the back door. Box elders flower. First groundhog killed along Grinnell Road. In Washington, D.C., today was the earliest cherry blossoming since the cherry trees arrived from Japan.

1991: Covered Bridge: Buzzards not here yet. Violet cress budding, many more bluebells up, some spreading out a little. Garlic mustard has just sprouted. New craneflies are spinning in the bushes. One touch-me-not has sprouted in the swamp spring. Moss an inch long, golden green, one ragwort heading up. A great blue heron fishing on Yellow Springs Creek. Geese loud below the ridge along the Little Miami. First woodcock of my life seen at the swamp brook: it rushed up into the air, and I could see its long beak for just an instant.

1992: Daffodils fully out in Cincinnati, honeysuckles twice as full along the roadway as in Yellow Springs, a tint of yellow green to the southern hills.

1996: A thunderstorm last night (the second so far this year) scared Buttercup, the family bulldog; she slept under the bed. This morning, temperatures were mild, light fog. The trees were wet, their black winter branches seeming to turn red from the spring glow. At school, a fly emerged in Lois's office, was crawling around on the window sill with a few lady bugs.

1998: Crows 6:24 a.m. No chorus yet at 6:00 a.m. At 8:00 a large flock of blackbirds came over the house.

1999: Sometimes a Yellow Springs March brings forsythia by equinox, sometimes just a few snowdrops. This March has been colder than most others in the past few decades. It's been a snowdrop March, reminiscent of the bitter third month of 1984.

That March, like this one, a child of La Nina, followed this year's pattern almost exactly. Both Februarys began mild, turned harsh at the end, and the cold stayed about four weeks. Six inches of snow fell on March 8th in 1984 - the same day that we had seven inches of snow here in 1999, four days earlier than the snow of March 1993, two days later than snow in 1996. March of 1984 brought more snow on the 10th, the 12th and the 13th; this year, snow was in the air for the 13th and 14th, but then moved to our south. On those days in 1993, a major storm missed us the same way.

This past week's mild temperatures were also presaged in the thaws during the third week of March in 1984, 1993 and 1996. If history continues to shadow the past, our weather will be less dramatic from here on out; but it will stay cool -- highs mostly in the 40s, lows in the 20s, some snow a day or so past equinox (like 1984 and 1996).

And by equinox, snow or no snow, the season will have brought the Virginia bluebells out of the ground, the foliage advancing on its own schedule in spite of the weather, wiser than La Nina, and pushing its warmth out into the climate, tempering its harshness like the hazy Yellow Springs sun.

As in 1984, Middle Spring and the first wave of wildflowers will most likely be about a week late in Glen Helen; the Bloodroot Moon will have to move towards its final quarter before the bloodroot actually blooms. But then, as history comes around again, everything will happen at once: hepatica, twinleaf, Dutchman's britches, snow trillium opening along the river, daffodils, full crocus, grape hyacinth, first tulips all over town.

2000: Robins chirping at 6:05 a.m., and the whinny of a screech owl, sounds linking night and day. First cabbage butterfly seen at 12:25 p.m., then I almost stepped on a grass snake out by the painted daisies. In the east garden, columbine is six inches tall. In the south garden, the poppy leaves are bushy and a foot high. The first great ragweed has sprouted. In the north garden, the money plant is starting to extend from its basal leaves. In town, I found a whole clump of puschkinias in full bloom near Allen Street. Two more cabbage butterflies in the afternoon along the bike path, another grass snake. Great mullein basal leaves are rich and fat, some plants already a foot across.

2003: First cardinal heard at 6:25 a.m. Pileated woodpeckers were calling at Antioch School through the morning. Snake sunning itself on the greenhouse window. Robins whinnying. Honeybees arrived at the full-blooming patch of crocus. Snowdrops emerging. Pussy willows almost completely out.

2004: Robins heard at 6:12 a.m., cardinals at 6:20, the morning clear, moon a fourth of the way up into the southwest, temperature right at freezing. As I worked outside this afternoon in the warm 50-degree temperatures, I saw the first blue-eyes blooming.

2005: First spring bird chorus heard at 6:14 a.m. Cardinals singing by 6:30. The first robin seen in the yard at 8:00. Red-winged blackbirds on the fences along the road to Washington Court House.

2006: The very first purple primrose opened in the east garden, and one scilla unraveled near the lungwort in the backyard today – in spite of the cool weather. *Cornus mas* seen open in Wilmington.

2007: *Cornus mas* opening around town, one bush on Stafford, another on Allen Street. Waterleaf is emerging, leaves about half and inch or so a cross. Ramps and tulips are up two to three inches, lungwort barely emerging. Resurrection lilies are at two inches, definitely behind the daffodils and grape hyacinths.

2008: The annual robin chorus began at 6:15 this morning, first as faint twittering, and then by 6:25 a strong and steady calling. For the first time this year, I saw a robin working the lawn about 7:00. The flicker was on Eric's tree again this morning when I went through the alley with Bella. In the yard, waterleaf has still not appeared. Grackles have come by most of the day.

2009: Bowling Green, Kentucky, loud robin song by 4:30 (CST) this morning at the campground. Robins were all over the place, mating and chasing each other when I walked Bella, and doves were calling. On the way to the interstate, we saw a star magnolia in full bloom. More daffodils and some forsythia noticed on the way through Kentucky, and Cincinnati had hundreds of daffodils open along the river. At home, snowdrops were in full bloom, and many crocus were open, several daffodils budded.

From Jeffery Goss, Jr., Springfield, Missouri:

When the seeds are beginning to blow from the seed heads of the later prairie asters, the next warm spell is the time to change the straw mulch over any under-mulch wintering leaf crops. It is also the time to harvest endive and January King cabbage.

When the migrating geese arrive at the Ozarks' lakes, it is the optimum time for parsnip harvest. (The migrating geese going north, that is)

When Ozark witch hazels are blooming, then the maple sap will run in a few days.

When the early daffodils are showing flower stems, then you should be done with all pruning in the vineyard.

2011: Jekyll Island, Georgia to Asheville, North Carolina: The tree line much more lush and green than a week ago (after five days in the 60s and 70s). And a large flock of turkeys feeding on the side of the major freeway between New York and Florida!

2012: Another clear, mild morning in the 50s, the robins beginning twenty minutes later than yesterday - 6:20. Privets along Limestone Street greening up. Willows all around the area suddenly bright chartreuse. Star and pink magnolias blooming from Springfield to Xenia. Crab apples ready to flower in Xenia. Snowdrops to seed, full pollen pussy willows, first yellow tulip against the south wall. Buds on the bluebells at home, April running away with the land.

2013: Another cold morning with frost. At 6:00, no birds, then distant chirping (but not the robin chorus singsong) at 6:07, then cardinals began to call at 6:12, crows coming in at 6:20. Grackles and doves and cardinals singing when I walked Bella around 8:30 into the steady south wind. In the Phillips Street alley, I found patches of aconites still bright yellow, having been protected by the wandering euonymus and a few outbuildings. And I discovered a great new patch of snowdrops, full bloom, hundreds of square feet, hidden in a backyard bordering the alley. In my east garden, the crocus stand tight, waiting for full sun and a little warmth to blossom. This afternoon when the temperature rose a little above 40, they finally trusted enough to open. When I was looking for henbit budding, I found that the first stonecrop had emerged. Tulip foliage is three to four inches now, daylily foliage two to three inches. A few of the aconites I planted last fall have yellow buds, but they lie limp like naked fledglings just emerged from their eggs.

2014: Cool and clear, Venus in the southeast very bright: Robins faintly at 6:00, cardinals by 6:10. Today's yard inventory almost exactly the same as last year's. Saw John Blakelock at the drugstore. He was excited. "I saw one sandhill crane," he told me, "just one flying north."

(I have recorded reports of sandhills flying south over Yellow Springs from late November to early January since 2003. But spring sightings have been less frequent. Liz was the first to notice the migration of Florida cranes north over Yellow Springs on February 27, 2011. Kit saw them last year on March 1. This year, John reported them on February 22 and March 16, Ed on March 14. Audrey saw them on February 23.

What I find most interesting about all this is that the appearance of the early winter cranes in our local consciousness is something new, and the appearance of the late-winter/early-spring cranes is even newer. Since we only aware of a minute number of events taking place in the world around us, and since so many of those events, even if seen, have no historical or personal context, the community tracking of the migrating cranes and the fleshing out of their visitations open wondrous, hidden windows and are reminders of how little we understand and what we still might learn.

2015: Clear and frost, Sagittarius due south, the Dipper turned deep into the middle of the sky, crescent moon bright in the east, the turning point of spring: First cardinal at 5:48 a.m., second at 5:54 another at 5:58, then a robin, then more robin peeping, but not sing-songing, and more steadily at 6:00 as I turned down High Street. I left Bella at the house and then went for a short run: I walked out at 6:08 into full robin mating singsong and whinnies, competing with the steady calls of the cardinals. I could hear song sparrows wedged in between the loud chorus, and then doves at 6:14. Crows and a pileated at 6:35, and off in the trees I could hear grackles – for the first time in the year. And another day full of sun, temperature into the upper 50s. Now everything comes up: hyacinths, daffodils (two with buds), iris, daylily foliage, bittercress, my reluctant few aconites, the first open white standard crocuses with honeybees, the first. Pussy willows finally break out.

2016: Robins were calling at 5:45 this morning, temperature in the 50s. When the sun came out in the afternoon, I walked the North Glen path to the Yellow Spring in my shirtsleeves. I was expecting the land to be full of new flowers, but really I only found the skunk cabbage fat and tall, violet cress and white hepaticas in full bloom, a few spring beauties, a spice bush with a just three flowers about to open, one lesser celandine. Some Dutchman's britches were bushy off the trail, but I saw only a few buds.

On the way back from Dayton, I saw a purple magnolia tree full of blossoms. At home, the pussy willow catkins are getting yellow with pollen, and the squills are now completely open, well ahead of the daffodils, which are coming in steadily. Japanese knotweed, red and young: some sprouts two inches. Canadian thistle leaves two inches, monarda sprouts all clustered together, maybe half an inch long. Sitting in the sun on the back porch, I watched a cluster of sparrows in vociferous, mating randori. In the evening, Rick reported that he heard the first toad sing in his pond, the earliest he's ever recorded it.

2018: The cold weather continues, but the four daffodils hold near the peach tree, doing well with lows in the 20s. The snowdrops are thinning quickly, though, and the snow crocuses are about gone. A few forsythia buds on the bushes near the east sidewalk show slivers of gold, and I found one grape hyacinth with its fat, purple buds. The finches feed every day in the backyard, but no sign of yellowing yet. In the North Glen, the skunk cabbage is prominent in the swamp, but only a few leafcup leaves have emerged on the hillsides, and the watercress has not returned. I did find a few touch-me-not sprouts, however, one of the few signs in the woods that spring equinox approaches. And Jill noticed a small, pale moth fluttering by us when we stood looking at the Cascades waterfall.

2019: Strong wind, clouds, 40s: lily foliage pushes out ever so slowly to about three inches. The dark basal leaves of winter cress in the fields by Ellis Pond spread a little in the sun. At this point in the month, the large winter flocks of geese have broken up, and only a few pairs remain in the fields across from the pond.

2020: Daffodil petals visible but still holding tight in the cold. Leslie and Bruce report many goldfinches with bright yellow plumage.

2022: More flies are out in the garden today. In the woods near the Indian Mound with Jeff: foliage of wild strawberries, ramps, dock, lilies, chickweed, creeping Charlie. At the Covered Bridge, similar foliage along with violet cress, several very new touch-me-not sprouts, sweet rockets, skunk cabbage, Monarda bed cut back in the north garden. A few tulips and daffodils planted last fall continue to push out.

2023: Cliff Fawcett reports a his first bluebird sighting...and it was on his bluebird house. Daffodil count is 103 in spite of morning temperatures close to 20.

See the Spring brings back its pleasures,
all the passions of its treasures,
and the sun calls out the flowers,
soothes the meadow with its colors,
plucks the sadness from the gray,
and the wildness from the winter day.

From the *Carmina Burana* (bf)

March 16th
The 75th Day of the Year

So forth issued the Seasons of the year:
First lusty Spring, all dight in leaves of flowers
That freshly budded and new blooms did bear.

Edmund Spenser

Sunrise/set: 6:46/6:43
Day's Length: 11 hours 57 minutes
Average High/Low: 48/30
Average Temperature: 39
Record High: 78 – 1945
Record Low: 8 – 1970

Weather
Today's temperatures are usually similar to those of the 15th. Highs reach the 70s five percent of the time; they get into the 60s fifteen percent of the time, into the 50s thirty percent, the 40s thirty percent, and into the 30s twenty percent. Historically, however, the 16th is a little wetter than the 15th, rain or snow falling half the time. Chances of morning frost are 65 percent.

Natural Calendar
When the mourning cloaks, the question marks, the tortoise shells and the white cabbage butterflies come out, catfish are getting ready to feed in the Little and Great Miami Rivers, and goldfinches are turning gold throughout the Valley. The great predawn chorus of birds begins near 6:00 a.m. Later in the day, flickers and pileated woodpeckers call. Winged ants will be flying then, and the first green-bottle flies. Garter snakes will lie out sunning.

When butterflies appear, spring picks up speed, the number of new plants increasing every day even though the air is cool. Hepatica, harbinger of spring, and twinleaf are pushing out. Toad trillium and Dutchman's britches are ready to open. The foliage of wild geranium, clover, and columbine is growing. September's zigzag goldenrod is two inches long. Leaves of the golden Alexander are an inch across. Scarlet cup mushrooms swell in the dark.

All the leaves and fungi and butterflies in the Ohio Valley are signs that sandhill cranes are migrating through the Rocky Mountains. The road to Savannah is green with leaves a third to half emerged. Wisteria is fragrant along the Georgia coast, and fields of rice show off their purple blossoms. In Alabama, it's time for redbud trees and pears to bloom. On the outskirts of New Orleans, winter cress is going to seed, and huge, squat yellow thistles grow beside the roads; in the French Quarter, azaleas and camellias are wide open, and yellow day lilies and the crepe myrtles are flowering.

Daybook

1982: First day of the year in the 70s. At the Covered Bridge, first snakes of the year basking in the sun along the river. Virginia bluebells just out of the ground.

1985: Four buzzards, two geese by the mill. Skunk cabbage huge and purple. The first touch-me-nots have sprouted in the runoff from Grinnell Pond. Some bluebells budding. Some roses bushes have full-sized leaves. Bees are out today. Violet cress budding.

1986: First cardinal heard at 6:22 a.m. Geese fly over at 7:48 a.m. Foliage of the small-flowered aster as strong as any spring leaves.

1989: First cardinal heard at 6:22 a.m. First buzzard seen on the way to work. Cedar waxwing killed when it flew against the window at Wilberforce. At South Glen, red-bellied woodpeckers call back and forth to one another.

1991: Clematis leaves emerging, a little behind the dodder. Pussy willows swell out, some crocus and snow drops already done. A cool to average March, but still some seasons ending already. Flicker mating call heard in the late afternoon.

1992: Buzzards circling the North Glen. Squills recovering from the heavy freeze, but snowdrops and aconite melted in the cold.

1994: Into Mint Hollow with Buttercup, maybe two-dozen or more buzzards circling overhead, swooping at what seemed considerable speed compared to their lazy summer circling. River high. At the edge of the bottom land, the first waterleaf seen, its foliage brand new, shiny, less than an inch in diameter. Garlic mustard, its late summer leaves killed by the hard winter, is growing back now from under the mulch.

1996: First waterleaf has just emerged by the pussy willow (which is just about fully out).

1998: Crows 6:20 a.m. Flicker 8:11 a.m. Buzzards are here today. Squills are open in front of the Community Service building on Whiteman Street.

1999: My yellow-bellied sapsucker is back, tapped at the siding at 9:15 a.m. Purple spring iris blooming in the snow.

2003: The full chorus of robins was singing this morning at 6:00 a.m. At 6:08, the first cardinal heard. Grackles join in by 7:00, the whole backyard alive with birds.

2005: Robins singing by 6:13 a.m., temperature 25 degrees, cloudy.

2006: Robins were singing at 5:50 this morning, full moon setting through high clouds. I heard the first cardinals at 6:20 from indoors.

2007: Walking Bella at 7:30 this morning, I heard the first blue jay bell call. Grackles and doves and robins and cardinals all were singing.

2008: Grackles come awake with sunrise, fly all about town cackling.

2009: Robin chorus this morning began between 5:50 and 6:00, very strong, temperature mild in the 40s. Around the yard: the pale green Lenten roses are in full bloom, ramps up three inches, hyacinths three inches, Resurrection lilies pacing the daffodils at seven to nine inches, peonies one inch, squills three inches, stonecrop one inch. Poppy foliage is coming along, but thin and short, no rhubarb yet, only one or two hollyhock leaves, daylily leaves to three inches, no primroses yet, but foliage present.

2010: Inventory in the yard and alley: The maple behind Mrs. Timberlake's yard has reddish flowers; two other maples in the alley have fat silver flowers. In Mateo's lawn: early clover leaves. Aconites remain in full bloom behind Katie's house. The snow crocus and standard crocus hold, petals closed against the chilly morning. Pussy willows completely emerged, fat, along the sidewalk.

The first wild henbit is budded there, and the first bittercress is budded in a crack on the back patio. Lilac buds are full green now. Daffodils six to eight inches, some buds straining to open. Grape hyacinth leaves five to seven inches, tulip leaves getting fat, seven or eight inches, large clumps or rockets, daylilies surging to nine inches, beautiful red veins on the tall ragwort leaves, allium growth to three inches, waterleaf up in places, lungwort up and budded, bluebells up, purple, ramps five inches, pachysandra strong, peonies and rhubarb remaining low at just an inch, spiderwort leaves up to three inches. First Lenten roses have opened, two white flowers, and the scarlet flowers all budded, small patch of blue-eyes by the trellis. Songs of the titmice, cardinals, doves and grackles dominate the neighborhood. This afternoon, several more bittercress opened, more bluebells came up. Honeybees, house flies (more hatching near the fallen box elder tree), and bumble bees were gathering pollen from the crocus. Walking Bella this evening at sunset, sky gold and violet, I heard robins and doves all along the way. The setting sun gilded the flowering maples at the park.

2011: Asheville to Yellow Springs: Robin chorus in the early morning. Mild temperatures through the mountains and piedmont, more green to the countryside than a week ago, more forsythia, more daffodils and pears well toward Lexington.

2012: Robins in the far distance at about 5:15, clear at 5:35, cardinal song at 5:45 this morning, another warm day. In the Glen, hepatica, white, violet, purple, in early bloom, violet cress and deadnettle in full bloom, two bloodroot flowers, leafcup clumping. In the yard, chickweed is suddenly in full bloom, viburnum and even the hydrangeas starting to leaf. Along High Street, the privets and lilacs and black raspberry bushes are leafing. Our bleeding heart is up two inches. Pussy willows are full of pollen. Maple flowers shedding along Limestone Street (had been shedding in Springfield three days ago). Red-bellied woodpecker calls off and on through the day here and in the woods. A lawn of squills near the college campus. Mid-season crocus are almost all faded.

2013: Sky open but full of cirrus plumes, temperature at 40 degrees. Faint chirps and twittering at 5:40 this morning, faint singsong from the robins at 5:50, full-throated singsong chanting at 6:00 with loud whinnies and peeping; finally the first cardinal broke in at 6:10. Bittercress and henbit have budded in the backyard. The pussy willows have all emerged, but they still hide a little inside their sheaths. In the south garden, the red stems of peonies, which have been holding back this cold March, have pushed out an inch. Some honeysuckle bushes have buds that are flushed and fat. Stafford Street maples are flowering, and Ed Oxley says he has squills and *Iris reticulata* in bloom, and I also saw some in the alley this morning.

2014: The air still. The full moon setting clear behind the back trees before dawn, then around 6:00, suddenly the raw wind came in, blowing all the leaves in the street southeast.

2015: Full robins and cardinals when I went out at 6:15 this morning. In the east garden, almost all the snowdrops are now completely open. Blue jay steady bell call just before sunrise. First carpenter bee noticed; it was looking exhausted on top of a white crocus near the pond. Large patches of full-blooming aconites seen along Davis Street this afternoon.

2016: The pachysandra opened overnight, whole stems of blossoms at once, two days before its bloom in 2012. When I fed the fish (the first time this year), all the creatures, large and small came up to feed. Jill's star magnolia started to flower today, and she told me about a whole lawn blue with scillas on Phillips Street. In the garden, several small, reddish English daisies are blossoming, the earliest and least conspicuous of the perennials. I saw a *Cornus mas* tree in full bloom on Stafford Street, and when we walked at the Covered Bridge just before sundown, we marveled at the brightness of the chickweed that covered the woods floor across the bottomland and up into the high ridge.

2017: Walk from the mill to John Bryan Park: chickweed thick and deep green in spite of the cold past weeks, ramp foliage three to five inches throughout, a few violet cress in bloom, a few clumps of lesser celandine found along the river, a large killdeer (average arrival date February 22) at the water's edge.

2018: Up before daybreak with Jill to listen, clear sky, moon dark, 22 degrees, the air still: No birds heard at 6:00, first cardinal sang at 6:04, first robins at 6:07, first song sparrow at 6:14. By the time we went indoors at 6:20, the cardinals were in full song all over the neighborhood, but the robin chorus was not happening. From Madison, Wisconsin, Tat sent a text at 10:32: "Sandhill cries just now along Wingra. Blue scillas up in a few places. Great morning…." From Chris a few mile north of Springfield: a photo of a harbinger-of-spring blooming through last year's sycamore leaves.

2019: Clear early morning, setting moon lighting up the yard and the bedroom, reflecting in the koi pond. I went outside at 6:14 into a full robin chorus (the first time so clear this spring), boisterous cardinals, mourning doves, song sparrows, black-capped chickadees, titmice, grackles and crows coming in by 6:30, all the birds so loud together that they drowned out the nearby road noise.

2020: Grackles were loud and raucous in the alley this morning around 6:30, all over the feeder yesterday. They have moved in to mate. Their fledglings will be out of the nest the first days of June. Ed Oxley called in the late morning, said his snowdrops and aconites were about done for the year (mine just starting to fade) and that he had seen a bird that looked like an eagle, except that it was all white!

2021: Rain overnight, temp in the 30s. First robins at 6:07, first singsong mating robins at 6:10, first cardinals and doves at 6:12.

2023: Mild in the 50s: I cut down tree-of-heaven saplings near the north garden. Daffodil count: 115 (not one open last year).Glory of the snow noticed in bloom by the back porch. In the. peony patch, deep red stalks about four inches high and leafing. At Ellis Pond, the willow tree is a pale yellow-green. Tat reports grackles mating in Madison, Wisconsin.

Journal

From time to time, I am visited by depressions, sometimes light, sometimes deep. One morning not long ago, I woke up to one of those darker moods in which nothing seemed right or meaningful.

Staring out the window and nursing my emotions, I heard the knocking of a yellow-bellied sapsucker on the siding of the house. She had been there before; a yellow-bellied sapsucker had appeared in the middle of spring to tap at my siding nearly every year for more than a decade.

She comes just once a spring on her way to somewhere. If she is not the same bird each year, then maybe a daughter or grand-daughter following a family tradition, taught by her parents that for good luck, or maybe for the taste of a certain kind of beetle emerging from the cedar just before equinox, she should stop and check the wood.

And that simple knock, which I would have missed had I been busy at more practical things, brought flooding in the whole optimism of spring. The isolation I'd been feeling dissipated immediately. The bird's presence and her history were all I needed to come back from what seemed to be a hopeless funk.

In my joy, I blew the whole incident out of proportion. I allowed the arbitrary act of a sapsucker to reassure me about the good order of the entire world. Things were not, as my mood had told me, out of sync and empty, but rich and all in place if only I would listen.

Perhaps, I thought, fortune was no more or less than this.

Maybe sense and virtue, immediate pleasure and lasting meaning, were as free and as accessible. And if the transient yellow-bellied sapsucker could wield the power of happiness, I might wield it, too.

To see spring,
watch the willows:
harps plucked
by the wind
rustle into notes
that reply to the sun,
pull up water to speak,
(and sometimes weep)--
the warp and woof,
root and reach.
Borrow ocher and
yellow-green,
having held water in reserve
until the sun looked their way.

"A Small Spring Poem"
Barbara Valdez

March 17th
The 76th Day of the Year

The first in time and the first in importance of the influences upon the mind is that of nature. Every day, the sun; and, after sunset, Night and her stars. Ever the winds blow; ever the grass grows.

Ralph Waldo Emerson

Sunrise/set: 6:44/6:44
Day's Length: 12 hours
Average High/Low: 49/31
Average Temperature: 40
Record High: 74 – 2012
Record Low: 0 – 1900

Weather
Today is typically one of the warmest days in March, with a five percent chance of 70s, fifteen percent of 60s, forty percent of 50s, twenty-five percent of 40s, fifteen of 30s. Skies are clear to partly sunny 60 percent of the time; a thunderstorm or flurries occurs five years in a decade. Chances of frost this morning: 45 percent.

\Natural Calendar
An hour or so before sunrise, the wandering stars of Capricorn lie in the southeast. Sagittarius and then Scorpius (easily identified by the red star, Antares, in its center) fill the southern sky. West of Scorpius, is boxy Libra. West of Libra, is Virgo, marked by Spica, the brightest of the western stars.

Mock orange leafs out, pacing the new honeysuckle foliage and the boxwood, the Japanese honeysuckle, lilac, black raspberry, multiflora rose and coralberry. In the greenhouse, tropical mother-of-millions blossom time ends just as day and night grow equal. In the late evenings, robins chant their vesper songs.

March 17 is equilux in most years, when day and night are equal. On spring equinox, the Sun is directly above the equator, but because of refraction of sunlight by the Earth's atmosphere, the actual equality of the day and night occurs on the 17th.

143

1985: East to Washington, D.C.: Solitary buzzards at various locations. Coltsfoot full bloom in western Pennsylvania, but missing at higher elevations. The length of day-lily foliage indicates that the region between Yellow Springs and western Maryland is at about the same point in spring development.

1986: Waterleaf shows half-inch leaf growth.

1987: Thin-winged moth at the door, one of the *Pterophoridae.*

1988: Blue jays loud, setting territories. Comfrey leaves are two inches long, the same as I recorded on my weather notes in 1987, 1986, 1985, 1983.

1989: Cardinal sings 6:20 a.m. Last aloe flower dies back. First day in the 70s. The very first honeysuckle leaves emerged today, and a few mock orange buds unraveled. Huge flock of buzzards seen above North Glen. New mallow and coneflower foliage noticed. Pussy willows fully out. Day and night were equal today. After supper, I went out to check the sun's position: it was setting behind the apple tree, 270 degrees on the compass, due west, just like it was supposed to be.

1990: The year is two or three weeks ahead of schedule. Pussy willow catkins have all fallen. Some parts of the lawn are long enough to cut. In Dayton, redbud trees are showing some pink. Willows are leafing, and maple bloom is well along. Japanese knotweed is four inches high at the garden wall, a mid-April length. Beggarticks have sprouted. The first periwinkle is blue.

1991: Scilla are up today.

1994: The pussy willows are just about all the way out, but the rest of the world seems back in February. Even if the weather warms up some, the year will be late, all the wildflowers at least a week or two behind. This cold March is more like a Chicago or Detroit March, and March in 1990 was more a southern Kentucky or northern Tennessee March. So Yellow Springs, like most everywhere else, contains numerous possible climates. In order to know what this day was like here four years ago, I would drive to Knoxville.

1995: The flowering period of mother-of-millions in the greenhouse is complete, timed almost exactly to equinox. The first spring iris, which opened on the 11th, is wilting in the sun and 60 degree temperatures.

1998: Puschkinias open. Snowdrops, early iris and snow crocus end.

1999: Cardinals by 6:11 a.m., crows by 6:17.

2003: Cardinals by at least 6:06 a.m., robin chorus in full song by 6:00. A mild and sunny day, high reaching 71. Snowdrops now open all the way in the east garden. One buzzard circling High Street about 3:00 p.m.

2005: Robin chorus by 6:05 a.m. Cardinals by 6:10. The koi began swimming in the pond today for the first time since December.

2006: Even though the temperature is only in the middle 40s, the midseason crocuses are in full bloom in the sun. Snowdrops and snow crocus seasons are just about complete for the year.

2009: Robins singing at 6:00 this morning, a cardinal heard as I sat by the fire at 6:15. Four grackles at the bird feeder at 8:00, the first I've seen since we've been back from our trip west. When I walked Bella, I saw that aconites have been blooming behind the Danielson's (Katie's) house in the alley. Achillea leaves about two inches long in front of Moya's. Our first daffodil opened up all the way this afternoon, one squill is showing blue, bittercress with its white flowers is open, the first honeysuckle leaves are coming out, lilac leaves are spreading now, the pussy willows are fully emerged, and the red hellebores have joined the green in bloom. Tulip foliage has put on two inches in the 70-degree afternoon. Grackles and doves calling at sunset.

2010: Honey bees, Eastern carpenter bees, bumblebees and small, thin bees with long, hairless abdomens all on the wide-open crocus flowers. Grackles active in the trees this evening.

2011: Home from Jekyll Island, Georgia, to a high in the 60s: The robin chorus began at 5:53 a.m. In the yard, the first daffodil was getting ready to bloom this morning, snowdrops and snow crocus still full in the east garden, standard crocus full bloom, Lenten roses full bloom, tulips, ramps, spiderwort and daylily foliage to four inches, peonies two inches, blue eyes flowering, one red rhubarb knuckle showing and a few scilla with blue buds, one bluebell clump emerged by the budding lungwort. By late afternoon, the one daffodil had opened up most of the way. Robins and grackles calling at dusk. The warmest day of the year so far.

2012: Another warm day, crocus complete in the Phillips Street alley, more magnolias open, Don's serviceberry trees and Peggy's pear tree straining to open, will probably come in today, along with the downtown pears. Red-bellied woodpecker insistent.

2013: Cold east wind today. Robin whinnies at 6:02, chorus by 6:10. Grackles mating on the side of Limestone Street, doves courting along Stafford, a pair of geese honking out their territory across from the skunk cabbage patch downriver from the Covered Bridge. In the woods, few signs of spring, just some tiny new leaves on a multiflora rose, no chickweed buds, no purple cress foliage. Throughout town, grackles and starlings continue to be active.

2014: Walking through the village this afternoon, temperature in the upper 30s, I found yards covered with snowdrops and occasional outcroppings of early and mid-season crocus. Peggy's lamb's ear has put out new soft leaves, about two inches long.

2015: Light overcast, dusky crescent moon rising, mild and a steady northwest wind this morning. Robins seemed unperturbed, whinnied at 5:58 and were in chorus by the time I went indoors (without hearing cardinals) at 6:15. But I have never had much luck with cardinals when the wind is up. In spite of the chilly temperatures today, the dark violet mid-season crocuses opened in the east garden, replacing many of the paler snow crocuses. And this evening, the wind weakening, I heard robin vespers.

2016: First robin whinnies heard at 5:45 this morning, the sky clear, wind calm, temperature near 40 degrees. The wind picked up through the day, with hard gusts and weather warnings. Two pairs of geese at Ellis Pond, weeping willows there soft, bright April green. Achillea leaves about three inches long by Moya's. front sidewalk. A few puschkinias are open near the pond. Another purple magnolia seen, this one along North High Street: the purples are ahead of the white star magnolias this year. And Ed Oxley called: He saw a "brown and orange" butterfly and the first violet today.

2020: I walked Ranger at 5:30 this morning, humid and cloudy, temperature in the 40s, the robins quiet until 5:52, when they all started up at once. No cardinals or doves heard by the time I went in a little after 6:00. No skunks smelled or seen so far this winter/spring. From Washington, D.C., Liz reports full bloom of forsythia. Leslie and Bruce report more courtship feeding by cardinals and house finches. And they saw the first green frog of the spring, and periwinkles in full flower.

2021: Bittercress is budded near the circle garden. Daffodils are coming undone in the north garden, the first one open just about all the way.

2022: The first. four daffodils opened in the north garden today. Pussy willow catkins fully emerged, but no pollen seen yet. Ditch lilies are three to four inches tall. Jack Blakelock reports antlions are active. First honeybee seen in the first deep purple crocus that just bloomed overnight in the porch garden. At Agraria, one *Veronica,* many bittercress, honeybees in the blooming deadnettle, very small hemlock, clover common and tight to the ground, a variety of cresses, green buds on the front lilac bush, a few honeysuckle bushes leafing, tree frogs chanting but no American toad song yet.

2023: Daffodil count in a chilly wind: 136. Reading about Aristotle's definition of time (the measurement of change) and Newton's concept of pure time that occurs no matter what. Then there is daffodil count, a blatant measure of change which no one else uses or pays attention to. Do daffodils come and go in pure time? Does counting them create time? Does not counting them reduce or eliminate time? At what point are enough events and objects eliminated so that time does not exist?

Journal

When the cold returns like it often does in the middle of Early Spring, it pushes me to withdraw even more than I usually do from people in colder months. But then I struggle with loneliness, and I ruminate about solitude and isolation.

Solitude is contained and confident; isolation is needy and implies that separation is insufficiency. Solitude implies context and self-reliance and safety.

To break isolation, I struggle to sever the ties of my insecurities and doubts, enemies of serenity. I try to allow approval and dependency and worry to fall away behind me.

In wintry solitude, I still keep the companionship of memory and affection. I hold to the good of the cold and the past. I carry gratitude and love with me into my personal retreat, invite them to support the walls of my seclusion.

Then the sun and the thaws become stronger, March deepens. Gold finches turn gold and daffodils bud. Crocuses and yellow aconites and snowdrops are blooming, and nothing about loneliness and solitude seems to matter any more.

March 18th
The 77th Day of the Year

He is bewitched forever who has seen,
Not with his eyes but with his vision, Spring
Flow down the woods and stipple leaves with sun....

Vita Sackville-West

Sunrise/set: 6:42/6:45
Day's Length: 12 hours 3 minutes
Average High/Low: 49/31
Average Temperature: 40
Record High: 78 – 2012
Record Low: 8 – 1941

Weather
There is a five percent chance of a high above 70 today, 15 percent for a high in the 60s, twenty-five percent for a high in the 50s, thirty percent of 40s, twenty percent of 30s, five percent for 20s. Completely overcast conditions occur half of the years in my record, but snow falls just five percent of the time, rain twenty-five percent. Frost strikes 60 percent of the mornings.

Natural Calendar
All of the seasons of the first half of March continue to develop as Periwinkle Season moves through the undergrowth and Violet Cress Season and Ragwort Budding Season start in the warmer corners of the wetlands. In the woods, Turkey Gobbling Season is announced, of course, by gobbling turkeys. In milder years, it is Honeysuckle Leafing Season, at least on the lower branches. And now it's Pussy Willow Pollen Season and the early time for Blue Butterfly Season. Weeping Willow Greening Season parallels Toad Trillium Emerging Season on the forest floor.

Daybook
1985: In Washington, D.C., forsythia is in full bloom (opened a week ago, my sister Tat said). Star magnolias are just opening. Blue periwinkle flowers seen. Returning to Ohio along the

turnpike, I saw only one small patch of coltsfoot blooming near Zanesville.

1986: Cardinal sings at 6:21 a.m. Snowdrops are still in full bloom throughout the village.

1987: My sister Maggie reports the first crocus blooming in Madison, Wisconsin, two weeks after Yellow Springs, supporting the rule of thumb that spring moves north at the rate of 25 miles a day. In Yellow Springs, box elders are starting to bloom, and red maples. First buzzards seen today.

1988: First groundhog seen feeding by the side of the road. Peonies are up an inch despite the recent cold. Purple and golden crocus are blooming through the snow. Daylily foliage strong in the Wilberforce hills. First pigweed is sprouting by the front crocus.

1989: First pigweed is up near the front walk, the same day as last year. Pussy willow catkin hulls are falling today.

1990: Cardinal sings at 6:16 a.m. The pear trees downtown have started to bloom, the earliest date since they were planted along Xenia Avenue. Daylily foliage at least half a foot high now.

1991: First daffodil seen on Dayton Street.

1992: Three mother-in-law plants send up flower stalks at the same time.

1993: Continued cold, ten degrees or so below normal every day this past week. With today's sun, though (even with temperatures never getting out of the 30s), the golden snow crocus opened in the east garden. A thin bud on one daffodil in the south garden.

1994: A small patch of blue-eyes is in full bloom along the stone garden wall, bright in the sun this cool and windy afternoon. At Jacoby, the first touch-me-nots have sprouted along the path where a spring crosses down into a brook full of cress. Moss has started its spring growth on the logs nearby.

1995: Along the streets, forsythia is just starting, the first daffodils and squills are blooming, a few tulips are budding, pansies have appeared in their beds. Motherwort swells into clumps, purple deadnettle is in full bloom. Perennials are coming up: lupine, daylily, phlox, queen Anne's lace, waterleaf, Virginia bluebell, bleeding heart, columbine, coneflower, yarrow, sage, sweet pea, mallow, buttercup, snow-on-the-mountain, New England aster, lemon verbena, the red pyrethrum. The early bushes and vines are leafing all around the yard: privet, common honeysuckle, Japanese honeysuckle, lilac, goldenrod, clematis, mock orange, black raspberry, multiflora rose. Garlic mustard and great ragweed have sprouted.

1999: First squills on Whiteman Street.

2005: Screech owl heard this morning at 6:00, robins barely audible in the distance. As I drove off for a walk with Bella and Mike, two robins, crazy with March lust, flew in front of the truck, mating. I barely missed them. Judy called at 9:30 to say that robins had arrived in Goshen, Indiana last week, and that the gold finches were turning gold.

2006: The screech owl was singing at 5:30 this morning, continuing until robinsong about 6:00. Throughout town, many daffodils are open, many forsythia bushes in early bloom. The kaufmanniana-like tulips in the south garden are almost all open, their buds drooping in the cold.

And so much happened before the cold weather moved back in this week. On the 9th, Mike reported, "The redwings finally showed up a week ago on Tuesday (February 28). I heard a killdeer for the first time Sunday (March 6), and I believe the mockingbirds might be back. Bluebirds were singing today." Casey also called on the 9th. He'd seen one buzzard, but he admitted that "one buzzard doesn't count" as the official return of buzzards for spring.

The next day, the problem was solved. Casey phoned again to tell me that eight buzzards were circling above Gaunt Park. "Old friends," he called them, and he described the birds to me as they rode the hard wind up and up. So I went out into the backyard of my house on High Street, and there they were, so high that both Casey and I could see them even though we stood a mile apart.

Mosquitoes typically appear with the buzzards. Sure enough, on the 11th, Jeanie and I found a mosquito flying around in our car. Blackbirds arrived on schedule last week, too, the week that robins began their morning predawn chorus just after 6:00 a.m. The starlings disappeared from their tree between High and Stafford Streets, their pairing up apparently complete for the year. Cardinals and doves were calling around 6:15.

As I drove to Dayton, I saw my first groundhog of the spring running through the brown grass. After two days of hard rain and highs around 60 degrees, the koi in our pond began to feed, moving about for the first time since December.

Then before the cold wave came through town in the middle of the week, I took inventory around the yard. Everything had changed since my last accounting at the end of February: Snow crocus and snowdrops full bloom, two jonquils open, purple deadnettle, small flowered cress, blue eyes all blossoming, first flowers on several forsythia bushes, mid-season crocus budded, daffodils eight to ten inches tall and well budded, daylilies five inches, tulips ten inches, ramps three inches, lungwort up with one-to-two-inch leaves, waterleaf with one-inch leaves, Canadian thistles three inches, peonies three inches and leafing, red quince leafing and buds cracking, rhubarb and hollyhock leaves to two inches, bleeding hearts up two inches, grape hyacinth seven inches, resurrection lilies six inches, buds cracking on the serviceberry trees, buds cracking on the lilacs, pussy willows coming out all the way, privet and mock orange bushes leafing, buds reddening on the crab apple, new garlic mustard sprouts coming on.

2007: Pussy willows fully emerged now, and I saw the first red primrose opening under Janet's redbud. All of the snow crocus are up, some blooming in the sun.

2008: Rain and flooding in the yard continues, the entire north side under water. Even the pond has been flooded, water flowing in from the peony and Jerusalem artichoke beds. The red-bellied woodpecker was calling when I walked Bella this morning, and grackles were moving through the trees, cackling. Cardinals sang, and robins hunted in the lawns. Finches were feeding on the bag feeders, still no brighter than a few days ago.

2009: Cardinal heard at 6:11 this morning; robins were up by 6:00. Another day near 70 degrees, sun and high clouds. In the alley at about 9:30, a cardinal was singing on the top of a budding red maple, the bird facing east and standing out in the sun against the bright sky. One more daffodil opened overnight, and I'm noticing more and more progress in the foliage. Japanese honeysuckle leaves are prominent along High Street. Korean lilac buds are swelling pacing the standard lilacs. The buds on our viburnum on the north side of the house, our crabapple and Don's serviceberry trees are all pushing out from their hulls. Puschkinias full bloom near the pond.

2010: Robins were singing when I went out at 5:50 this morning, a cardinal heard from inside the house at 6:15. Another day in the 60s, continued full crocus season. Two daffodils along the north stone fence have pushed through to show their bright yellow, will both bloom tomorrow. The grass is quite green now and beginning to have uneven growth.

2011: Robins began to sing this morning at 5:50. Several squills opened all the way, and bittercress was budded. One more daffodil bloomed, and several more are on the way. The cats cornered a small grass snake in the garden. After putting up with their stalking and patting it, the snake made a run for the porch and found safety under a blue tarp there.

2012: Robins late at 6:15 this morning. The heat wave continues: Daffodils full bloom, the first dead-headed; squills and grape hyacinths and lungwort full; the pachysandra suddenly in flower, lanky bittercress; full deadnettle; Peggy's pear starting to flower, our peaches starting, too; Don's blue windflower is open beside several of his blue hyacinths; apple trees are leafing; Korean lilac leafing; red quince buds fat and red and set to come out; grass ready to mow; bees and cabbage butterflies about; wrinkled rhubarb leaves have formed now; peony stems are four to eight inches, one up to a foot and leafing out; the blue flag iris foliage is catching up with the peonies; waterleaf has spread all over the ground; raspberry shoots have emerged, some bushy to a half a foot; box elder in flower; redbuds showing purple buds; one weeping cherry in full bloom along Stafford Street.

2013: Grackles courting in the cold rainy morning. Ramps are up two to three inches, and the lungwort is struggling to put out a few short leaves. No bluebells yet under the mock orange bush. No waterleaf along the west border. No color on the finches. But the flowering maples (that traditionally mark the end of sugaring season) do not lie: Michele Burns wrote from Flying Mouse Farms here in Yellow Springs: "John believes syrup season is over, but there is a chance more will come. So far we've made 220 gallons of syrup. That's a record for us."

2014: Walking before sunrise with Bella, I heard the first cardinal at 6:01. The first robin chirping began a minute or so later, and the full robin singsong chorus built up over the next fifteen minutes. Another cardinal joined in at 6:14. I am guessing that the differences in song time from year to year are most likely the result of morning temperatures, the wind and the character of the season. Casey called around 7:45 to report he had seen the first redwing blackbirds along Grinnell Road - the first sighting this year. And Annie commented on the extreme, robust plumpness of one of the robins she had seen. In the garden around Jeanie's redbud tree, the first tiny waterleaf leaves have emerged. In the circle garden, the allium leaves are about three inches tall. Jeff, returning from southern France, said that magnolias were in full bloom there. On the way to have supper at Ella's, I met Michele from Flying Mouse Farm, who said that sugaring was about over for the year.

2015: Frost, thin, thin crescent moon rising just shy of Limestone Street, clear sky, Sagittarius south, low and long bank of violet altostratus in the northeast: First robin whinny, announcing the chorus, at 5:57, the robin singsongs coming in a minute later, then a song sparrow pitched higher but in tonal sync with the robins; cardinal at 6:02 over on Stafford; doves at 6:12 at least, and by then the song sparrows were piercing the chorus on High Crows at

6:27, eastern frontal banks of altostratus breaking apart and glowing roseate, cut by gold contrails, geese at 6:33, and more song sparrows through the neighborhood.

2016: I was late this morning: robins were already whinnying at 5:45, sky clear, first quarter moon down, no wind. Rick sent a note today saying that when he and Mary left the Florida panhandle last week, the redbuds were blooming and the maples were coming in. This afternoon, Dennie sent a video of a frog croaking in a pond near Hocking Hills, about a hundred miles southwest of Yellow Springs: "There were colonies of them in wet spots along the bottom of the gorge near Old Man's Cave!" At home: the beleaguered rhubarb now has two leaves, one of them three inches long. And Jeanie's primrose by Janet's redbud has a purple blossom.

2017: Sweetgum seed ball falling increases, more on the ground now than in the branches. Small groups of robins, five or six birds together, hunting in the village lawns. Black buzzards seen eating roadkill along Dayton-Yellow Springs Road.

2018: In the side yard: two patches of full-blooming violet windflowers. In the porch beds, full flowering, purple mid-season (Dutch) crocuses. Two beds of daffodils seen open in town. From Spoleto in Italy, Neysa says that daffodils are blooming there and that the almond trees are in bloom. In Madison, Wisconsin, Maggie reports a few scilla sprouts in spite of ice and snow on the ground.

2020: Ed Davis and I walked to the Glass Farm wetlands this morning, coming into a flock of boisterous red-winged blackbirds. At Ellis this afternoon, the weeping willow's branches were glowing yellow, and its leaves were pale green and about a half-inch long. Maples were shedding in the rain, and the north edge of the pond was red with their flowers. On South West College Street, the first pachysandra seen in bloom. And all around town, the first forsythia bushes were flowering.

2022: A third mild day in a row. Before sunrise, a chaos of robin and doves and song sparrow and cardinal calls. Yesterday's first four daffodils have become twenty this afternoon. The first canna lily roots and seeds, planted indoors during the last week of February, are sending up shoots. From Goshen, Indiana, 200 miles northwest of Yellow Springs, Judy reports riotous croaking and calling of frogs and toads at a nearby pond.

2023: Cold wind, high only in the lower 30s, today's weather is a five to ten percent phenomenon. The day is so raw and gray, but the daffodils and the scattered forsythia flowers mark the time as the middle of March in which the beauty is ragged and marginal. The aconites and snowdrops should still be flowering, but the foliage is defiantly green, making patches of transition in the alley and yard. Holding to the daffodils and the gusty wind, I say to myself, "This is March. This is March! This is where I am."

Like the moment just before someone first told you they loved you:
Spring is like that.

Catherine O'Kane

March 19th
The 78th Day of the Year

Daffodils, that come before
the swallow dares,
And take the winds of March
with beauty.

William Shakespeare

Sunrise/set: 6:41/6:46
Day's Length: 12 hours 5 minutes
Average High/Low: 50/31
Average Temperature: 41
Record High: 81 – 2012
Record Low: 6 – 1885

Weather
The 19th is cloudy one year in two, with rain or snow coming one year in three. Highs in the 70s or 80s are recorded five percent of the years, 60s in 20 percent of all the years; 50s come 15 percent of the years. Forties are the most common of all on this date: 40 percent of the highs remain there. Colder temperatures occur too: 15 percent of the afternoons reach only into the 30s, five percent don't rise above 29. Frost strikes one morning out of two.

Natural Calendar
In average years, clematis leaves emerge beside new growth of the dodder. Comfrey leaves reach two inches long. Motherwort swells into clumps, and purple deadnettle is usually in full bloom. Snowdrops and snow crocuses have often turned to foliage. Waterleaf leaves, about an inch or two across, begin to cover the ground of their habitats. Lamb's quarter, beggarticks, pigweed and amaranth sprout as periwinkle flower petals continue to unfold.

Daybook
1984: The yellow-bellied sapsucker is rattling on the cedar siding of the west wall. This week last year, he did the same thing.

1985: Water striders mating beyond the third fishing hole. Snow trillium found in bloom near the swinging bridge. New forget-me-not sprouts are up; some black raspberry buds are opening. Garlic mustard seeds have sprouted.

1986: Cardinal singing at 6:16 a.m. Grackles are back in the yard, loud and active at 7:00. Pussy willows fully emerged.

1987: Large flock of buzzards seen over the North Glen.

1989: At Jacoby Swamp, some skunk cabbage leaves are nine inches tall. Garlic mustard has sprouted under the mulch. Forsythia buds are bright yellow, ready to open. In front of the house, crocus budded and bloomed in one day.

1990: First live groundhog (as opposed to road kill) seen today in the middle of a wheat field. Many more killed along the roads all week.

1993: First red-winged blackbird of the year seen today along Wilberforce-Clifton Road, two weeks late. Still no buzzards sighted over North Glen, a similar pattern in cold March of 1984.

1998: First carpenter bee. Full bloom of the late crocus.

1999: Faint twittering of robinsong at 6:00 a.m. Stonecrop pushes through the mulch in the east garden.

2003: Ten days after the end of the long freeze, all the snow is gone, the pussy willows are completely out, the first of the crocus patches have already wilted, and the daffodils are budding.

2004: The eight inches of snow that fell a few days ago is melting quickly today. The bamboo straightens up as the weight of the snow falls away. The crocus emerges and blooms again.

2006: At 5:30 this morning I went out to get firewood and heard the screech owl calling. At 5:50, one cardinal sang but then was quiet. Robins peeped off and on at that time, but no chorus until later. Cool weather continues.

2008: The Danielsons' aconites are open this morning, in spite of the gray sky and heavy rain. Their entire side yard is golden. In our north garden, tulip foliage is getting fatter, the plants almost looking like young skunk cabbages.

2009: Aconite season has ended in the alley, and some of our snowdrops have wilted. The grass in the north yard is clearly greener, glowing in the morning sun. Two more daffodils have opened in the backyard. When I walked Bella this morning, grackles, blue jays, doves and cardinals were calling, robins in considerable numbers flying and chirping and hunting worms. The peach tree has started putting out leaves, veronica and spiderwort foliage has started, the rhubarb is finally out of the ground, privets are leafing, the roses and hydrangeas have some soft buds, the remaining winterberry berries are dark and decaying, coralberries brown and shriveled. By the pond, the first early red dwarf tulip was open, and a mosquito buzzed around me in the woodshed (the first of the year having attacked me near Peggy's yard two days ago).

2010: To Bowling Green, Kentucky: No changes in the landscape noticed until about 30 miles from Louisville, when we saw the first clumps of daffodils, then a few weeping cherries and a star magnolia half in bloom. Robins were mating in the campground streets, grackles loud in the trees. Here the bittercress is much taller than at home.

2011: Robins at 5:45 this morning, seven daffodils blooming in the yard, full bloom of all crocus and snowdrops, with some fading noticed.

2012: Pussy willow catkins and early star magnolia petals falling, red quince in bloom, the first hosta coming up, river birch buds greening as they push out. Lawn is definitely long enough to mow. Dutchman's britches, snow trillium, swamp buttercup, flowering in the Glen, toad trillium fully formed, redbuds almost in bloom along Xenia Avenue - full purple, and toads singing tonight in the neighborhood (Casey reporting that his toads started the evening of the 17th and sang all day today). The first patches of the Great Dandelion Bloom noticed on the way to Dayton.

Exploding Zeitgebers in 2012: A note for *the Yellow Springs News,* March 19, 2012:

The week ahead is supposed to be the sixth and final week of Early Spring in Yellow Springs, but temperatures in the 70s over the past weeks have accelerated so many of the seasonal markers that the village has entered Middle Spring, three to four weeks ahead of average years.

Zeitgebers for the end of March often include the first blossoms of hepatica, twinleaf, bloodroot, violet cress and Dutchman's britches. Cabbage butterflies typically appear in the last week of the third month, and forsythia flowers usually usher in April. This year, however, wildflower season opened in Glen Helen by March 12, with the blossoms of hepatica and violet cress. Daffodils opened in town on the 8th, blue squills on the 10th, puschkinias and grape hyacinths by the 11th.

At the end of March's second week, the acceleration increased, and the village reached and surpassed markers ordinarily associated with the first weeks of April: Forsythia bushes turned yellow overnight on the 13th. Bluebells were up and budded by the 14th. Cabbage butterflies and carpenter bees were out on the 15th, the same day that star magnolia blossoms appeared along Xenia Avenue. The first weeping cherry bloomed on Stafford Street, and the first bloodroot near the Cascades on the 16th. Pollen formed all over the pussy willows on the 17th, and the first peach and box elder and pachysandra bloomed that same day. The pears opened downtown, and redbud buds were emerging as the first red quince flowered on the 18th.

Still, in spite of this explosion of zeitgebers, local seasonal markers have been this far advanced an average of once every six or seven years ever since records were started in 1883. My own notes go back thirty years, and, for example, forsythia bloomed on March 3 in 1983, daffodils and hepatica on March 6 that year, tulips and bluebells on the 13th. I tracked similar patterns in 1990 (when the downtown pear trees all burst into bloom in the first week of March) and 2000. Statistics on temperatures in February and March going back to the 19th century show that the same zeitgebers must have been observed in Yellow Springs during the mild Early Springs of 1976, 1973, 1946, 1945, 1938, 1935, 1929, 1925, 1921, 1918, 1907, 1903, 1898 and 1894.

2015: Temperature at 34, partly cloudy, light wind: One cardinal at 5:49, then nothing heard until 5:56 when the first robins started to whinny; then at 5:58 cardinals started; at 6:04 the first dove and the robin song developed to the chorus singsong; by 6:11 strong robins, cardinals, doves; crows at 6:25; a nuthatch heard when I went back outside at 6:35. Around lunchtime, I noticed that the pale brown bamboo leaves, killed by the hard winter, had started to fall to the pond.

2016: I look back at this day in 2012: Last week, I thought that the March of 2016 would pace the progress of 2012, but the remainder of the month is forecast to be cool, and blooming times will most likely settle into their more typical pattern; I will see. Still, the lawn could be mowed to even it out, and the grass near the rocks at the edge of the north garden needs to be trimmed back.

2018: Michele from Flying Mouse Farm reports that the trees are still giving up their sap and that John is making syrup. I finished spading up most of the annual patches this mild, 60-degree afternoon, transplanted some Resurrection lilies and a clump of snowdrops. Ice storm forecast for tomorrow, snow on the 21st.

2019: Tulip foliage up an inch, mock orange leaf buds greening, straining to open before the honeysuckles. Snow crocuses, aconites and snowdrops still in full bloom in the dooryard. In the west garden, the first bright blue squill is opening. I heard the first cardinal at 5:53 this morning (the sky clear, frost on the car windows), then lots of robin whinnies, then the full robin chorus, then the song sparrows and doves a little after 6:00. When I came out an hour later after breakfast: blue jays, crows, sparrows, grackles. At midday: the first two honeybees were in the violet, large-flowered crocuses.

2020: At Ellis, the grass was long enough to be spongy as I walked today, very green and almost ready to cut. Along Limestone Street, the privet bushes are greening with small leaves. Jane writes that her Carolina wren has built its nest in her old bicycle helmet. Heavy night rains, and the Little Miami River overflowed into the lowlands near the covered bridge and even across Grinnell Road.

2021: Jennifer Berman reports sighting an American Tree Sparrow at her feeder.

2022: Cold in the 40s, cloudy and windy: 30 daffodils in bloom across the north garden.

2023: A low in the middle teens bends the daffodils (118 counted). High not reaching 40. Deep blue sky with rugged cumulus clouds, raw March. Grackles feeding in the early morning. This cold snap holds back the movement of the month, prolonging the progress of the warm winter, helping to fit this March into the broader March history here. The forecasts for the cherry bloom in Washington D.C. had been for close to today. (The average bloom time is the last week of March or early April.), but cooler temperatures may move it well into next week.

Shepherd sprouts are the earliest, then dandelions, then mustard. Then come poke, lamb's quarters, then pigweed.

Myrtle Brown, Yellow Springs, Ohio

March 20th
The 79th Day of the Year

It is the first mild day of March:
each minute sweeter than before,
the redbreast sings from the tall larch
that stands beside our door.

William Wordsworth

Sunrise/set: 6:39/6:47
Day's Length: 12 hours 8 minutes
Average High/Low: 50/32
Average Temperature: 41
Record High: 83 – 2012
Record Low: - 3 – 1885

Weather

This is one of the wettest days in an average March, with rain coming 45 percent of the time, and snow another 20 percent. Despite the precipitation, some sun shows through the clouds two thirds of the years in my record. High temperatures are in the 70s or 80s five percent of the time, in the 60s twenty percent, in the 50s another 20 percent, in the 40s about 25 to 30 percent, in the 30s twenty percent. Today is the last day of the spring on which the chances of a high just in the 20s reach five percent. There is also a possibility (one or two percent) of highs climbing above 80 for the first time since October 31st. Frost occurs one morning out of two.

Natural Calendar

White cabbage butterflies are the surest sign of the collapse of Early Spring. And once you notice the familiar white cabbage butterfly, then you know the more elusive mourning cloak butterflies and the question mark butterflies and the tortoise shell butterflies and the tiny blues are flying, too.

When you see cabbage butterflies, then you know that gold finches are turning gold, and you may soon see ants working on the sidewalk.

When cabbage butterflies appear, then catfish have begun

spring feeding and breeding. Green bottle flies have hatched and termites swarm, looking for new sweet wood to eat.

When cabbage butterflies are out, then soft sprouts of touch-me-nots have emerged in the wetlands and the branches of weeping willow trees are turning pale yellow-green as their buds expand. In the city, *Cornus mas* shrubs produce golden blossoms, promising forsythia within a week.

When white cabbage butterflies are out, then Middle Spring's hepatica and violet cress and spring beauties are open. Twinleaf is pushing out in the sanctuary of the woodlands. Toad trillium and Dutchman's britches are ready to open there, the entire spectrum of wildflowers surging to encounter April.

Just before dawn, the stars of Capricorn lie in the southeast. Sagittarius and Scorpius (with the red star, Antares, in its center) fill the south. West of Scorpius is boxy Libra. West of Libra is Virgo, marked by Spica, the brightest of the southwestern stars.

Daybook

1984: Covered Bridge. This spring is slow and cold, but parsnip and dock are finally growing at the swamp beside the early ragwort and the sweet rocket. Red-winged blackbirds whistle in the trees, ducks are scouting the banks of the misty river. There are buds on the violet cress.

1985: First periwinkle and dandelion seen blooming. Two more daffodils are out at Fern Albertson's (in front of the Methodist rectory). Raspberry leaves starting, dock strong, horseradish leaves are an inch long.

1986: Junco at the bird feeder. Still here.

1990: First fly in the house.

1991: Cardinal sings at 6:19 a.m. Snowdrops wilting now in the warm sun, aconites just a little stronger. Crocus wide open, peonies the length of my index finger and unraveling a little, purple deadnettle early bloom, perennial phlox are up an inch, bushy around the old stalks. The first great ragweed sprouts.

1993: This spring is even later than the spring of 1984, the progress of mid-February continuing to stall in a month of snow and cold.

1994: Out along Yellow Springs Creek, hazy sky, temperature into the 60s, the water sparkling, the ground cover starting to rise ever so little now, the tiny waterleaf and sedum protruding, lots of leaves of violet cress poking through the autumn mulch, wild onion with lanky new spears, tight clusters of garlic mustard coming back, sweet rocket strong with fresh new foliage, one or two honeysuckle buds pale green. Two geese held their ground against me on a small peninsula formed by the wandering creek; Buttercup and I gave them plenty of room. In the east garden, the first full bloom of the snow crocus. In the south garden, mallow has small leaves. A few daffodils have buds, the first standard purple crocus opened today, and as Jeanie and I worked in the yard, two more bloomed. Queen Anne's lace has started to come back, as have the yarrow, silver sage, columbine, bleeding heart, and red sedum. Jeni called from Jacksonville, Florida: she saw the first baby ducks on the local pond just a couple of days ago. The canopy is half filled in, she says, and azaleas are in full bloom.

1995: Throughout town, silver maple blossom season is ending for the year, flowers falling to the streets. Beside them, all the snow crocus lie wilted. At the Covered Bridge, with the wind blowing hard and warm, buckeyes are starting to unravel, the first violet leaves are spreading, a few toothworts have buds, the first cabbage butterfly is out, and the first violet cress is blooming.

1998: Crow seen with nest material in its mouth. First daffodils are opening in town.

1999: Crocus full bloom through town. Honeybees with pollen on their legs at the purple blossoms in the backyard. Light chirping of a few robins at 6:00 a.m. Then at 6:10, the first cardinals. Crows eight minutes later.

2003: Buzzards sailing the sky over the freeway as I drove to work this afternoon. At home in the north garden, daylily foliage has shot up to three inches.

2004: Robins quiet at 5:45 a.m., full song at 6:00. Doves came in at 6:10, cardinals at 6:15. Clematis and Japanese honeysuckle leaves have started. Lilac leaf buds unraveling.

2005: Robins strong at 5:35 this morning, a sudden surge in volume, a full half an hour earlier than just a couple of days ago. At Antioch School, I heard the first blue jay bell call.

2007: The first blue squills noticed opening in King's Yard downtown this morning. Willows yellow-greening along the freeway. Small white-flowered, cut-leafed cress blooming in the dirt where I dug up bamboo last August.

2008: One flicker call heard and the red-bellied woodpecker's "brrrt." Finches still feeding strong, but coloring unchanged. The first red nubs of the rhubarb are visible today, the ramp leaves are starting to unravel, and the Dutch iris spears have come up in the past few days. The front garden's snow crocus have all opened up in the sun this morning.

2009: Even with cold temperatures in the 40s, honeybees continue to visit the pond to drink.

2010: To Montgomery, Alabama from Bowling Green, Kentucky: Forsythia in bloom at the Alabama border, then more April: a patch of dandelions and ground ivy. Fifty miles north of Birmingham: chickweed, pink magnolia, white clover at a rest stop, apples and full pears at Birmingham, the lower bush line greening. Large and small buttercups, black medic, the red Southern clover, and the first upper trees are greening.

2011: Robins in full song when I went outside at 5:44 this morning. The first red *Iris reticulata* is in bloom by the pond.

2012: Between Yellow Springs and Xenia, all flowering trees except the crab apples and dogwoods are in full bloom, three to four weeks early. Along Dayton Street, the serviceberries are finally starting to open. Darkening of forsythia petals is occurring as the unusually warm weather holds. Henry Myers called this morning to say he and his wife heard toads singing when they went for a walk yesterday morning. Four pink tulips planted last fall opened overnight in the north garden.

At the dairy outside of town, two purple azalea bushes completely open. From Madison, Tat reports forsythia in full bloom, at least a month ahead of normal. On my evening walk, strong robin vespers. Lawn mowed for the first time to level out old crocus, wild onion and longer clumps of grass. Looking back at my records from 1983, 1990 and 2000, I can see that even though the first half of March was very mild those years, the heat did not last through the end of the month, and so the flowering did not continue to accelerate like it has this year. And if the warmth occurred in the upper Midwest in those years, it did not stay as long or as intensely as it is staying this year.

2013: At 5:57 this morning, the first robins started chirping and whinnying along Stafford Street. At 6:00, they were in full, rhythmic song. At 6:05, doves were calling on Limestone Street, and three minutes later cardinals on High Street. At the feeder today, a faint flush of gold on one finch. Catherine reports a red-breasted nuthatch at her feeder – the first in years.

2014: Cloudy, cool, windy this morning when I walked Bella, starting at 5:50. There was no birdsong at all until the robins started chirping at 6:11, gaining momentum every minute. But no cardinal sang by 6:15, and I went inside. This is the second morning in which I noticed that the wind delayed the morning songs. From the house, I heard the red-bellied woodpecker call at exactly 7:00.

2015: Cool, light rain/mist, no wind: Robins whinny at 6:03, singsong slow to develop; cardinal at 6:08, reluctant, it seems to me, then gathering some momentum.

2016: My second tier of aconites is still bright yellow, either a later variety or just delayed by their age or depth. Tonight: loud, close thunderstorms for at least an hour, hard rain, the yard and front sidewalk flooding.

2019: Maggie and Tat report seeing their first robins in Madison, Wisconsin. Maggie found scilla foliage in the preserve near her house. Here in Yellow Springs, an entire patch of scillas open downtown.

2020: Jill's daffodils near the street have opened, and many of mine have finally come in all the way. No worms noticed on the roads or sidewalks after last night's heavy rain. Ron reports hearing a yellow-rumped warbler. Forsythia full flower now, pacing the daffodils. Flooding all over the yard and in patches throughout the village.

2021: Update after several days of sun: full blooming daffodils and mid-season crocuses in the garden, snowdrops and snow crocus fading. Peony stalks three inches high, ramps four inches high, Virginia bluebells three inches by the mock orange bush. A great patch of scillas all blue in King's Yard downtown. No forsythia noticed yet, no pollen on the pussy willow yet. Some maples ready to open. Robins vespers at last light.

2022: Jill's aconites are done flowering, and the snowdrops and snow crocuses in my dooryard are disappearing quickly. Many bods on the ancient forsythia bushes are starting to unravel, an equinox bloom. Thirty daffodils open this morning, many more budding, more tulips coming up, more lilies, the first two blue squills.. The cup plants that I put in last fall have developed basal leaves. More honeysuckles and Japanese honeysuckle vines are leafing, winter collapsing all around.

Journal

Even though average blooming dates of certain spring shrubs seem to have moved back about a week in the past thirty years, the familiar structure of the seasons is not so different in the first decade of the 21st century than that of the 1980s. In spite of changes, I continue to enjoy the similarities that continue to appear.

Probably the most striking changes that I have noted, thanks to many observers who have shared their observations, concern birds. In the last century, sandhill cranes did not fly over Yellow Springs like they now do every November and December. Phil Hawkey was the first to report them in 2004, and every year afterwards, village residents have seen or heard them.

When my family and I arrived in Yellow Springs in the 1970s, the appearance of turkey vultures in March or late February was a sign of spring. Then, just in the past decade, the sightings became earlier and earlier until it was clear the vultures were no longer leaving the area during the late fall; they were spending the winter here. And in 2004, the first black buzzard (a variety of vulture that rarely ventured north of the Ohio River in the 20th century) was reported in the Glen, and by 2009, small flocks were overwintering in the county, along with their turkey vulture relatives.

In reviewing my journal for this column, I have been reassured to see once again that what has happened before will happen again. It is comforting to see that each week and even each day has its own agenda for weather, flowers, insects, grass and trees, even as that agenda may be slowly transformed by climate. As I piece together my own life, I realize that its fragments accumulate around natural history, threads of excitement, disappointment, idealism and love weaving in and around snowstorms and starlight, robins, anemones and lilacs.

And what if all of animated nature
Be but organic harps diversely framed,
That tremble into thought, as o'er them sweeps
Plastic and vast, one intellectual breeze,
At once the Soul of each, and God of all?

Samuel Taylor Coleridge

March 21st
The 80th Day of the Year

And so we celebrate
renewal of the world:
happy are they
who find their love therein,
their heart's desire.

Manuscript of Benedictbeuern
(bf)

Sunrise/set: 6:37/6:48
Day's Length: 12 hours 11 minutes
Average High/Low: 51/32
Average Temperature: 41
Record High: 86 – 2012
Record Low: 9 – 1885

Weather
The traditional first day of spring is partly to mostly sunny 90 percent of the time, making it one of the two brightest days in the month. Chances of precipitation are low: rain falls just 20 percent of the days, and snow another 15 percent. Fifteen percent of the days reach 70 or 80 degrees, ten percent 60s, twenty-five percent 50s, twenty percent 40s, twenty-five percent 30s, five percent 20s. Frost occurs two mornings in three.

Natural Calendar
The Sun is directly above the equator on March 20 or 21, but day and night are equal (equilux) on March 17. Now. Scilla foliage pushes out in Wisconsin; aconites and snow crocuses flower in Chicago, and star magnolias bloom in Cincinnati as the Sun reaches equinox and enters its Middle Spring sign of Aries. Sandhill cranes continue to congregate for migration north along the Platte River in Nebraska, while some flocks settle in for the spring in the lakes of Madison, Wisconsin.

1987: Comfrey emerging, and earliest horseradish leaves, first forsythia flowers, first pussy willow pollen, first bee.

1990: I was waiting, and a cardinal began to sing at 6:00 a.m. sharp. Shepherd's purse late blooming on Corry Street. Tulips budding everywhere, pear trees in flower downtown.

1991: Box elders opened today in Yellow Springs. Then we went south toward Jekyll Island on the Georgia coast. At Cincinnati, the grass was greener, and *Cornus mas* was open, first forsythia, many honeysuckle leaves. Fifty miles into Kentucky, willows were greening, and there were fields of daffodils, patches of red maples flowering. Toward the Tennessee border, more trees were coming in, giving sometimes an orange, sometimes reddish tint to the horizon. Two hundred seventy-five miles from Yellow Springs, the first cabbage butterfly seen. Thirty miles from Knoxville, three redbud trees in bloom; in the city, crab trees and pears were completely out, forsythia full bloom, dandelions full, daffodils gone in certain patches. We seem to have come at least three weeks in 300 miles. It's April 15th here, Yellow Springs Time.

1995: Most all spring iris gone now, but it's the first day for the pink wood hyacinths.

2000: Asparagus up an inch in the garden. The first lungwort flower is open. Bleeding hearts have pushed up another inch, are getting bushy. Cressleaf groundsel and achillea have put on a couple inches in the past cool week. The first tulip bulb has formed. Squills and daffodils still full bloom. Quince ready to leaf. Across the countryside, a faint touch of green from honeysuckle bushes, and the city tree line is tinged with red from the flowering maples. On Dayton Street, the pale snow-on-the-mountain is pacing the waterleaf at home. At night, a black wasp sat dazed on the back of the couch, as though waking from a long sleep.

2003: Robins chirping at 5:40 this morning when I got up. In the south garden this afternoon: sweet Williams are getting new leaves, poppy foliage has grown bushy, peonies are two inches out of the ground now, a small spring iris has bloomed, and the midseason crocus are coming in.

2005: Dropping Neysa off at Don Gasho's house to deliver her taxes, I noticed that one of the daffodils on the south side of his house was just starting to open, the first seen so far this year.

2006: Cold weather continues, holding spring where it left off ten days ago. The bittersweet berries continue to thin, now down to maybe just ten percent. A few blue privet berries hold, even as the buds crack and green up. Coral berries hang on, mostly shriveled and dark. Birds are quiet this chilly morning as a storm moves in.

2007: A high in the 70s today. The first daffodil and forsythia buds show yellow. Rhubarb and peonies have put on an inch since a few days ago, some aconites and snow crocus are done blooming, the koi in our pond are hungry, lilac buds are greening, the sounds of blackbirds and grackles fill the days. Blue eyes open in the vegetable garden area. Tat in Madison, Wisconsin, reports that her chipmunks became active around her porch two days ago.

2009: Robins at 6:00 this morning, cardinals at 6:08. Bluebell foliage in the south garden is up three inches; above it, the first mock orange leaves are coming out. In the north garden, the first mint is pushing out, blue-eyes and wild deadnettle blooming beside it. In the east garden, the snow-on-the-mountain leaves are coming up. Along the west edge of the property, pachysandra has been budded for over a week.

2010: Montgomery, Alabama to Dauphin Island, Alabama. Pears leafing and losing petals all along the road, soft wind, clouds, rain. First redbuds in bloom about 150 miles north of Mobile, yellow Jessamine flowering about 50 miles north. At the island, we saw a brown thrasher (larger than a wood thrush, nervously thrashing around in the leaves for insects), collared doves (and listened their calls, which were more intense than those of the mourning doves). Flock of cowbirds seen, and dozens of tiny yellow-rumped warblers working the ground around the camper for seeds. Found spiderwort, sow thistles, wild strawberries, azaleas with red buds.

2011: Soft robinsong before 5:00 a.m., temperature in the middle 50s. A gentle April day, tulips pushing up, honeysuckles and mock orange leafing, more daffodils in bloom. All the aconites in the alley are past their best. High close to 70 this afternoon, and I sat out watching the sun move down over Dayton. Tonight, strong robin vespers at 8:00 p.m.

2012: Cardinal heard at 6:00 this morning. More heat in the 80s today, redbuds and box elders now all the way out, and serviceberries in the first day of their peak bloom. Almost all the pussy willow catkins have fallen. Pears downtown full. Two male cardinals seen jockeying for territories in the alley this morning, birdsong loud and raucous all around me, cardinals and grackles and robins and sparrows. More magnolias falling, pink and star, some daffodils fading, lungwort, pachysandra, squills, daffodils, deadnettle full, very lanky bittercress, blue eyes almost gone. Virginia bluebells and violets flowering. Some peonies over a foot tall, leaves fully formed. First of the lily trees has emerged. River birches and magnolias leafing. The graceful, flowing box elder flowers complement the violet glow of the redbuds. Lace vine leaves are an inch across, filling in around the trellis. Constant cardinal song in the morning, and fierce steady sparrow chattering, not the summer-like chirping. Carpenter bees humming around the porch, nesting. The first small blue butterfly seen fluttering through the southwest garden.

And tonight I came to realize that writing down what happened each day was not so much repetitive as it was affirming, broadening each day's texture through the years. What happened today on March 21st in 2012 fleshes out the history of what I have seen on March 21st in all the years that I have watched. Each day enfolds on the other, not only sequentially but also along the radii of the repeating cycles, tying together space and time, motion and stasis, presence and absence, body and spirit.

2014: Mid-season crocus are now opening up throughout town, a few even in my yard. More bees on the blossoms in the sun. At North Glen, almost no new foliage up at all, but moss is in full bloom.

2015: Very clear, no wind, no frost: I walked outside at 5:49 to the first robin chirps. A song sparrow was warming up, too. The robin chorus got underway at 5:53. (It seemed like a long time between the first calls and the chorus; of course, it wasn't.) It took the cardinals until 6:05 to join. I heard crows off in the southwest at 6:11. In the noon full sun, the east garden's mid-season crocuses are all open, deep purple or white. The paler snow crocuses still in bloom. Two blue squills noticed this afternoon downtown, and I heard a red-bellied woodpecker call, the first time this spring that I've noticed it.

2018: Cold weather remains the rule, holding the progress of the year at about four daffodils and several patches of mid-season crocus. Two inches of snow with a raw wind here, and a major storm across the East.

2019: Under the influence of full moon, perigee and the March 20 cold front: wet and chilly today. First robins chirping at 5:40, first cardinal at 5:50.

2020: The North Glen is full of people going to see the thundering cascades waterfall.

2021: Cascades: small clumps of white hepaticas along the river, only a few bushy outcroppings of Dutchman's britches foliage. One housefly seen, and a mosquito (Jill having avoided the first one yesterday) pestered me as I sat out on the porch after our walk.

2022: Forty-two daffodils in bloom today, many, many more budded for later in the week.

Community Spring

The spring equinox occurred at 11:33 a.m. on the 20th, and late that afternoon, several dozen women, men and children gathered at Agraria, an experimental farm near Yellow Springs, to celebrate. After rain and chilly winds on the 19th, the sky was cloudless, the low sun intense, the air gentle.

Emily lit a fire in the fire circle and told a Native American story about the passage of the seasons, and participants were asked to observe, feel or remember at least one fragment of spring as they made a slow, meditative walk in silence.

Returning to the circle, the meditators, one by one, created community spring.

Josephine's poem captured the physical feel of the still expectant earth, the furrows of the field and the uneven paths, *lumpy and bumpy.*

A few people shared memories (their words in italics): *Spring was the time to throw off our winter coats and go in to the woods to play...for me, the skunk cabbage was the the most important marker for me... this morning, I watched a robin gathering grass for its nest...*

As the number of observations grew, so did the sense of place and time. People told what they experienced or wrote their impressions on note cards:

The angle of the sunlight in the late afternoon was invigorating...bird song...soft earth... red stems of dead nettle... verdant yarrow... velvety leaves of honeysuckle...edible dead nettle... the start of evening primrose...wild onions growing...dandelion leaves...soft breeze...no clouds... fermenting Osage fruit...ants around a tapped tree spigot...insect galls...thick moss on a stump... honeysuckle leafing out...dark green fern starting...hard shelf mushroom... clover... tiny buds... warm sun... sap running... smell of earth and the campfire...red buds on trees and shrubs...bird song piping... a milk jug on a maple tree... red little leaves among the grass...moss really thick on the north side of trees... fresh air... watery path... distant field... walnut in the mud... white, yellow and reddish brown fungus on fallen branches and logs becoming re-animated...oneness...possibility...new awareness... presence, being together, awakening... deer tracks... fallen trees... chirping birds... lots of mud!...brown branches seemingly dead, but soon to spring to life...cherry bark... grape vines... elm bark... buds swelling... blooming flowers... creek unfrozen... sounds of water... warmth of spring sun upon my face.. rebirth of plant life... pairing of ducks and geese, sounds of woodpeckers looking for grubs...brown mushroom on the ground... the combination of decay continuing as new growth begins... even though the trees look bare, and the flowers aren't yet blooming, the air and sun feel like spring....

And an appreciation: *It's neat to experience spring with people. This is how the world grows and leads.*

And one person knew that Orion was setting in the west with the equinoctial sun; he said farewell to the winter sky and first day of spring: *Good night, Orion.*

To chart the minutes of this hour, when time itself is so mysterious a thing – it's very difficult indeed, too much responsibility to wrap your head around. Much as if you were called upon to create the very fabric of the cosmos.

Bonnie Nadzam

March 22nd
The 81st Day of the Year

When daffodils begin to peer
With hey the doxy over the dale,
Why then comes in the sweet o' the year
And the red blood reigns in the winter's pale.

William Shakespeare

Sunrise/set: 6:36/6:49
Day's Length: 12 hours 13 minutes
Average High/Low: 51/32
Average Temperature: 42
Record High: 84 – 1907
Record Low: 5 – 1885

Weather

Today's high temperature distribution: 80s five percent of the time, 70s five percent of the time, 60s twenty-five percent, 50s ten percent, 40s forty-five percent, 30s ten percent. The sun shines five days in ten; rain falls 25 percent of the days, snow just once in a decade. Frost occurs 60 percent of the mornings, but this morning is the last morning in the spring when odds for a freeze rise so high.

The Week Ahead
The storms of Wintry Time will quickly pass,
And one unbounded Spring encircle all.
\

From James Thomson, *The Seasons*

The last quarter of March brings dramatic changes. Today, for the first time since October 22, there is a five percent chance of highs to reach 80 degrees. And on the 31st, those chances double. On the 23rd, the odds for morning frost are about one in two, but on the 29th, those odds fall to just one in four. In the warmest years of all, frost can be gone until October or November (but an average season brings 20 more dawns below the freezing mark). Through the 28th, cold afternoons in the 30s still happen one year in ten or 15, but then on the 29th and 30th, chances of such cold drop to less than five percent for the first time since the end of October. The 25th through the 28th are the driest and sunniest days of the week, each bringing a 60 percent chance or better of a break in the clouds. The 29th is the day most likely to bring overcast conditions -- the sun is absent on that date 65 percent of the time, and rain falls 50 percent of the time. The likelihood of a thunderstorm is six times greater this week than it was last week. And tornado season usually begins now, and lasts through the summer. Ohio has an average of 12 twisters in a year, but not one has ever come to Yellow Springs.

Natural Calendar

The final week of Early Spring brings May Apple Season on sunny slopes, and the first days of Leafing Out Season for willows, mock orange, and buckeyes. Forsythia Blossom Season starts at scattered locations this week.

Field Corn Planting Season and Oats Planting Season get underway in Lower Midwestern fields by the end of the month. Sweet Corn Planting Season and Lettuce Planting Season open in the garden.

If temperatures rise to the 60s for a few days, Middle Spring Wildflower Season arrives in the woods, with bluebells, twinleaf, bloodroot, small-flowered bittercress and hepatica budding and then bursting into bloom. And American Toad Calling Season coincides by the 31st with the first days of Duckling and Gosling Hatching Season.

Daybook

1986: Cardinal sings at 6:08 a.m., skies clear, 18 degrees.

1987: First cabbage butterfly in the garden. Raspberry leaves sprouting. No worms found yet.

1988: Depart from Yellow Springs for Tuscaloosa, Alabama. First greening near Cincinnati, Louisville much the same. By Bowling Green, Kentucky, 220 miles south, a rapid shift in the color, hills brightening toward Tennessee, a week to ten days ahead of Yellow

Springs. At Columbia, Tennessee, 400 miles south, two to three weeks from Ohio, the first flowering tree noted, honeysuckle leaves emerging. In south central Tennessee, flowering crabs clearly in bloom, grass and pastures green. In northern Alabama, the first tree line glowing with flowers and leaves. Redbuds in bloom below Huntsville, common along the road. In Birmingham, 500 miles south of home, it is late Middle Spring, the end of April, the canopy yellow green and opening, full flower of redbuds, crabs, pears. In Tuscaloosa, pears are late full, and leaves full, some flowers fading. In all, we traveled into spring at the rate of three or four days per 100 miles.

1990: North to Wisconsin. The landscape, greening from a warm spring, remains constant through central Indiana and Illinois. Bloomington, for example, seems to be at the same point of the season as Yellow Springs. An hour below Rockford, however, a decided shift takes place back toward February. I've noticed that on other trips too, that the Rockford area is the upper limit for the mild climate of the Ohio Valley. In Madison, there were robins and red-winged blackbirds. Tulips were three or four inches, daffodils higher, maybe six inches. Honeysuckles barely starting to leaf.

1991: At the southern North Carolina border, rhododendrons are blooming, and the first purple azaleas. A flock of robins and a swallowtail butterfly outside of Asheville. Near Columbia, South Carolina, and the beginning of the coastal plain, I saw the yellow trumpet vine that I came across last year in Mississippi (Jessamine), a vine with opposite, narrow leaves, full bloom. Dogwood also open. From here now, the first low trees begin to leaf, and then the taller ones as we drive towards Charleston.

Turning south along the coast, the leaves become thicker and thicker until, above the Georgia border, the roadsides are red, yellow, gold, and green with leafing and flowering trees, short and tall canopies. Just above Savanna, red clover in the roadsides, and white-headed thistles. Some cress or rape, patches of ragwort, white sweet clover on the causeway (the mark of early June in Yellow Springs). Jekyll Island: blackbird mating rituals. Azaleas full bloom, toadflax, spiderwort, white thistles full bloom through the dunes. Pokeweed three feet tall, tadpoles in the brackish water a few hundred feet from the coast. Monarch butterflies seen. Darners mating.

1992: Peak of robin migration, small flocks and pairs throughout town.

1993: The temperature got into the middle 50s today, the golden crocus in the east garden were full bloom, one of the paler yellows opened, and the violets almost opened. At the Covered Bridge, some touch-me-nots had sprouted, the hemlock had its first bright new leaves, violet cress was still small, a week away from budding even with a strong warm-up. No moss seen growing.

1994: First groundhog seen by the side of the road.

1995: Spiderwort has emerged an inch or so in the south garden.

1996: March continues cold, but more daffodils are budding, even in the snow, and their leaves seem to be getting taller. Spring iris, aconites, crocus, snowdrops survive temperatures below 20 degrees to open in the sun. Henry Myers called this afternoon to talk about the green frogs in his garden pond. The pond, he said, is right by the kitchen window, and he and his wife watched them until the first week of December last year. This year, they were active the third week of February, the first stage of Early Spring.

1999: At 5:58 a.m. singsong robin calls. At 6:07 a.m., crows. At 6:15, a cardinal.

2000: Rhubarb is up an inch or so, red nubs and tight, small, dark green leaves. The first carpenter bee of the year must have lost its way, died on the back porch last night. Snowdrops have pods now; the flowers must have all died back more than a week ago. One patch of Glory-of-the-Snow is in full bloom in the south garden.

2003: Grackles in the back trees at 6:30 a.m., their cackling and chatter directly following the robin chorus. Peewee heard at South Glen. Mike reports an Eastern Towhee this morning.

2005: Peony stalks have grown an inch in spite of the cold weather. They are up to two inches in places now. The snowdrops continue at full bloom; the snow crocuses suffer from the cold, wilt and then are replaced by other snow crocuses.

2007: Aconites definitely finished for the year at the Danielson's. Crab apple and lilac buds are unraveling. The willow tree in the alley has started to leaf, foliage maybe half an inch long and bright green. The yellow primrose by the redbud has larger buds today. Small red tulips have small buds near the fish pond.

2009: Robins and a cardinal were singing when I went outside this morning at 5:53. The afternoon was warm and sunny; we cleaned up the pond, at least 50 fingerlings counted, then we planted a pair of bittersweet vines, three larkspur plants, three salvias, three veronicas and a catmint. Noticed that our Virginia bluebells had buds. The first carpenter bee seen in the middle of the afternoon checking out the siding.

2010: Dauphin Island, Alabama: Virginia creeper a third of its full size, dock tall and budded, small star of Bethlehem plants (*Ornithoglum umbellatum*) and black medic throughout roadsides and lawns. Squirrels mating, gulls mating, collared doves mating. Most deciduous trees are budded, just starting to flower.

2011: Snowdrops and snow crocus suddenly declining. In the alley this morning, grackles and doves and titmice were steady and loud. By the back porch chickweed has suddenly come into full bloom. Full puschkinias and squills are following the crocus season, daffodils gaining momentum throughout town, apples, lilacs, Korean lilacs leafing, peonies three inches, daylilies four inches, purple coneflowers three inches, some tulip foliage six to eight inches, a few rhubarb leaves formed, viburnum buds swelling, some hydrangea branches budded. Dead nettle is starting to flower, the yellow primrose showing yellow, a few ferns showing green at the base. The willow at Antioch School is a pale yellow green. In the warm afternoon, Jeanie and I cut back the butterfly bushes and the hydrangeas, cleaned out last year's stalks and stems. A large frog or female toad spotted in the pond. At dusk, robin song loud and steady, whinnying and chirping and peeping.

2012: More tulips opened: the old orange ones by the south wall, and the new ones by the pond. Lil's maple flowering. Oakleaf hydrangea leafing. Then, to the Covered Bridge: Buckeyes in full leaf, skunk cabbage leaves about seven to ten inches long. Toothwort, Dutchman's britches, small-flowered buttercup, swamp buttercup, late twinleaf and bloodroot, violet cress, purple and pale lavender violets, early wild phlox, well-budded ragwort, toads singing down river, the undergrowth as well as the middle canopy pale green. One orange *polygonia* butterfly seen, and blues followed me all down the path to the valley pasture. Toads were singing south toward Jacoby, but Casey called to say that all of a sudden, the thunderous chant of the toads that had started on the 18th suddenly ceased in the middle of the day. Maggie writes from Madison, Wisconsin that the squills and daffodils are still holding at full bloom, many trees flowering.

2013: I got up early to walk Bella, and I heard the first cardinal at 5:54, and then a minute later, a robin chirped, and two minutes later the whole robin chorus was singing. This afternoon, the sky having been clear all day, the temperature rose into the lower 40s, and most of the aconites that I planted last November (and which had come up so much later than the established plants) finally opened to the sun.

2014: Robins and cardinals very thin this morning, some kind of change in the morning chorus. Doves, however, were really strong at 6:20. Ramps three inches in the backyard. Lungwort finally pushing out a little. Aconites early bloom in the yard.

2015: I went outside with Bella at 5:43 this morning (clear sky above, rose broken altostratus in the east, near frost, very light wind from time to time, barometer rising): The robins had already begun to chirp and whinny. I waited for the singsong chant to start: 5:51 a.m. The first distant cardinal: 5:53, the first cardinal on High Street, practically right on top of me: 5:56, and then maybe the rattle of a song sparrow getting ready. I went back inside to put on my running shoes, left Bell because of her arthritis, went running to the calls of crows at 6:18, then to the rattle of woodpeckers, accompanied for half an hour by the robins and cardinals and song sparrows, back near home at 6:43, sun just up, to the first grackles. A red-bellied woodpecker heard off and on through the day.

Inventory in the yard: First blue-eyes, first bittercress, some tulips to six inches, squill foliage up all the way, not budding yet, many aconites, snow crocus and many mid-season crocuses in bloom, pink lungwort budded, leaves very small, Resurrection lilies pacing the height of the daffodils and tulips, up to six inches, hyacinth foliage showing all around the circle gardens, red peony stalks starting now, up half an inch, more budding Lenten roses, daylilies really starting to emerge now (so absent just three days ago). Pruning in the yard: pink quince, redbud, honeysuckle.

2016: Robins at 5:49 this morning, frost, clear. A few tulips budded in the south garden. Pussy willows are full of pollen. From Goshen, Indiana, Judy says that she only has a few crocuses there. The pink and star magnolias that opened several days ago were burned badly by the sudden cold. At Jacoby, the smallest buckeye trees are leafing, narrow, sleek, red with birth.

2017: After hard rain yesterday, the river is wild and loud in North Glen. Skunk cabbage is very fat and high near the stone steps. All along the Cascade walk, I found scattered white hepaticas and violet cress. Some touch-me-nots had sprouted, as well as some common ragweed. Inventory in the yard: lungwort with very small flowers, and some of the plants seem to have disappeared over the winter; some aconite patches continue bright; more bluebells are up, around half a foot, about as tall as the ramps, five or six inches; peony stalks are half a foot and leafing a little; in the circle garden, the miniature jonquils are tall and open, but the standard varieties are flopping (except in Peggy's yard); tulip foliage six inches; daylily foliage hurt by the recent cold days, but some standing tall; squills still deep blue; almost all the standard crocus are gone – only two white ones remain; honeysuckle leaves definitely turning the undergrowth green now; pollen beginning on the pussy willows; weeds taking over, crab grass and chickweed and bittercress filling in all around the perennials. Jill's violet windflowers have opened, her two daffodils barely coming undone. From Spoleto, Italy, Neysa says violets are in bloom everywhere.

2018: The cold weather continues throughout the East and Lower Midwest, but daffodil buds continue to swell just a little, and from New York City, Jill sends a photo of Tompkins Park full of daffodils in bloom, with patches of snow in the background.

2019: In Nebraska, record flooding has most likely disrupted the sandhill crane gathering.

2020: At Ellis, silt drifts along the shore reflect the heavy rain and flooding of a few days ago. At their Talus Drive home, Leslie and Bruce report seeing a brownish color lacewing, a queen bumblebee, the first house fly and violet leaves fully formed.

2021: Casey called: A white egret "was sailing toward the bridge by the bike path" past Ellis Pond. The earliest I've had a report of egrets there was April 12, 2015 by Mary Sue. This morning, I saw the first forsythia blossom open along the old fence line, a lonely blossom from a hedge that once produced a sold gold border to the land. When Jeni and I were near the north garden planning perennial plantings, the first cabbage butterfly of the year fluttered by. At John Bryant Park, the first honeysuckles were just starting to leaf out.

2022: Fifty-two daffodils at home, full bloom around town, and forsythia hedges suddenly gold.

The trees are still leafless; indeed the aspect of that valley is not of April -- save where the hepaticas push up out of the bed of leaves; but the delicate fragrance of the blossoms is always faintly manifest and the air is April's with the warm sun slanting down the slope to renew the earth as sight of these delicate flowers struggling forth invariably renews me every spring.

August Derleth

March 23rd
The 82nd Day of the Year

All the afternoon there has been a chirping of birds,
and the sun lies warm and still on the western sides
of swollen branches.

Amy Lowell

Sunrise/set: 6:34/6:50
Day's Length: 12 hours 16 minutes
Average High/Low: 53/32
Average Temperature: 42
Record High: 83 – 1907
Record Low: 5 – 1885

Weather
Of all the March 23rds, ten percent of the days can be in the 70s or 80s, thirty percent in the 60s, twenty-five percent in the 50s, thirty percent in the 40s, and just five percent in the 30s. The sky is mostly clear six years in a decade. I have rarely seen snow on this date, but rain falls 35 percent of the time. After today, the average chance of frost declines from about 60 percent to 40 percent. On the 29th, chances drop to 30 percent.

Natural Calendar
The sun's eyes are painting fields again:
Its lashes with expert strokes
Are sweeping across the land.
A great palette of light has embraced the earth.

Hafiz of Shiraz

By March 23, the cardinals are singing about thirty to forty minutes before sunrise. Sometimes, up to an hour earlier than the cardinals come the first notes of the great predawn chorus of robins. Later in the day, red-bellied woodpeckers, flickers and pileated woodpeckers call in the woods. Foliage of wild geranium, clover, and columbine is growing. September's zigzag goldenrod is two inches long. Leaves of the golden Alexander are an inch across. Touch-me-nots and ragweed sprouts. Scarlet cup mushrooms swell in the dark.

Before midnight, Leo and Regulus are overhead. The Pleiades and Taurus lead Orion into the far west. The Big Dipper protrudes deep into the center of the sky. By six o'clock in the morning, the stars have become a prophecy of Late Summer, August's Vega almost overhead, Hercules a little to its east, the Northern Cross to its west.

Daybook

1983: First grape hyacinth flower found.

1984: Mill Habitat: Buzzards have finally returned, three circling "Buzzard Bend" above the dam. The ground still very bare, only a few violet, rocket, sedum, henbit and parsnips growing, a few sprouts of comfrey, a few branches of columbine.

1985: The black raspberries are sprouting leaves today in the side yard. Waterleaf is growing in the lawn, small one-inch leaves.

1986: Cardinal sings at 6:09 a.m.

1987: Cardinal sings at 6:09 a.m. The first question mark butterfly came to the stone wall this afternoon.

1988: South from Tuscaloosa to New Orleans. Redbud in bloom well into Mississippi, then fading by Louisiana. Jessamine seen above Birmingham. From Picayune south, the canopy really opening, high oaks filling. On the outskirts of New Orleans, winter cress was going to seed. There were huge, squat yellow thistles along the side of the road. Downtown, many trees had leaves emerged, half size, the tree line yellow green most everywhere. Azaleas and camellias were in full bloom, some yellow daylilies out. Throughout the city, wisteria, tulips, iris and phlox have passed their prime. A few crepe myrtles were blossoming. Frogs were croaking.

1991: Jekyll Island, Georgia, walking the beach: Low tide with the full moon overhead, high tide with the moon setting in the west;

low tide with the moon directly below the earth; high tide with the moon rising from the east. Do we all have a four-cornered day, a pattern of six-hour highs and six-hour lows?

1993: The cold finally broke today: high of 60 degrees. I heard the first flicker calling. The first groundhog of 1993 was out along Grinnell Road, switching its tail back and forth. Finches were chasing each other through the trees. The purple crocus in the south garden came up and budded overnight. Lemon verbena was growing, and maples were flushed red. At the mill, the river was rushing over the dam. Daylilies just beginning to emerge from the ground.

1994: Snow crocus peak in the east garden. Some of the gold finches are pale yellow now. A pair of chickadees has been building a nest all week in a hole in the old poplar.

1995: My star magnolia opens a bit at Wilberforce.

1998: Today, impatient for spring, I headed south a little after six in the morning. Red-winged blackbirds were out singing just past town. In Kettering, the freeway grass showed just a tint of green, pink and gray and violet sky, golden sunrise, layers of shine. Crows. A few patches of snow   Blue sky with cirrus at 43 miles south, and the grass was greener. By the time I had gone a hundred miles from Yellow Springs, the honeysuckle leaves became prominent on the roadside bushes. Calves appeared on the hillsides an hour from Louisville. And the grass continued to grow brighter, just above Louisville, the daffodils were open – they were all but a few closed at home when I left.   On the other side of Louisville, forsythia was in full bloom (only a couple of bushes had opened in Yellow Springs, and they had been badly hurt by the severe frost of middle March). And 181 miles, three hours from Yellow Springs, the roadside grass was bright green.

Shepherd's purse appeared a little south of Louisville, and the pears were open in early bloom. A flock of great blue herons going northwest seen 20 miles south of Louisville. Then more maples started to come in, redbuds open near Bowling Green, and then dandelions well into their mid-April season just before

Bowling Green. At the Tennessee Border, 333 miles from Yellow Springs, henbit, chickweed and small flower bittercress bloomed at the rest stops. At Nashville, the honeysuckles were maybe a third of their full foliage. By Franklin, Tennessee, 388 miles from home, pear trees were leafing, flowers gone. Crab apples and cherries in bloom, pink and violet and white.

Near Huntsville, Alabama, winter cress in bloom and wild roses and blackberries well leafed out, and the middle canopy had patches of green. The high trees, though, were still bare, the mistletoe still standing out like green squirrel nests. Box elders flowering a few miles north of Birmingham, and daffodil season had ended there. Then more patches of spring in the high trees, and the lower growth very green. Apple trees full bloom below Birmingham. Full redbud bloom 50 miles from Montgomery, 610 miles from Yellow Springs, and most trees were budding. Azaleas were in bloom, and cow vetch, white clover, black medic, corn salad, small creeping bluets.

Montgomery: honeysuckles all open. Dock has red blossoms. Almost all the trees in flower. Tree line full gold and green 648 miles, 11 hours from Yellow Springs. And through the city, red clover, lush and a foot tall full bloom, canopy rich, redbuds and dogwoods full, roadside grasses four feet high. Lanky winter cress and rape full bloom. Sudden extravagance in the grass and treetops, water willows fully leafed, fields of spring beauties. I had come a week of Yellow Springs time for every 100 miles or so, one day for every 10 to 15 miles.

1999: Crows 6:13 a.m. Comma butterfly slow and stiff in the cold, loving the sun, surrounded by cardinal song.

2000: To Jacoby with Gus and Buttercup, the two family bulldogs: A pre-pubescent late afternoon, warm in the low 60s, the Early Spring accumulating. We cut across the swamp through the soft matting of new chickweed. April was budding with the wild phlox and geranium leaves. Leafcup bushy and six to eight inches. One skunk cabbage with leaves, the others full bloom, some with thick bright basal leaves, but less like foliage than part of the flower itself unfolding. One buckeye sprout had fully developed leaves; the larger trees were just starting to come undone. Hillsides glowing with fresh plants. A mourning cloak butterfly flew by at the end of our walk. The wheat fields such a bright green on the way home. Hemlock along the roadside, boot high and fat. The first tulip, pale yellow, was open in the south garden when I arrived home. Tonight, a toad was singing hard and long in the pond.

2001: Robins singing in the dark, 5:50 a.m. Cardinal at 6:16, then crows. Blue jay bell call at 8:10. First yellow poplar bud cracks.

2003: Mike Miller's friend reports that ramps (a variety of wild onion) are three inches tall in southern Ohio. In the south garden, blue eyes (*Veronica*) are open in the sun.

2004: Ramps (planted last summer in the backyard) are about two-inches tall. Peonies are between one and two inches. I saw the first daffodil in bloom at Evadine's this afternoon.

2007: After a mild night of hard rain, the koi swim around in the pond, invigorated by the warm temperatures and the rising water. This evening, I saw that the first forsythia flower had opened.

2008: Osage fruits have all been eaten or have rotted, the absence punctuating the arrival of the sun into Aires.

2009: Dove and robins heard when I walked outside at 5:50 this morning. When I took Bella, our border collie, out at 9:30, I found the first few forsythia flowers open on the south side of the yard. Grape hyacinths are turning blue in the north garden. In the Dakotas, a tremendous blizzard has shut down roads and services. At Fargo, sandbaggers are attempting to stop the Red River from flooding the town.

2010: Dauphin Island to the Florida panhandle on the ferry: Light haze, blue sky: Redbuds full and trees flowering all across the panhandle. Small "Innocence" bluets, white and blue, and one old dogwood and several azaleas in bloom at the campground along I-10.

2011: Snow-on-the-mountain leaves are up now; maples are flowering at Dayton and Stafford Streets, the hulls of the flower buds all over the street. Violet-blue Glory-of-the-Snow seen along Stafford. The first forsythia flowers are opening in front of our house and along Winter Street. Pollen has appeared on the pussy willows. In the backyard, Virginia bluebells and lungwort are fat and budded. Flicker or pileated woodpeckers calling throughout the day.

2012: Cardinal sang at 6:10. The barometer drops slowly as rain and the end of the heat wave approach. Casey says the toads that sang so loud on the 18th and 19th are still silent. Sweet cherries in full bloom here and at Casey's, but he says the pie cherries there aren't open yet. First morels found in the region, first May apples are up, too.

2013: Walking Bella starting at 5:45, cold about 25 and mostly cloudy: Robin chirping at 5:50, robin chorus started at 5:55, a cardinal at 6:00, a dove just a few seconds later. By the time I was back at the house at 6:05, the whole chorus was underway. I checked outside at 6:20, and several dozen grackles were up in the Lawson's tree squawking and grackling; they'd been up for maybe five or ten minutes. Spring storm Virgil is approaching now from the southwest, snow and winds forecast for tomorrow.

2015: Gray, chilly morning, barometer falling, northeast wind, snow forecast for the afternoon. Robin chirps at 5:50, but I didn't stay to hear the chorus. Iris foliage up at least six inches in front of Lori's shop downtown. Don's daffodils on Dayton Street are well budded.

2016: Mild, partly cloudy, light breeze: Cardinal at 5:47, first robins at 5:49. Nettles about two-inches high near the primrose bed. The box elder tree along the west edge of my property is in bloom.

2017: John Bryan State Park in afternoon sun, temperatures in the high 50s: the bottomland was speckled with hepaticas, violet cress and spring beauties, clumps of lesser celandine in flower and bluebells almost budded along the river, some foliage of toothwort and a cluster of snow trillium – more than I've ever seen – showing through the mulch toward the hills, ramps bushy and long, maybe some eight inches. And I saw the first polygonia/question mark butterfly of the year, a small one, flying low through the honeysuckles.

2018: Sun and cold: Two finches at the feeder, definitely turning gold, maybe half. Along the road to Cedarville, the wheat fields are emerald green, sprouts about three inches high.

2019: In the dooryard, snowdrops are wide open, a few past their prime. Two bees were working the open crocus, and Leslie reported first bees today, as well. In the porch garden, I found phlox foliage that had been hidden by mulch as it paced the new leaves of the autumn sedum. Jill shared a photo of a daffodil blushing gold, captioned: "Almost."

2021: I went out jogging at 5:25 this morning, mild 44 degrees, overcast. One cardinal sang out at 5:29, and then robins began their full chorus at 5:33, cardinals gradually joining. When I returned and sat on the back porch, cardinals were drowning out the robins, and I heard the first doves at 6:11. Red quince buds show a little red today, Japanese honeysuckle leafing out, privets budding, unraveling.

2022: Fifty-two daffodils blooming in the yard today, honeysuckle leafing starting to turn the undergrowth spring green.

2023: Today's daffodil count is 130, the plantings holding at the level of last week, but so many are drooping from the past cold weather. Pussy willows have pollen, quince bushes showing no sign of buds.

So it is ... important often to ignore or forget what men presume that they know and take an original and unprejudiced view of nature – letting her make what impression she will on you – as the first men and all children and natural men still do. For our science so called is always more barren and mixed up with error – than our sympathies are.

Henry David Thoreau

March 24th
The 83rd Day of the Year

The fair profusion that o'erspreads the spring;
Flings from the sun direct the flaming day;
Feeds every creature; hurls the tempest forth;
And, as on earth this grateful change revolves,
With transport touches all the springs of life.

James Thomson

Sunrise/set: 6:33/6:51
Day's Length: 12 hours 18 minutes
Average High/Low: 52/33
Average Temperature: 42
Record High: 87 – 1910
Record Low: 4 – 1974

Weather

Highs in the 70s occur ten percent of the afternoons, 60s come 20 percent, 50s fifty percent, 40s fifteen percent and 30s just five percent. The 24th is typically the second-wettest day of March, with precipitation recorded 55 percent of the time (of which only ten percent is in the form of snow. Skies are completely overcast on this day about half the years.

Natural Calendar

On March 24 in the chilliest years, the Ohio landscape is uniformly brown all the way from Toledo in the north to within 30 miles of the Kentucky border. In the Cincinnati valley, grass shows just a little color, a sign that the next season is approaching. West toward Louisville, time runs parallel to the Ohio River. The land is locked in the last minutes of Early Spring. Wildflowers are budding; only a few are more advanced.

Bowling Green, Kentucky, just over 200 miles from Yellow Springs, provides the first major step away from winter. The hills and lawns are bright green. By Nashville, another 100 miles south, yellow forsythia is blooming. Willow leaves have formed. Daffodils are common. After six hours of driving, the equivalent of twelve days have passed. It's the middle of Ohio April.

Crab apples blossom 50 miles further south in Columbia, Tennessee. Winter wheat is five inches tall. Plowing is well underway. Corn and oats are in the ground. Maples are flowering. The very first redbud opens forty miles north of Huntsville. In Birmingham, 500 miles from southwestern Ohio, the canopy is thickening. The air is rich with the pollen from magnolias and Bradford pears. Foliage is fully developed on a few trees by Laurel, Mississippi. Dogwood is common below Hattiesburg. Fleabane flowers in the waysides. Daffodils are almost gone. A little past Picayune, Louisiana, the undergrowth is completely green, and the high oaks are filling in.

On the outskirts of New Orleans, winter cress is going to seed. Downtown, in Jackson Square, azaleas and camellias are in full bloom. Throughout the city, wisteria, tulips, iris and phlox have passed their prime. A few crepe myrtles and yellow daylilies are out. Frogs are croaking. East toward Jacksonville, Florida, summer dock, clover and thistles are flowering. Gaillardia is ready to pick near the beach. Pokeweed and cattails are three feet tall. Nine hundred miles from Ohio Valley, it's May.

Daybook

1982: Saw the first question mark butterfly along with the first mosquito of the year. First new leaves seen on strawberries and raspberries. Blue-eyes open. Hepatica, harbinger of spring, and twinleaf are blooming at the Cascades, toad trillium and Dutchman's britches ready to open (all these identified for the first time today). Mints are growing. The first bluebells blossomed on the ridge. At the river, five snakes were lying together in the sun. Waterleaf found growing, a small rooting taken home and planted.

1985: To Cincinnati: magnolias barely opening at the conservatory.

1987: First carp and white sucker caught this morning on dough balls. First polygonia butterfly, probably a question mark. Downstream, a deer with a bad front leg limped across the river, eluded a beagle that had followed it from South Glen. In town, the daffodil season is completely here. Forsythia now early bloom. Magnolias open more at Wilberforce.

1988: East along the coast toward Jacksonville, Florida: summer dock, clover and thistles are flowering. Blanket flower is ready to pick near the beach. Pokeweed and cattails are three feet tall.

1989: Fishing at Caesar Creek. Carp leaping around the lotus pads. Caught five small ones. Sixteen geese counted on Goose Island. *Cornus mas* is yellow along the road south.

1991: Jekyll Island to Yellow Springs: Privet in bloom, beach oxalis. At home in Ohio, the forsythia has started to open, daffodils, scillas, star of Holland blooming, first tulip open. Snowdrop, aconite, and crocus seasons have ended in the yard. Waterleaf is up. Peony sprouts have doubled in length. New garlic mustard seeds have sprouted everywhere, and more ragweed. More honeysuckle, and Japanese honeysuckle have leafed out. The star magnolias on the east side of my building have come undone at Wilberforce. Suddenly the stagnation of Early Spring has ended, the rush, the multiplication of Middle Spring is underway.

1992: News lambs, maybe a week old, in the fields seventy miles west of Yellow Springs. Red-winged blackbirds mating on the fences, calling all the way north through Illinois, on the last trip to see Dad.

1993: Some robins twittering, like waking calls, at 5:30 a.m. Cardinal sings at 6:02. At South Glen today, a patch of snowdrops near the entry to High Prairie filled with honeybees. Nothing else in bloom, but there were a lot of flies out, the garlic mustard was growing, turning the forest floor green. Flickers and cardinals loud all day in town and in the Glen. At High Prairie, the oaks still hold their October leaves. A few box elder seeds still hang on their branches near the red barn. At the bird feeder, the finches seem to be turning, the breast of one or two lighter now, just slightly yellowish; the upper feathers seem brighter, the wings darker. Burroughs, in his journal of April 14th, a hundred years ago, says that "the yellowbirds (goldfinches) are just getting on their yellow coats...."

1995: Drive into Dayton in full sun, temperature in the 50s. Magnolias are in full bloom toward the city center. Crab apples are leafing everywhere, willows glowing. At the bird feeder, gold finches still mostly brown, just a hint of gold in their upper bodies.

1999: First robin chirps at 5:43 a.m.

2000: First pink peach tree flower here at home. Along High Street, early cherries or plums in full bloom. Toads in the pond singing, intense, through the evening. Walking south through town, toads from a different direction every few blocks.

2001: My nephew John reports the first flock of robins in Lanesboro, Minnesota: temperature 16 above zero, wind chill of 40 below.

2003: First small jonquils open in the west garden. Korean lilac and standard lilac starting to leaf. Bleeding hearts are three inches tall. Snowdrops declining, snow crocus gone, mid-season crocus full bloom. Catmint coming back strong.

2004: Light rain and 45 degrees: Robins, doves, cardinals and the back-yard wren all vocal at 6:03 this morning. Very low branches of some honeysuckle bushes are putting out leaves. Pansies set out in the east garden. Mid-season crocus full bloom, but many snow crocus and snowdrops remain. John reports the first robin in Lanesboro in southern Minnesota.

2007: After several mild, wet days in the 60s, nights in the 50s, the first three daffodils opened in the yard. Under the redbud, the first pink primrose bloomed. Flicker calling yesterday afternoon and this morning. The first pink lungwort has blossomed by the ramps. The first small red tulip unfolded by the pond. First pink purple deadnettle and purple periwinkle are flowering. The first Canadian thistles are about an inch long, and violet leaves are about half an inch across in large clusters. Bleeding hearts are reluctant, still hidden. First Dutch iris spears noticed. First honeysuckle leaves noticed, and the Japanese honeysuckle buds have revived from the deep cold and are leafing out. Full bloom of late crocus. End of snowdrops and snow crocus. Waterleaf is strong and spreading. One hunting spider seen near the woodpile. I found a carpenter bee lying sideways in a big blue crocus. Greg called and said he's been seeing skunks out in his yard since the 18th. He saw a raccoon last week and heard reports that a golden eagle was sighted in the Gorge.

2008: Yellow Springs to Hendersonville, North Carolina: The cool spring has kept back development throughout the region. Cincinnati showed no real change from Dayton except for one small patch of half-open daffodils. A few pear trees seen in bloom near Lexington, but the undergrowth showed no change until southern Kentucky. At a Kentucky rest stop, henbit and some dandelions were in bloom. Pear trees continued to appear in northern Tennessee, and some red and orange flowering of the canopy through the Smoky Mountains. Huge roadside plantings of daffodils along I-40 are in full bloom, both white and yellow varieties. Knoxville showed little change, and we didn't see the first redbud in bloom until well along toward Ashville. The campground in Hendersonville had a huge weeping cherry in full bloom, many of its petals falling when we were there. Walking Bella on the grounds, I saw a patch of spring violets.

2009: Many robins still in all the lawns, a flock of grackles cackling, cardinals and doves calling as I walked Bella in the alley this morning. Monarda leaves are showing now in the north gardens. At Jacoby, skunk cabbage is blooming throughout the lowlands. Buttercup and ragwort foliage is common, and touch-me-not sprouts are up but quite small, only having emerged in the past few days. Along Clifton Road, bright green wheat fields. In the woods and at home, garlic mustard seeds have opened in dense clumps. Snowdrops are almost all gone. Quince buds are reddening. A star magnolia is opening on Xenia Avenue. Before sundown, I transplanted cattail roots to the pond, and I dug the Resurrection lilies from behind the lilacs for moving out into the brighter north garden.

On March 24th, Jeffery Goss wrote from Springfield,

Missouri: "A few days ago the fruit trees came into full bloom (peach and apricot), and the grass is becoming deep green. The smell of the air has also changed from a winter smell to a spring smell." He added the following about pollen: "I check the pollen counts by beaming a flashlight straight ahead in the night sky, and watch the amount of pollen dust in the air."

2011: Jeanie and I were talking about the grackles today, how they had replaced the starlings. The latter had come in late winter, stayed a while through February, then disappeared after the grackles arrived with Early Spring. Crows flew over the house this morning at 6:18, geese at 6:30.

2012: Cardinal sang at 6:10 a.m. Cloudy, soft, humid morning, redbuds, honeysuckle leaves, daffodils, tulips all glowing in the yard, grackles, starlings, cardinals, sparrows feeding, chirping. Magnolias and serviceberry flowers falling. The High Street star magnolia has lost all its petals. Don's pie cherry tree is open this morning. Lil's maple, Jerry and Lee's maple, and Mrs. Timberlake's maple are all in flower. Hostas and Asiatic lilies are up two to three inches in some places, the hostas leafing out to eight inches in others. Oakleaf hydrangeas have one to three inch leaves, peonies are budded, redbuds are in full bloom, actually becoming pale with age, Irish bells - small white bell-like flowers on daffodil-like foliage in full bloom, river birch leaves fully formed at half an inch, the viburnum well leafed and budded, box elder flowers losing their glow, blueberries leafing, paulownia leafing, tree of heaven and rose of Sharon leafing, rhubarb stalks three to four inches (big enough for pie if I had a larger patch to gather from), scilla in decline, daffodils and grape hyacinths probably at their peak or a little past. Rue anemone and red cap mushroom reported in the area. Peas and nine star-gazer lilies planted this afternoon.

2013: A very gold finch at the feeder this morning with at least half of its color, pacing Peggy's daffodils, which are just starting to emerge. This evening, fat, wet snow arrives as the crocuses are trying to open, covers them all up.

My notes from a talk at the Unitarian Fellowship today, which

I wrote up for the newspaper:

Community Spring: 2013

I was fortunate to attend a spring gathering in the village this past Sunday, and I asked those in attendance to write down brief images of the season. Here is what some of them wrote:

From Joy: "March 10 to 15: Saw a beautiful bluebird hanging around my (new) wildly-colored primitive birdhouse, high on a post in my side garden. It took my breath, and made me happy."

Jewel: "Black ants coming into the house. Turkey buzzards soaring. Changes in light."

Esther: "Tiny purple irises, snowdrops, robins, early crocuses – white, yellow, purple, primrose buds showing, buzzards, alliums, bitterweed, and a spider in my tub."

James: "I saw approximately six squirrels chasing each other over the length of several telephone wires, a heron fishing in a lake near my house, and a wolf spider crawling about on my floor."

Peg: "At about 10:00 a.m. on the way to the Unitarian Fellowship, I saw a buzzard picking at a skunk carcass on Hilltop Road."

Ron: "White-tail does, heavy with fawn, punctuating the soft, downy soil with cloven hoof-prints that soon will fill with tiny happy salutations of crocus."

Steve: "Violets springing forth in front of this church… on the Day of the Dreaded Eight-Inch Snow!"

Susan: "A yard of Robins!"

Holly: "Dead skunk on the side of the road. Several buzzards circling my house. Two gray squirrels chasing each other."

Kevin and Eden: "In the Glen Saturday: Water striders, skunk cabbage coming up, belted kingfisher, maybe a flicker, and a fly."

Dick: "Phoebe pairing, turtle doves mating, henbit blooming, barred owls calling each other, male cardinals doing territorial calls."

Kieran: "I noticed it was starting/trying to get warmer."

Mike: "Most may observe non-human changes, such as in plants, animals, the atmosphere, etc. What I see most evident this season is the human *excitement* about the coming new season. I am reminded that cultivating anticipation and celebrating others' eagerness is another small way to honor the mysteries of the circles of life, especially among my fellow persons."

Unsigned notes: "On January 18, witch hazel at Kennedy Arboretum started blooming." "Russet-breasted towhee at the feeder in late February. Animals more active – including domestic ones."

And from Flying Mouse Farms on the 18th, Michele wrote: "John believes syrup season is over, but there is a chance more will come. So far we've made 220 gallons of syrup. That's a record for us."

2015: Cold in the low 20s this morning, almost an inch of snow on the ground from yesterday's snowbursts, but when I went outside around 6:15, the cardinals and robins were in full song. I stood a while listening to them gather more momentum; then at 6:21, a loud crow call, and the volume of the songbirds collapsed for a few minutes, then came back some.

2016: Breezy, warm morning, cardinals and robins starting together at 5:48. In the south garden, the pale yellow early tulip that Jeanie and I planted in the 1980s opened overnight. Now the bluebells are budded, cracking a little, and I disturbed a small grass snake as I weeded in the north garden.

2018: More sun, more wind, more chilly temperatures in the mid 40s, but more clumps of daffodils have opened (Peggy's all in full bloom), and one for forsythia bush on Elm Street is covered with long, golden buds. From New York City, Jill sends photos of bedding plants on the street and a flowering crab apple huddled against the south wall of a skyscraper. From Madison, Wisconsin, Tat says that she heard sandhill cranes down by the lake this afternoon about 2:30.

2021: Forsythia bushes throughout town are slowly opening under warm sun with 70 degree temperatures, light wind. Daffodils everywhere. At Ellis Park, a second cabbage white butterfly, and maple flowers covering the north end of the pond. This evening: more robin vespers.

2022: Seventy daffodils in bloom, mid-season crocus strong, ramps bushy, many new tulips up two inches, several honeybees in the flowers.. A beekeeper reports that maples near her property were flowering last week. The star magnolia across the street is starting to flower - just in time for a cold snap in a couple of days. At Ellis Pond, I saw a fish jump...twice, and willow leaves were at least half an inch long. From New York City, Jill reports redbuds and dogwoods in bloom, at least ten days to two weeks ahead of southwestern Ohio.

These are thy wonders, Lord of love,
To make us see we are but flowers that glide:
Which when we once can find and prove,
Thou has a garden for us, where to bide.

George Herbert

March 25th
The 84th Day of the Year

The year holds one moment, which may last for a week, when tree and bush and vine are on the breathless verge of leafing out. It is then that one can stand on a hilltop and look across the valley and see the scarlet and orange maple blossoms like a touch of pastel crayon across the treetops.

Hal Borland

Sunrise/set: 6:31/6:52
Day's Length: 12 hours 21 minutes
Average High/Low: 53/33
Average Temperature: 43
Record High: 84 – 1929
Record Low: 1 – 1974

Weather

Chances of rain decline from yesterday's 55 percent down to 35 percent. Snow comes just one year in a quarter century. Highs rise above 70 on ten percent of the days, reach only 60 on 25 percent, only 50 on 15 percent, just 40 on 35 percent, just 30 on 15 percent. The sky is clear to partly cloudy 65 percent of the years. Average high temperatures are now above 50 in the northern part of the Lower Midwest, above 60 along the Ohio River.

Natural Calendar

The first blue periwinkles open among last year's fallen leaves. Summer's lizard's tail is sprouting in the river mud. Daylily foliage is at least four to five inches high now. Burdock leaves are two inches long, comfrey three inches. Ramps (native wild onions, famous throughout Appalachia for healing and seasoning) are three to four inches tall, their foliage unraveling and bushy along the rivers. Forsythia begins to flower in years that are normal or a little above normal. Butterflies sometimes appear.

Daybook

1982: Leaves starting on the mock orange, first tulip budding.

1983: First tortoise-shell butterfly seen at Jacoby Swamp. First green-bottle fly (a day earlier than last year). Moss is an inch long (same length, about the same date last year). Black raspberries are leafing. June's cinquefoil leaves are the size of my thumbnail.

1984: Bluebird seen. A few touch-me-not sprouts at Jacoby, despite the long, cold March.

1985: Periwinkles blooming in Celina.

1986: Halley's Comet seen from the Indian Mound at 5:00 this morning. Birds singing well before 6:00. In the afternoon at Jacoby (first afternoon in the 70s this year): tortoise-shell butterflies seen, snake in the river, huge two inch water bug, water striders mating, purple deadnettle full bloom, green-bottle flies, flocks of bluebirds, robins and red-winged blackbirds, more honeysuckle leafing, buds on Dutchman's britches, bees. Neysa reports hepatica open in the Glen, *Cornus mas* on the college campus.

1988: New Orleans: Wisteria full bloom, tulips late full bloom at Longview, some crepe myrtles just opening, phlox and iris late full bloom, large dayflowers common, elm leaves nearly full size. ⌈1⌉ ⌊SEP⌋

1989: Motherwort and great mullein are up four inches. Winged termites are out, and the first cabbage butterfly. Peony leaves unravel from their ten-inch stalks. First lilac leaves open just a little, crocus full bloom now, first tulip seen. Late home bluebells up nearly an inch, first forsythia flowering, First pollen on the pussy willows, robins, cardinals, red-winged blackbirds very loud. In the greenhouse, a few mother-of-millions still in bloom.

1990: Wisconsin to Yellow Springs: Red-winged blackbirds all along the freeway south. Illinois so much greener than Madison; 60 miles makes a significant difference. Meadowlark seen, ducks, blackbirds. Cloudless, unbroken sky. First bushes leaf out at Bloomington, Illinois, and some color comes to the willows. Box elder in flower a few miles from Indianapolis, tree line clearly flushed approaching Ohio.

1991: Jekyll Island to Yellow Springs: Spring has moved north almost a week since we came through a few days ago. The road to Savannah is green with leaves a third to half emerged; the orange and red of buds have faded from the coastal Georgia tree line. Wisteria has bloomed, fields of red rice are flowering, will soon be purple like in northern Florida. Into South Carolina, the canopy thins. Pears have leafed, flowers mostly gone. An apple orchard that had only been ready to blossom near Spartanburg on the 21st was bright violet today, acres of color. Through the hills, glowing emerald pastures between the brown and orange trees. Redbuds just showing into northern Tennessee. Red-orange flowers showing on the hillsides from Knoxville well toward Lexington, Kentucky, but then the changes stopped, and the season returned to Early Spring: late Yellow Springs March.

1993: One finch definitely turning gold today. Waterleaf is up in the pussy willow garden. Hundreds of flies have hatched, rest on the old greenhouse tomato plants I put outside. Pussy willows fully emerged. Crocus full bloom throughout the village. The first blue windflower in the south garden. Mock orange buds extending a little, lilac buds brightening.

1994: At Mint Hollow, Dutchman's britches are up, foliage an inch wide. Smooth basal leaves of snow trillium found. Pileated woodpecker calling from the mill. In the east and south gardens, a few snow crocuses have fallen over, but most are still full bloom, the regular crocus full beside them. Now spring picks up speed, the numbers of new species increasing every day, even though the air is cool.

1995: The first mourning cloak butterfly came to the south garden, several cabbage butterflies out today in the sun. First tulip opened, a yellow one. Daffodils, grape hyacinth, pink wood hyacinth, scilla, Glory-of-the-Snow (*Chiniodoxa forbesii),* and puschkinia were in full bloom.

1997: To Kentucky on a mild and windy day. The grass was immediately greener fifty miles south near Cincinnati, and the honeysuckles were far more advanced, forsythia in full bloom – whereas in Yellow Springs, the blossoms were only half emerged. By the time we reached Lexington, pussy willows were full of pollen; a magnolia was in full bloom a little southwest on Interstate 64. Then as we approached Elizabethtown, about two hundred miles southwest of the home, redbuds gradually came into bloom - we could watch the progression from budding redbuds to blooming redbuds over the course of maybe 30 or 40 miles. And then flowering crabs and pears leafing and losing their flowers 40 miles below Louisville. On the evening news: cherry blossoms are all blossoming in Washington D.C.

2000: Downtown, all the pears are coming in early. Along Dayton Street, last year's crab apples falling to the sidewalk, pushed off by new leaves. Now the pond plants are all in motion, the purple loosestrife showing about an inch or so, the water iris multiplying, the lake rushes sending up three inches of new foliage. In the north garden, the Dutch iris leaves are showing three to six inches, and the red quince buds are fat and showy. Burdock leaves are two inches long by the street. One fleabane has opened in the southeast corner of the yard, right up against the house. East garden periwinkles blooming. Daffodils and grape hyacinth still full. St. John's wort has new basal growth. Box elders are in flower. In the pond, the koi are splashing, and the toads are singing through the day. Out in the countryside: a few clumps of dandelions. Daffodils and full bloom flowering pears everywhere.

2003: Robinsong at 5:30 a.m., probably started by 5:15. At 5:50, the first cardinals. At 6:17, the grackles and blackbirds began to sing, and the robin chorus faded. Geese flew over honking at 6:30. In the 70 degree heat this afternoon (after two weeks of mild temperatures): pussy willows get pollen, first forsythia blooms, clematis leaves half an inch long, redbud buds are purple, achillea leaves up to six inches, scabiosa three inches and clustered, oregano returning, first rhubarb leaf is six inches tall. Aster leaves are one inch long, tulip leaves full size, daylilies up to a foot tall, first honeysuckle and privet leaves, purple deadnettle flowering, hollyhock leaves four inches wide, new euonymus leaves, waterleaf, lemon verbena, sundrop, snow-on-the-mountain, and phlox leaves are an inch long, peony stalks to five inches and leafing (but still red), squills and hyacinths budded, small, mouse-eared chickweed flowering, puschkinias open, resurrection lilies six to eight inches tall, spring iris still in bloom.

2004: The small jonquils in the west garden opened this morning. *Cornus mas* blooming at the college. Resurrection lilies only two inches tall.

2007: Small jonquils and yellow primrose opened last night. Peonies to five inches tall. Flicker sings at 8:00 this morning. Mock orange and quince leafing. Buds growing on the largest redbud tree, but not on the smaller, younger trees. Our crab apple tree has just started to leaf. First hosta spears appearing. Poppy leaves well developed, maybe six or seven inches long. Resurrection lilies to four inches. Geese flew over this morning near sunrise. Puschkinias opened this afternoon as the temperature approached 80 degrees. Not a single butterfly of any kind seen yet this year.

2008: Hendersonville, North Carolina to Jekyll Island, Georgia: More redbuds appeared in bloom as we drove south, and many weeping cherries. The high trees showed bright red, orange and golden flowers almost immediately after Hendersonville, and Jessamine appeared abruptly at Columbia. The coastal plain showed far less inhibition from the cool spring than did the mountain and piedmont areas, and leafing became common in the undergrowth and canopy even before Columbia. Full-blooming wisteria appeared a little before the I-95 intersection. The large white thistles, the red clover, the tall red blooming dock-like plant (very common), white clover, tall prickly sow thistles, what appeared to be bright yellow cressleaf groundsel, and an abundance of black medic type ground cover appeared in the roadsides. The causeway to Jekyll was lined with pink cosmos, and on the island itself, azaleas appeared to be late in their cycle. Back in Yellow Springs, Don Cepollini left a message saying this was the week of the mass sprouting of garlic mustard.

2009: The winterberry vine in the alley is getting new leaves. The bamboo along the south wall keeps its beige leaves. It will be another month or so before they are replaced with fresh growth.

2010: Florida panhandle to Jekyll Island, Georgia: High, gray sky, soft breeze, temperature in the 60s. Through the countryside, live oaks were yellowing. At the campground, live oak leaves trickled through the trees and undergrowth, clattered like raindrops on the camper top and on the windows, the ground covered in leaves - this is their major leaf-fall time. In the residential part of the island, old men were out raking piles of the leaves. Lawns were dry and brown, full redbuds but azaleas are just budding – the spring has been so cold. At the beach, a great cloud of birds appeared far out at sea, but they were so numerous that they seemed like an island appearing through the haze. They moved almost all the way across the horizon, then around and back again, disappearing down into the ocean.

2011: I was up early to listen to birds, but it was quiet until about 5:55; then, a few chirps, then gradually all kinds of robins, cardinals, grackles, starlings, titmice and sparrows loud, boisterous.

2012: Cardinals singing above the robin chorus right at 6:00 a.m. In the alley: a dogwood and an apple in bloom, fleabane budded. Don's pink magnolia has kept many of its flowers. In Dayton, dandelions and white clover in full bloom, apple blossoms common, snowball viburnums blooming throughout the area. Downtown in Yellow Springs, a purple lilac bush completely out. A few small ants seen in the attic (starting their spring wandering?).

2013: Four inches of snow overnight, all the flowers covered, the sounds of the village muted, the bamboo bent over the pond. About three dozen grackles mobbing the bird feeders. They are obviously still in flocking mode.

2014: Walking with Jeff along the river near Cedarville, the only sign of Early Spring was the mass of tiny garlic mustard sprouts planted by the water that had risen high into the bottomland. Jeff talked about seeing pink magnolias and some blossoming fruit trees in Spain a week ago, but no flowers. At 12:21 this afternoon, Casey called: "A flock of bluebirds along Tarbox Cemetery Road." This afternoon when I walked Bella down Stafford Street, I saw that the red maples were in full bloom (and probably bloomed as the sap ended at Flying Mouse Farm).

2015: Flying Mouse Farm: Michele reports that sap has stopped running. In the Phillips Street alley, one large patch of aconites is finished, a smaller patch still new like mine. Several dozen squills open across from the bittersweet vine – but none in my garden. Near the old mock orange, I found the tips of the bluebells just starting up. The peonies are maybe half an inch tall. The first waterleaf came up today. I looked for flowering daffodils on a walk downtown but didn't see any. Jeni reports that Portland is in the middle of Middle Spring, with tulips and fruit trees in bloom. The weather warming: I saw Princess, the white koi, jump way out of the water, frisking or trying to catch an insect.

2016: Jill sent a photo from her yard: a fat bleeding heart in bloom, the earliest I've recorded.

2017: As I depart for Spain: warm 70s. Early blue hyacinths open. Fruit trees straining. In Chicago, cold like San José in Costa Rica when I came through in June of 1961 from Panama, surprised to see women in coats, rain glistening on the black streets.

2018: More sun, more wind, more chilly temperatures in the mid 40s, but more clumps of daffodils have opened (Peggy's all in full bloom), and one for forsythia bush on Elm Street is covered with long, golden buds. From New York City, Jill sends photos of bedding plants on the street and a flowering crab apple huddled against the south wall of a skyscraper. From Madison, Wisconsin, Tat says that she heard sandhill cranes down by the lake this afternoon about 2:30.

2019: Tat reports that the first red-winged blackbird has arrived at the Madison wetlands, and Maggie (also from Madison) sent a picture of a patch of full-flowering aconites – the first of her year. In the alleys here, though, the aconites plantings have become dull and gray with age. On the way to Jill's house, we saw the small bittercress with white specks of buds. In my backyard, waterleaf has emerged, leaves an inch across, and a few new weed sprouts have come up in the bare ground.

2021: A third white cabbage butterfly seen, this one along Limestone Street. Snowdrops completely gone in the dooryard. Blue eyes *(Veronica)* blooming at the property line, bittercress blossoming all about. The star magnolia on Dayton Street is suddenly in full flower.

2022: Forty degrees, mostly cloudy, the fourth-quarter moon ghostly in the southeast, Venus bright behind above the trees. Robins whinnied on Stafford Street at 5:34 this morning, gradually increasing but no real singsong. The first cardinal heard toward Phillips Street at 5:48.

2023: Tornadoes in the South, ten inches of snow in Madison, Wisconsin. Here, temperature in the 50s. The barometer is at 29.45, the new moon is waxing through its third day, and the wind is hard, gusts rattling the greenhouse windows. Several inches of rain last night, rivers high and flooding throughout the area. Now the pussy willows, heavy with pollen, are falling in the stormy day. Daffodil count is 132 this afternoon, so many of them drooping from the rain and recent chill. Scilla, glory of the snow and grape hyacinths are all full flower, as is the star magnolia (which probably opened several days ago) across the street.

> *We felt the stir of hall and street,*
> *The pulse of life that round us beat;*
> *The chill embargo of the snow*
> *Was melted in the genial glow;*
> *Wide swung again our ice-locked door,*
> *And all the world was ours once more.*

John Greenleaf Whittier

March 26th
The 85th Day of the Year

Ye fostering breezes blow!
Ye softening dews, ye tender showers descend!
And temper all, thou world-reviving sun,
Into the perfect year!

James Thomson

Sunrise/set: 6:29/6:53
Day's Length: 12 hours 24 minutes
Average High/Low: 53/34
Average Temperature: 43
Record High: 81 – 1907
Record Low: 12 – 1955

Weather
Chances of a day in the 70s or 80s are 15 percent, of 60s twenty-five percent, of 50s thirty percent, of 40s ten percent, of 30s twenty percent. Rain occurs 25 percent of the days, snow just five percent. Frost comes half the mornings, the last time this spring that a freeze is so likely.

Natural Calendar
In central Minnesota, robins arrive; between Tennessee and Wisconsin, red-winged blackbirds nest along the fencerows; sugaring is in full swing throughout Vermont; on the Platte River in Nebraska, the sandhill cranes have assembled and are waiting to depart for Canada until around April 10.

In South Carolina, fragrant yellow jessamine is still in full bloom along the roadsides; in Huntsville, Alabama, redbud trees and decorative pears bloom. Foliage is fully developed on the box elder trees in Laurel, Mississippi. Dogwood flowers are common below Hattiesburg. A little past Picayune, Louisiana, the undergrowth is completely green, and the high oaks are filling in.

Throughout New Orleans, daylilies and wisteria blossom; rice fields flower red and purple beside the Gulf; azaleas and pale yellow Cherokee Roses fill Jekyll Island in southern Georgia.

213

In wilderness areas of the Southwest, late March brings the peak of wildflower season if rain has been sufficient. Golden corydalis, desert phlox, desert chicory, spiderwort, popcorn flower, thistle poppy, fiddlenecks, deer vetch, desert anemone, scorpion flower, strawberry hedgehog cactus and pincushion cactus are typically in bloom.

Daybook

1981: First daffodil seen today in town.

1984: Virginia bluebells, two inches high, discovered beyond the Covered Bridge. Ragwort has buds at the swamp. Crocus finally blooming along Elm Street.

1985: Bryan Park Gorge: After a mild March, the foliage of wild geranium, clover, and columbine is growing. Touch-me-not sprouts are big, but still just have two leaves, like at the end of the cold March last year. First yellow jacket seen today, lots of flies, two orange polygonia butterflies, first spring beauty, harbinger of spring, and violet cress blooming, more snow trillium. Scarlet cup mushroom found. First green-bottle fly lights on my hand. Summer's lizard's tail starting to sprout in the river mud. Toothwort, bluebells, and Dutchman's britches budding. Daylilies four to five inches high now. Toad trillium up. Hills full of white and purple hepatica. September's zigzag goldenrod is two inches long. Leaves of the golden alexander are an inch across. Snake seen basking in the sun. Deep blue squills have opened in town. New strawberry leaves in the garden.

1986: First cardinal sings at 5:50 a.m. River chubs are growing small horns, their heads turning pink: mating time. Two herons sighted down from the bridge, and Rebecca calls to report the arrival of the first heron at her pond. First leaves are starting on the skunk cabbage. Violet cress is blooming. First forsythia flowers in the yard. Star of Holland blooming in the lawn. Lilac and mock orange buds seem to be extending, getting ready to leaf.

1987: First star magnolia bud coming undone. New garlic mustard sprouts. Leaves emerging on the willows. Two carp caught mid morning.

1988: New Orleans to Jacksonville, Florida: Bright red clover all the way along the highway into Florida. Hop clovers high and full bloom. Many tall, white thistles and yellow thistles. Cattail foliage is waist high. Blue toadflax common. Dock flower stalks three feet.

1989: The first box elder is flowering. Violet foliage is the size of a squirrel's ear. Bluebirds seen nesting at South Glen. Tall coneflower stalks are up two inches. Buzzards drifting in the high clouds.

1990: Periwinkles and daffodils are in early full bloom, and dandelions in patches. Hosta is three inches tall. Peonies are 12 to 18 inches, leafing. Black raspberry leaves have come out. Lilac foliage half an inch long, honeysuckle closer to an inch, the very end of pussy willow catkin fall.

1991: The landmarks of early Middle Spring: *Cornus mas*, scilla, Glory-of-the-Snow, first forsythia. The lower honeysuckle leaves are out. The grass is green. Red maples continue in full bloom. Patches of purple deadnettle full bloom in pastures and roadsides. Raspberries and roses are leafing, magnolia buds cracking.

1992: Buckeyes unraveling even in this cold gray spring.

1993: To Caesar Creek: Water temperature too cold for crappie fishing, the lake was low and almost deserted. Caught one carp in two feet of water up river. One of the most beautiful days, a blush to the landscape, hazy sunny, warm out of the shade, but a cool north wind down the unprotected main channel. Cardinals and flickers called through the afternoon. Swallows chattered and circled the boat. Two buzzards, the first I've seen this year, soared above the oaks.

1994: Juncos still feeding in the south garden. Walking at Grinnell Pond this afternoon, I heard a tremendous racket to the east over the river valley, turned out to be a flock of hundreds of crows in a kind of conference. About half a mile away from me, they screamed and rose up, flapped and landed again in the high oaks.

1995: Pussy willows full of pollen, the first catkin fell to the grass in the wind this morning.

1998: Worms mating in the lawn this morning (55 degrees). Daffodils, a third open. Scilla, Glory-of-the-Snow, and many daffodil patches in full bloom.

2000: Dead nettle noticed blooming in the east garden.

2001: Flock of robins seen at Washington Court House, 30 miles south of Yellow Springs. The migration to the area continues.

2004: Robins were loud when I checked at 5:45 this morning. Doves began at 5:58, cardinals at 6:04. At South Glen, Mike and I found one purple cress plant and one white hepatica in bloom. Wild roses were leafing. Through the afternoon, squills, forsythia and white magnolias joined the growing ranks of daffodils.

2005: Ramps three inches, peonies three inches, daffodils ten inches and budded, tulips six to seven inches, rhubarb and waterleaf finally pushing through. Some new garlic mustard sprouts have come up just in the past few days, the first sprouts of the year.

2007: More daffodils opened overnight, more mid-season crocus wilted. The small red tulips are in full bloom like yesterday. Squills in full bloom, too. Pussy willows fat and completely full, but no pollen noticed. The pink spirea bush is getting small leaves. Now there are four dead squirrels up at the same place on High Street that one died last year.

2008: Jekyll Island: Yesterday walking along the beach, we saw a brown pelican and a black-headed tern, the tern hunting into the wind, diving into the waves to find its food. A dolphin played in the water of the sound. Throughout the island, live oaks are in bloom, their catkins long, many leaves starting. In the shorn grass along the inland waterway, small, white bluet-type flowers are in bloom, their leaves opposite and round, almost like chickweed leaves. I saw one red trumpet vine in bloom, the small yellow oxalis, the flax-like violet flowers with pansy-like blossoms, tall with opposite, thin, grasping leaves, and the ubiquitous black medic. In the undergrowth, a shrub with clusters of four-petaled flowers. As the tide went out, holes of ghost shrimp were revealed, easily identified by the shrimp droppings.

2009: Robins full song at 5:55 a.m., the morning gray and mild. One goldfinch, definitely turning yellow, at the feeder this afternoon.

2010: Jekyll Island: Squirrels mating. Walked the beach at low tide: sea slugs found, several sand dollars, a large live whelk. No Cherokee roses blooming yet, but camellias in full bloom.

2011: Aconite, snow crocus, snowdrop and standard crocus seasons are complete. Maples have started to flower. Pussy willows are full of pollen, forsythia and *Cornus mas* are opening in town, leafing has begun on honeysuckle, spicebush, lilacs, mock orange, crab apples. Quince buds are red. Daffodils gain momentum, even in the cold.

2012: A cardinal at a little before 6:00 this morning. Cooler weather now, frost expected tonight, full April throughout the county, snowball viburnum to apples to pink and white dogwoods. This afternoon, the wisteria on the trellis started to open, the first violet flowers. Working on the pond, I found fresh bamboo shoots six inches high.

And for the Yellow Springs newspaper, I wrote another update on the extremely warm March:

This week would be the first week of Middle Spring in an average year. Even though natural history suggests that forsythia should just be starting to bloom and that wildflowers should just be beginning to open in the Glen, the events of the past several weeks have literally moved the season close to the end of Middle Spring.

Although cooler weather will eventually bring the landscape back into a more normal sequence, all of the current markers in southwest Ohio are similar to those one might expect to find near Columbia, South Carolina or Savannah, Georgia in the first days of April: forsythia losing petals; pussy willow shrubs leafing - instead of growing pollen on their catkins; magnolia, pear, plum and cherry flowers falling; crab apples in bloom - instead of starting to leaf; dogwoods opening; dandelions in full flower or going to seed; white clover in the waysides; some lilacs and azaleas completely open; daffodils, scilla, bloodroot, twin leaf, violet cress and grape hyacinths dying back, mid-season tulips replacing them; peonies and viburnums budding; rhubarb stalks long enough for pie; tree of heaven, rose of Sharon and hydrangeas leafing out; buckeye trees with leaves half size; morel mushrooms swelling in the dark, the foliage of the understory almost completely green - instead of only starting to leaf out, and the high canopy slowly filling in.

Even though the warm Marches of 1983, 1990 and 2000 brought an early acceleration of flowering similar to what occurred this year, the heat did not last as long, and the season did not continue to advance as far as it has in 2012. March of 1907, however, did match the recent dramatic weather, and it was followed by one of the coldest April's in our history. On the other hand, the third months of 1945 and 1946 came close to the temperatures of March 2012, and their Aprils were mild.

2013: Snowy and cold today, but the crocus stick out and even seem like they are struggling to open up a little. The lone daffodil that has stood half open for over a week is patiently holding half open. I heard a song sparrow this morning, and blue jays were boisterous around the yard before noon. The new aconites finally emerged in the afternoon, bright, tight buds peering out from the snow.

2015: Another round of below-average temperatures, clouds, rainy. But a purple and several pale yellow hellebores have opened along the south fence, and red peony stalks have come up a little farther. I talked a few minutes with Rick at the gym: he said he saw the first daffodil open this morning in a sheltered south corner of his neighbor's house. Bright, bright orange sunset through the trees this evening.

2016: Frost and sun, third quarter moon in the high west: The first robin chirp at 5:31, the first cardinal call at 5:40 and robins in early song, doves at 5:53, and by then at 5:58 the birdsong was so loud that I couldn't be sure if a song sparrow were calling. A couple of red tulips seen opening in front of a house on the way to Jill's. In the east garden, pussy willow catkins, heavy with pollen, started falling overnight.

2017: Madrid, Spain: Partly cloudy in the 50s, then intermittent rain. On the way from the airport, trees definitely leafing. In the old city, pear trees in late flower and leafing, redbuds full and late and some transitioning to leaves.

2018: Virginia bluebells have tiny buds tucked among their dusky blue leaves. One small purple hyacinth is opening, hidden by a shrub, on Davis Street.

 For my column in *the Yellow Springs News*: As I write this column, the sky is bright but the wind is chilly. The average temperature so far this month has been 35 degrees, unusually low, it seems. But when I started writing almanacks for the *News* in 1984, the March average was 30.9 degrees, and my first predictions, based on the mild Marches of 1982 and 1983, were too optimistic.

 There have been 21 Marches with averages of around 35 degrees or below since 1883, when temperatures were first recorded in this area. There have only been two Marches as frigid as the third month of 1984: the March of 1885 (30.6 degrees) and the record-setting March of 1926 (26.7 degrees).

2020: Sun and close to 60 degrees: the first cabbage white flies over the circle garden, and my first honeybee visits the the daffodils in the north daffodil patch. The first hyacinths seen open, and Jill's star magnolia is in early flower, one pink magnolia tree near the Glass Farm starting to open. The red quince near Limestone Street is unraveling. Periwinkles, star of Holland and pachysandra are all blooming. Pansies have appeared in village dooryards. Daffodils and scilla are at the peak of their seasons.

2021: In Cedarville, buds of one of the old pink magnolia tree were starting to open. Multiple tornadoes cause many fatalities across the South. Pale violet windflowers open at Jill's. Glory-of-the-Snow blossoms are full at the back porch garden, following in sequence the decline of the mid-season crocuses. According to news reports from Kyoto, Japan, cherry blossoms have reached their peak there today, the earliest date on record. The previous record had been set in 1409, when they reached their best on March 27. Records have been kept there since 812 A.D. Since 1800, the peak period has been moving backwards from late April to mid and early April.

2022: Raw in the 30s and windy this morning, the first cardinal heard at 5:48 a.m., then scattered robin calls, song sparrows in the alley, doves by 6:00. Flurries throughout the day. From Umbria in central Italy, Neysa reports "daffodils everywhere." I noticed pansies planted in front of a house on Dayton Street: years ago before I watched the world, the pansies were the sign of spring.

2023: Pure sun and 60 degrees. In Xenia, ten miles south of Yellow Springs, honeysuckles were greening the undergrowth more than here, and fruit trees were obviously budded. Daffodil count: 120, and I saw periwinkle flowering by the fence. All about the northeast garden area, grape hyacinths have sprung up and are in full bloom.

Journal

The field of Nature being beyond the power of any one man to cultivate in full, let everyone begin with his own parish, and till that area intensively.

Gilbert White, *Selborne*

The parish phenological observer, one who watches what-happens-when in the local world of nature, gathers and collates scraps of information, and there are never enough scraps. To the parish phenologist, all the pieces are useful pieces, all the pieces have meaning, and all the pieces eventually become interconnected.

The cause for someone's practice of phenology may just be the need to focus. Or perhaps the drive to list and compare the elements of the seasons is a search for contemplation. The natural history of any region offers an infinite number of primary sources, and the process of collecting and cataloging can be the occasion not only for compulsive distraction but for making associations and philosophy.

No recorder is ever truly indifferent to the project he or she undertakes. The note taker ultimately becomes selective. The selectivity creates a specialization, and a kind of private curriculum appears from the continuing act of watching. Sometimes that curriculum becomes science, sometimes autobiography.

The concept of awareness is fundamental to a whole range of psychological and spiritual events in a progression towards some kind of fulfillment or awakening or relationship. Phenology is one form of journey to the center, a method of penetrating and cultivating consciousness. If, in meditation, the meditator watches thoughts like leaves carried downstream in a river, one can, in phenological rumination, substitute specific leaves or flowers or birds. Absorbed in the year's metronome of fauna and flora, the mind can empty itself of other issues.

Awareness of natural events also provides simple mantras for daily living, in which the whole swell of the year becomes a koan for contemplating the parish and for puzzling out personal space there.

March 27th
The 86th Day of the Year

Now Spring returns with warming breezes,
Now wild March skies
Retreat before the soft west wind.

Catullus (bf)

Sunrise/set: 6:28/6:54
Day's Length: 12 hours 26 minutes
Average High/Low: 53/34
Average Temperature: 44
Record High: 83 – 1910
Record Low: 11 – 1955

Weather
I have noted more thunderstorms on this date than on any other in March: 20 percent of all the years. High temperatures reach the 70s fifteen percent of the time, the 60s fifteen percent, and the 50s thirty percent, 40s thirty-five percent, 30s five percent. Completely overcast skies come only one day in four. Chances of snow fall to less than five percent, but rain strikes one day in three.

Natural Calendar
The entire land sets out to work,
All beasts browse in the fields.
Trees, herbs are sprouting.

Egyptian hymn

When forsythia shrubs are in bloom, then the first buckeye, apple and peach leaf out. At dusk, the first frogs and toads sing. Killdeer court, and woodcocks call near sunset with a nasal sounding "peent." Barn swallows arrive at barns, and the first baby barred owl hatches.

When forsythia blooms, then farmers seed the first of the oats and field corn. In town, the lawn is almost long enough to cut.

Nettles, chicory and leafcup are eight inches tall, peonies, Asiatic lilies and columbine four to five inches. Ragwort and garlic mustard are forming clumps; some sweet rockets and money plants get ready to send out their flower stalks.

Japanese knotweed catches up with the rhubarb (just about big enough for a small pie). Water rushes and purple loosestrife, water lilies and pickerel plants suddenly produce foliage in the ponds and streams, where small diving water beetles hunt for food.

Daybook

1983: Burdock leaves have come up this week. Quince is budding. Pussy willow pollen getting old and sagging. Box elder flowers turned to leaf buds. Ragweed sprouts have been up for several days now. In the woods, honeysuckles are pale green. Cold snap a few days ago has killed all the precocious star magnolia blossoms; forsythia half-damaged from the frost.

1985: First purple hyacinths seen in town. First forsythia in the yard.

1986: Cardinal sings at 5:55 a.m.

1987: First violets, chickweed, spring beauties, and wild strawberries blossom in the lawn at Antioch. One carp caught in the river about three o'clock, the water finally warm enough, no other bites.

1988: Jacksonville, Florida: Gaillardia full bloom at the beach. Pokeweed three feet high, not blooming. No flowers on the pennywort.

1989: Cincinnati: Daffodils near full bloom, things not much different from Yellow Springs. Star magnolias open in Eden Park (pacing my magnolia at Wilberforce), and some Bradford pears, a few flowering crabs. At South Glen, the warm days have brought out the heavy scent of the earth. The trees and fields are bare, but the land smells like spring.

1990: Jacoby: Buckeyes are beginning to leaf out. Cowslip leaves are two inches wide. Nettles are six inches, perfect for harvesting. Multiflora rose bushes turning green. First ginger is unfolding, one yellow-flowered toad trillium, patches of spring beauties and violet cress, one small-flowered buttercup, first Dutchman's britches in bloom. Toothwort and bluebells budding. Skunk cabbage leaves nine inches long, six inches wide. Wild geranium leaves tinted with orange in the sun, green out of the sun's rays.

1991: Pollen suddenly all over the pussy willows. Very first blue hyacinths show. First large white hyacinth. Rhubarb boot high.

1993: Bleeding heart just emerging, leaf heads purple against the ground. Phlox now have four or five shoots – there were only two a couple of days ago. Six lupine leaves came out on our one plant overnight. One finch almost yellow at the feeder this morning.

1995: First periwinkles seen open at Wilberforce. Chickweed in full bloom in patches of the college campus. I had seen it too along the north side of a building downtown a week ago.

1998: The pond fish came up to swim today. Water bugs were diving, water striders hunting. Algae began rising to the surface when the water got up to 60 degrees. Water rushes, pickerel plant growing now. In the south garden, anemone and hyacinth open. Forsythia full bloom. A spotted skipper in the house fluttering against the greenhouse walls. Scilla full bloom on Limestone and Whiteman Streets.

2004: At 5:15 this morning, robins were in full chorus in the rain. At 5:55, I heard a screech owl, and then the doves began to call, cardinals joining at 6:02. To Cincinnati at 8:00: A green flush to the roadside grass all the way south. Willows pale green, forsythia full bloom, honeysuckle bushes greening the undergrowth. Hemlock at least two feet at Mt. Healthy. In Cincinnati, roses were sending out shoots. Pink hyacinth was coming in at the Monastery of St. Clare. Spring beauties were in full bloom on the monastery grounds, toothwort was budding, and ramps were three inches tall. I saw cabbage butterflies and Asian lady beetles.

2007: Pussy willows suddenly full of pollen after two days in the 80s. Three cabbage butterflies seen today.

2008: Jekyll Island: Clear and mild, steady light wind, highs in the middle 70s, cirrus clouds in the afternoon. Woke to red-bellied woodpeckers and cardinals – more red-bellies than I've ever heard. Walked the North Beach and the marsh paths this afternoon, found a white or pale yellow star grass, a violet with divided leaves (perhaps a palmate violet, a coast violet, a birdsfoot violet or a three-lobed violet). Two monarch butterflies seen there. A blue spiderwort bloomed by the bathhouse. As the tide went out, thousands and thousands of pinkish gray slugs or fat, short worms were left lying on the sand, apparently unappealing to the birds. We watched two pelicans fly up and down the sound, dropping occasionally into the waves for fish. Cormorants disappeared under the water, reappeared far from where they went down.

2009: One-inch growth on a hosta in the alley, but no signs of hosta growth at home. In the North Glen this afternoon: the very first Dutchman's britches were flowering – most plants just have foliage; very early bloodroot and purple cress seen; hepatica that must have started blooming up to a week ago was relatively common downriver from the Cascades. In the wetland area, a few skunk cabbage plants were getting leaves. Along the path, new leafcup foliage was clumped, and aster leaves were an inch to three inches long. At home, the first yellow tulip opened against the south wall. Small ants have started to appear on the bathroom sink, beginning their springtime cleanup ritual (according to an exterminator we talked to a year or so ago).

2010: Jekyll: Azaleas starting at the beach access. Live oak leaves pushed by the wind like flocks of small shore birds.

2011: North Glen: Hepatica early open, violet cress and Dutchman's britches budding, leafcup leaves about three inches, skunk cabbage with very early leaves unraveling, one bloodroot bud, very small, pink wood betony foliage an inch high, trout lily leaves two inches long. The woodland area lags behind the town – which is already in the first days of Middle Spring. One small ant in the kitchen.

2012: Cardinal heard at 5:50 this morning. Temperatures were in the upper 20s last night, but the breeze never died down, and I don't see frost damage. Since all of the magnolia petals have already fallen along Xenia Avenue, there is no apparent collapse of the progress from the warmth. As I walked down Stafford Street, a south wind rolled pear petals down the pavement in front of me.

2013: Grackles all about the yard this chilly afternoon.

2015: Frost and clear, no breeze: Robins had already begun their chanting when I went out at 5:50. Cardinals and song sparrows at 5:57, crows at 6:03. Today's inventory around the yard almost exactly the same as the 28th of last year, maybe a little ahead.

2016: To Old Man's Cave in southeastern Ohio: An exceptionally warm day in the middle 70s, we drove through the brightest landscape, the green glowing in each pasture and through the undergrowth, some high tree-lines, probably the box elders, lacey green from leafing. Coltsfoot open here and there. One azure butterfly seen in the park's gorge, water striders in the river, and the first cabbage butterfly near my back porch. Forsythia and daffodils were open everywhere. Pears were flowering in Yellow Springs and throughout the countryside. Weeping cherry trees and even a pink-flowered apple were in bloom. Redbud buds were purple here, and John Blakelock called with reports on the toads singing in his pond: "They had a false start the last couple of weeks," he said, "but they're serious right now, they're committed to it." More of the thirty-year old yellow tulips opened in the south garden, and two new red tulips bloomed in the north garden. And Mary Sue sent a note saying that she had seen a bright yellow goldfinch today.

2019: At 5:50 this morning, the robin chorus was the most robust I've heard it so far, cardinals competing. Doves and black-capped chickadees and song sparrows joined at a little after 6:00. On the bathroom vanity, small ants have come with spring. In the garden, peonies are three inches. Bittercress is fully open. No pollen seen on the pussy willows. Daffodil buds in the garden are still waiting for warmer afternoons to open, most daffodils at about six inches, but walking Jill downtown after lunch, I found the first two daffodils just coming undone in a sunny spot across from St. Paul's church.

At the old mill along the river, henbit and bittercress in bloom, honeysuckle branches leafing for the first time, foliage of rockets and Dutchman's britches bushy, ramps common four inches high, clumps of ragwort leaves, scattered squills and hepatica in flower, one spring beauty hidden in the mulch. I looked for snow trilliums well into John Bryan Park, then with Jeanie's help, I found the first in a hollow formed by earlier spring flooding. Further back toward the mill, I found a patch of five snow trilliums across from three sycamores, close together, that stood against the river bank.

From her property on Talus Drive, Leslie reports the first butterfly today, a mourning cloak, and the first housefly. She also saw small-flowered bittercress in bloom.

2021: Full late Early Spring, more pink magnolias opening, daffodils at their best, some standard hyacinths in boom, maples shedding. Outside my studio window, the branches of the honeysuckle and mock orange have clusters of bright leaves an inch long. When I jogged this morning at first light, the morning chorus was intense and rich, included pileated woodpeckers, red-bellied woodpeckers, mocking birds, song sparrows, chickadees, blue jays, roosters, geese, late crows – along with the robins and cardinals and Carolina wrens. Late in the afternoon, Jill and I went to Pearl Fen. Well into the woods, we found Dutchman's britches in bloom and the largest patch of bloodroot – all open and bright – that I've ever seen.

2022: Grape hyacinths flowering, hidden among the wild rose of Sharon. Japanese knotweed has started to emerge in the north garden, its red sprouts invading the patch I usually reserve for zinnias.

2023: Daffodil count is 142 today, even as the earliest ones are fading. Scilla, periwinkles, grape hyacinths and the first purple henbit create complement the daffodils now, making a new phase of Early Spring in the yard.

Journal

I've been thinking about the simple (simplistic?) phenology "laws" I put together several years ago, one of them being that if something in nature happens once, it will probably happen again (without which supposition no one could make any sort of plans). But looking back over my notes, the most obvious principle might be that if something happens once in nature, it has probably happened before. For example, the hepaticas and bloodroots, bluebells and violet cress that grace Glen Helen now are flowers from history.

Uncertainty about the future that accompanies the Anthropocene does not affect what has already happened. If the present is tentative, and if the future is in grave danger, at least their antecedents are not. And so the enjoyment of what happens in this instant (these leafing skunk cabbages, these blossoming cowslips) has deep roots in time and need not be dismissed as threatened or ephemeral. The past is not undone.

I look deeply into the repeating mirror of the mirror of recollection that recreates near identical images and happenings back and back not only through the years of my lifetime but so far beyond, hundreds of years, into an imagined infinity. So I am here in all of time, firmly settled in the passage, no matter what lies ahead.

I depend not only on the likelihood that spring will come again because it is coming now; I depend on the certainty of all springs that ever were.

It was a day "borrowed" from Eternity, so glorious it was; a day when we experienced again all the sights, sounds and odors of Early Spring that we had longed for ....

Charles Burchfield

March 28th
The 87th Day of the Year

There grew pied Wind-flowers and Violets,
Daisies, those pearl'd Arcturi of the earth,
The constellated flowers that never set;
Faint Oxlips; tender Blue-bells, at whose birth
The sod scarce heaved....

Percy Bysshe Shelly

Sunrise/set: 7:28/7:57
Day's Length: 12 hours 29 minutes
Average High/Low: 54/35
Average Temperature: 45
Record High: 85 – 1910
Record Low: 16 – 1955

Weather

Today is typically one of the warmest days in March, with highs in the 70s occurring 20 percent of the time, 60s twenty-five percent, 50s twenty-five percent, 40s twenty-five percent, and 30s the remaining five percent. Precipitation falls on 40 percent of March 28ths, but almost never in the form of snow. Sunny to partly cloudy skies are accompanied by frost six years in a decade.

Natural Calendar

As Early Spring moves to a close, gall mites start working in the ash trees; pine weevils and moths infest the evergreens. Bluegrass billbugs become active at this time, laying eggs when temperature warms at the end of March.

If the land is dry enough, farmers seed the first field corn in southern Ohio counties. Commercial potato, sugar beet, carrot, and red beet planting begins along Lake Erie. The first winter wheat is jointing in a mild spring, and oats seeding has begun.

In Washington, D.C., the cherry blossoms often come out at the end of March and the beginning of April. Monarch butterflies have reached the Deep South, moving across Texas, then to Louisiana and Georgia. Some have flown north to

Oklahoma and Arkansas, laying eggs all along the way.

Daybook
Spring does not happen alone,
just for me or you,
nor is it just for now,
this event or that one only,
this morning or this afternoon,
these bluebells, these indigo buntings
along the river....

Hepatica Sun

1985: Covered Bridge, 70 degrees: Very first bluebells, chickweed, bloodroot, small-flowered bittercress blooming. First new ginger leaves up. Ground coming alive with sprouts and new leaves. Twinleaf with buds. Soft, red buds on the buckeyes. At home, pollen begins on the pussy willows.

1986: Forsythia in full bloom now, and enough honeysuckle leaves have emerged to give some patches of woods a green shading. Wasp seen in the sun at Antioch School.

1987: Cardinal sings at 6:01 a.m. Hepatica is in full bloom in North Glen.

1988: Jacksonville north to Asheville: The lush green fades a few miles past the Georgia border, leaves turning to flowers, Savannah full flower. Less color between Columbia and the North Carolina border. Then near Asheville, whole apple orchards in flower, redbud in bloom throughout, late daffodils.

1989: First dandelion seen at Wilberforce. Burdock up. The apple tree in the backyard is leafing.

1990: Young opossums killed on Wilberforce-Clifton Road, maybe four to six weeks old, born about the middle of February.

1990: Carp are biting at Caesar Creek (caught three).

1991: First wasp in the office. Bradford pears are budded. First spring beauties seen at the corner of Grinnell and Wilberforce-Clifton. Early periwinkles at Brush Row. Mock orange leafing out. Japanese knotweed leaves are an inch long, which means the ginger is just up at South Glen. Pollen getting old on the pussy willows.

1993: First squill and first large hyacinth budding in the south garden. One small light blue grape hyacinth blooming in the east garden. Snowdrops half gone. Under the bird feeder, a courtship dance by a male cardinal, wings outstretched, female attentive.

1998: Apple and peach trees leafing now. Full pollen on the pussy willows. Japanese knotweed, comfrey and phlox are up an inch or so. In the woods, along the river, snow trillium in full bloom. Wild phlox about two inches.

2000: Starlings building a nest in the wooden sign outside the dentist's office this morning. A huge weeping cherry blooming in Xenia, and some white-flowered apples pace the pears.

2004: Euonymus vines in the backyard have put on an inch or sow of new growth. Maples seeds are sprouting in the lawn. Pussy willows are full of pollen.

2007: In the North Glen this morning with Jeanie: Some May apples had emerged, many leafcup, sweet rocket and garlic mustard clusters. Very few wildflowers were open – some hepatica, violet cress, bloodroot and Dutchman's britches. Compared to the progress in the village, the wildflowers have remained conservative in their development. Skunk cabbage leaves are three to five inches long, about the same length now as dock leaves in the garden. Full pollen on pussy willows. Full cherry blossoms in the alley. One finch seen half golden, mottled.

2008: Jekyll Island: Warm and sunny. Walk from the campground down to the historic district this afternoon, maybe four to five miles in all, the wind gentle and steady. Webworms seen in one tree, already crawling outside their web. (We had seen them from the road near Columbia on the 25th.) Wild grape noticed for the first time. Oxalis, yellow and violet common, as was the flax-like flower. One obvious zeitgeber was the thin bamboo that grows along the roads and bike paths. New bamboo sprouts had emerged maybe a week or two ago, some of the spears three to four feet. Cherokee roses in full bloom near the Jekyll Island Club, and more dogwoods and azaleas seen, and one crab apple in full flower. Plantings around the historic houses were mostly bright, tall snapdragons. As we walked, cardinals (redder here and with a different accent), doves and mocking birds heard. Slash pine, the giant trees with squares or shingles of bark, identified. Several orange and yellow lantana plants found coming up from the dock walk in front of the Club. On the news tonight, pictures of full bloom of cherry trees in Washington D.C.

Thomas Merton's Kentucky journal from Easter Sunday, March 28 of 1948: "All the apple trees came out in blossom Good Friday (the 26th). It rained and got colder, but today is very bright with a pure, pure sky. The willow is full of green. Things are all in bud."

2009: The robins were starting to sing when I went outside at 5:38 this morning. Across the street, the high buds of the star magnolia have opened, and a few buds on Don's pink magnolia are breaking. Through town and the yard, daffodils are multiplying, blossoms held by the cool gray days. The Internet reports that in Washington D.C., a few cherry trees are opening, tulips and "a few of the other trees" (probably pear and plum) are starting.

2010: To Hunting Island in South Carolina from Jekyll Island: Wind and rain, but soft throughout the day: Definite leafing taking place north along I-95, much greener than a week ago when we came down through Alabama. At Beaufort, pink magnolias, forsythia, azaleas, redbuds, camellias and pears in bloom – well ahead of Jekyll.

2011: Cardinal loud at 5:59 a.m. One small ant seen on the kitchen counter and another on the bathroom sink. They are starting to clean up for spring.

2012: Warmth returns, high above 70 degrees, as I fill the new water garden (box elder flowers the first contributions to the pond). More tulips are blooming, the lilac in the backyard opening, more wisteria flowers opening on the trellis, pachysandra flowering complete, euonymus vines finished leafing, ferns growing to six inches, bells of Ireland still flowering, daffodils definitely in decline, white bleeding hearts in bloom. As we walked on Xenia Avenue, the wind blew down the pear petals, whisking them across and along the street, grackles cackling all around us.

2013: Finally all-day sun, the temperature getting to 50 degrees, the crocus in the east garden opening back up and the new aconites in full, broad bloom. (All the established aconites have already completed their season in the alley.) Under the northeast redbud tree, two of Jeanie's primroses, a yellow and a red, are budding. In the garden by the west redbud, waterleaf is starting to emerge, leaves just a fraction of an inch. Henbit blooming, but tight. Peggy's daffodils continue to open, but my one that has been half open through the coldest days seems stuck in *media res*. A patch of scilla has replaced aconites in the Phillips/Stafford Street alley. Flies and bees are in the flowers, the first time I've seen them this year. Lilac buds along Dayton Street soft green, serviceberry buds expanding now and turning pink. One ant noticed crawling on my desk this afternoon.

2014: A cardinal sang outside my door at 6:02 this morning. Inventory at the end of a cold March: Snowdrops and aconites still in full bloom, many snow crocus still coming in, mid-season crocus open throughout town when the sun comes out and the temperature reaches 40, red maples still blooming, tulip foliage to six inches, peony stalks to two inches. Daffodil and naked lady foliage about the same at three to five inches – and I picked one broken daffodil that was half open, the first seen in the yard this spring. Waterleaf in the southwest gardens has developed a little this week, but it is still only an inch across. Ramps up three inches. In the weedy north gardens, crabgrass, bittercress and wild onions are filling in between the daylily leaves, the first bittercress in flower along the south wall. One blue squill has flowered against the north wall, and both the pale and the violet Lenten roses are open wide. The rhubarb is still just a red nub, barely showing, by the raspberry patch.

2015: Clear and cold in the lower teens, frost: I went outside with Bella at 5:39, no sound of birds. The sequence began at 5:47, the first robin chirping, the calls increasing to whinnies until the first High Street cardinal called out at 5:53, then the first song sparrow at 5:54, then a couple of crows at 5:56, doves at 5:58. Bella didn't really want to walk, the cold at her arthritis maybe. We went inside, and I built up the fire. When I went out for wood at 6:20, the tufted titmouse, piercing and steady, had joined the choir. I found large white moth sitting in a flowerpot near the sprouts under the grow light in the attic.

2016: Chilly and raw, rain overnight. The first cardinal sang at 5:36, waking a nearby robin. I found a carpenter bee trying to get out of the greenhouse this afternoon. He must have come in yesterday when the temperature was in the 70s (40s all day today).

2017: Madrid, Spain: Cool and sunny, sycamores and buckeyes (some with three-inch leaves), a few trees in bloom, wisteria in full bloom, tiny grass daisies full, regular daisies and pansies full, a large patch of dandelions in flower, a forsythia bush fresh gold: one star of Bethlehem in the grass by the *Retiro*: this is Yellow Springs middle April.

2018: Through the chilly rainy days and nights, the buds of the daffodils in the circle garden swell and show more yellow, and then the first one opening in the late afternoon. Along Dayton Street, bittercress has come into bloom.

2019: First robins at 5:40, cardinals and the full robin chorus at 5:45, song sparrows and doves at 5:55, crows a little after 6:00. At breakfast, Jill spotted a camel cricket behind my chair, the first cricket in a long time. High in the upper 60s this afternoon, the purple bluebell sprouts just barely showing under the ancient mock orange bush. The first daffodil and bittercress came a day earlier this year than last year.

2020: High in the low 70s today. One small tan moth seen fluttering to the circle garden. Bittercress getting lanky in the alley.

2021: Waterleaf, leaves an inch or two across, has covered the ground in the south garden. Leaves are coming out on the crab apple trees at the park. Don's serviceberry trees are well budded. A box elder tree on Limestone Street is in full flower. The news from Washington, D.C. is that the cherry blossoms there reached peak bloom a few days ahead of schedule. Some sources say that the blossoming time has moved back about a week in the past 100 years. Last night's full moon (with perigee) created tides high enough to free a huge tanker that was stuck in the Suez Canal.

2022: A substantial flock of black buzzards feasting where the geese spent the winter.

2023: Waterleaf leaves appearing near the squills. In Don's front yard: deep purple wood hyacinths and some violet windflowersI walk the yard, counting daffodils (about 150 today), suddenly realizing that the snow crocus and the standard crocus, the bittercress and the snowdrops and aconites have all disappeared, leaving empty floral spaces, empty spaces where markers blossomed. And lanky snowdrop foliage. Pussy willow catkins on the road, their fluff and color matted and spoiled. How simple it is to know that this space is what is here now, this space tied inextricably to season. Is all space-time simply awareness of the combined nature of movement and locale, or of local movement? And a snapshot of the landscape can be confusing; it is a picture of time-space/time.

The early garden\: potatoes, onions, peas, lettuce, spinach, cabbage, carrots, radishes, marking their straight rows with green, before the trees are leafed.

Wendell Berry

March 29th
The 88th Day of the Year

The Time hath laid his mantle by
Of wind and rain and icy chill,
And dons a rich embroidery
Of sunlight poured on lake and hill.
No beast or bird in earth or sky,
Whose voice doth not with gladness thrill,
For Time hath laid his mantle by
Of wind and rain and icy chill.

Charles D'Orleans (William Cullen Bryant)

Sunrise/set: 7:26/7:58
Day's Length: 12 hours 32 minutes
Average High/Low: 54/35
Average Temperature: 45
Record High: 82 – 1910
Record Low: 14 – 1887

Weather
Afternoon temperatures come up past 70 degrees 25 percent of all years - making a typical March 29th the most likely day of Early Spring to see such warmth. Sixties come another 25 percent, 50s fifteen percent, 40s thirty percent, 30s and 20s just ten percent The likelihood of morning frost drops from 40 percent to 25 percent. Rain comes half the time, and the chances of mostly overcast conditions are 60 percent.

Natural Calendar
If spring equinox in the third week of March is a solar gauge of the sun's position in the sky and a popular dividing line between periods of dormancy and growth, other temporal milestones in the natural world create more immediate borders to the landscape's different stages of flower or decay.

One of the local events of Early Spring is tapping maple trees for sap. On the Flying Mouse Farm in Yellow Springs, the tapping usually gets underway by the second week of February and ends in the third week of March, bracketing the flowering of snowdrops, aconites and crocuses, the emergence of pussy willow catkins, the arrival of red-winged blackbirds and grackles, and opening of the pre-dawn chorus of robins, cardinals, song sparrows, titmice and doves.

Although cold or warm Februarys and Marches may add or subtract days from the local equation, the first blooms of bulbs, the running sap, and changes in bird behavior are clear events of Early Spring almost everywhere. No matter where the traveler may go, the sight of one familiar Early Spring marker suggests the likelihood that the other parallel markers might be found.

Along much of the 40th Parallel, Middle Spring is usually the season most people associate with the arrival of "real spring." At this time of year, there are many more visible markers to observe and collect, making the passage seem more in keeping with the sense that "real spring" should bring mild weather and green leaves.

Among signs associated with Middle Spring are flowering shrubs like forsythia, then tulips and blossoming fruit trees. In parks and preserves, the sequence of wildflowers offers a clear and annotated pathway through this middle season.

And the fact that these signs are based on regional recording of periodic change does not limit their use in identifying similar seasons elsewhere. The parochial is the gnomon of the broader world. For the casual observer, the character of the landscape at any latitude or altitude takes shape in its relationship to familiar, local events; it also expands the role of sequence and stages in finding home across the planet.

Daybook

1979: First forsythia blooms.

1981: First forsythia blooms.

1982: Dandelions blossoming in the sun. Bleeding hearts up.

1984: First small leaves on the raspberries.

1985: First lilac leaves are out. Box elders flower. Two crabapple trees getting leaves. Some small pink tulips open along Limestone Street. Blackbird seen making a nest. Squirrels seem to be defending their nests.

1986: Mock orange leafing, box elders beginning to flower.

1987: Rhubarb six inches high. At South Glen: geese and ducks seen at nesting sites, first bluebells, twinleaf, spring beauties. First May apple up, toad trillium. Violet Cress and Dutchman's britches full bloom. Bloodroot common. Shrub line greening. Pussy willow catkins almost all fallen. More magnolias blooming. First buckeye leafs out. New ginger leaves just up. Fishing at sycamore hole, chubs and shiners caught, and one three-pound carp.

1988: Asheville to Yellow Springs: Redbud and flowering crabs throughout the Knoxville area, and an increase in budding trees into the city. Last redbud open seen 30 miles north of the Kentucky/Tennessee line. Into northern Kentucky, only forsythia blooming and honeysuckle leafing. The grass was half green; a week ago it was completely brown here. In Cincinnati, forsythia was in full bloom and roadside grass deep green. In Dayton, forsythia just starting to open. At home, pussy willows were getting pollen. Garlic mustard and pigweed had sprouted in front when we were gone. Peonies were now six inches, daffodils full bloom, mock orange, Japanese honeysuckle leafing, box elders poised to flower. News report says cherry trees are in full bloom in Washington DC, putting them at the Knoxville stage.

1989: Rhubarb four inches high. Pussy willow full of pollen.

1991: A sleepy cabbage butterfly came inside today, hiding in a bouquet of south-garden daffodils.

1993: Cardinals and other birds full song at 5:45 a.m. At dawn, I found the delphinium up an inch or two. It wasn't there yesterday.

1994: In the last day or so, the palmate lupine leaves have come up strong, and the first shoots of comfrey. The first raspberry bush is starting to leaf. The honeysuckles in the woods have opened a little, and the buckeye buds have loosened.

1995: Saw finches with full summer color today, their heads and breasts almost completely yellow.

1996: Puschkinias have been open for four or five days now, and I saw the first blue scilla blooming close to the earth. The crocuses are at their peak, pussy willows fat and fully emerged. Along the north garden wall, one purple deadnettle has flowered. No daffodils yet this cold year.

1998: First Bradford pears flower in the heat. News reports of cherry trees full bloom in Washington D.C. Hibiscus flowers in my greenhouse. American toads have started to sing after dark along the river.

2000: To Cincinnati: In Dayton, the honeysuckles were leafing, and high trees were about a fourth unraveled, pale, translucent, the fields all bright beside them. Thirty miles south at a rest stop, the apples were budded, one quince almost out. Then in Cincinnati, 55 miles south of Yellow Springs, redbuds and all the apples were in bloom. So many of the city trees were fully April green. Red and yellow tulips in front of a gas station, maturity of daffodils everywhere, and the honeysuckle leaves were full size. Four deer seen killed by the side of the road.

2004: Cardinal woke me this morning at 5:45 – now a sudden acceleration in their (or my) rising time. Puschkinias opened in the east garden today. I noticed privets leafing ahead of the honeysuckle along Limestone Street.

2005: Inventory today includes more foliage of waterleaf, dense and bushy celandine and poppies, rhubarb and peonies stronger, scillas and mid-season crocus suddenly in full bloom, the first purple deadnettle, Dutch iris foliage up about three inches, garden phlox, catmint and butterfly bush up half an inch to an inch, allium up three inches, the first daffodil in the yard and the very first forsythia flower bud cracking, red quince leaves just starting to unravel. The year continues to pace the progress of 1996.

2007: Pear trees downtown are opening.

2008: Jekyll Island to Spartanburg, South Carolina: Little change observed along I-95. The high canopy is blooming and leafing all along the Georgia coast. In South Carolina, the change is more dramatic from when we came through on the 25th. Now redbuds, rare a week ago, are open all the way to Spartanburg, and Jessamine, first seen in Columbia on our trip down, was common now all the way through the Piedmont. Wild cherry trees are in bloom along the road, and webworms, only seen once on the 25th, are now common to the mountains. At the welcome center to South Carolina, fleabane seen with violet flowers, and a six-petaled star grass, violet with a reddish center. By Spartanburg the flowering and leafing have receded, and the tree line is mostly bare.

2010: Hunting Island, South Carolina: Grape leaves about half an inch at the campsite. Seashells found: Large pin shell, Atlantic coquina, Eastern oyster, minor jackknife, cockles, piles of Atlantic abra, knobbed whelk, lightning whelk, many sand dollars, hooked mussel, disk dosinia.

2011: Robins very faint when I went out at 5:45 this morning. A cardinal sang at 6:00 sharp, and geese flew over at 6:12. But there have been no crows for quite a while. I missed the point in the year at which they stopped coming into the neighborhood. When I walked Bella this morning, I noticed that the grape hyacinths at the corner lot were all blue in bloom. This evening, small ants appeared on the bathroom sink, once again beginning their cleanup ritual at the end of March.

2012: The first cardinal heard at 5:36 this morning. No crows noticed today. In the yard, the white lilacs are in full bloom, violet ones gathering momentum, ground ivy and fleabane and celandine in bloom, grass getting too long, violets taking over, redbuds still holding full, downtown pear tree flowers almost all down in yesterday's wind, serviceberry trees now leafing, box elder flowers almost gone, bluebells and hepatica in the yard full. Helianthus leaves found as I weeded in the garden, the plants so strong last summer, very late and tentative now, buried under bittercress and deadnettle and violets. Reports of morel mushrooms throughout the area.

2013: When I went outside this morning at 5:45, the robins and cardinals were already in full song, quite a change from a week ago when I strained to hear them at 6:00. Juncos seen on the ground under the feeder today. Bluebell foliage has just emerged, deep purple and an inch tall, under the mock orange bush in the backyard, tulip foliage is six inches high, and peony stalks have put on another half inch. At Ellis Pond, the weeping willow buds are slowly producing tiny leaves. Red-winged blackbirds sing near the water.

2015: Frost, orange and completely clear sky, Sagittarius edging a little west, no wind at all: I went out with Bella at 5:40, no birdsong. The first wave of cardinals started singing at 5:43. Robins were chirping at 5:46, their chorus at 5:48, doves at 5:49, song sparrows in the background, then the lazy crows at 5:57.

2016: Frost and clear: Robins began at 5:31. Crows have been absent from the mornings for several weeks. Two thin-leafed autumn hostas have come up strong over the past few days, are five inches tall already. Patches of dandelions seen at various locations on the way in to Dayton. One peach flower opened on Jill's tree.

2017: Botanical Garden in Madrid, Spain: sun and temperature in the upper 50s: forsythia, tulips, bridal wreath, old daffodils, yucca with tall stalks, iris, pink camellias, red flowered buckeyes (*Aeschylus Pavia*), early strawberries, fat golden heads of euphorbia, *Brummera macrophilia*, lilacs, peonies with spreading green leaves, white bleeding hearts, orange geums, violet geraniums *Macroorrhizum*, frilly pink rhododendron, pink camelia, yellow-flowered holly, huge pink flower clusters on the *Prunus deregulate*, pink magnolia, scraggly shepherd's purse to seed, bright red *Rhododendron macrophilia*, *Viburnum Davidii* with mixed color flower clusters, a spring version of virgin's bower, dramatic jasmine branches hanging and covering the entire trunk of a tree with yellow flowers.

2018: Soft 50s, misty, benign, the ground soaked, daffodils unraveling, bluebells up to three inches loving the rain. In front of the house, the sidewalk is blocked with puddles. Water has pooled in pockets on the lawn.

2019: My first daffodil opened overnight, and Peggy's first one, too. Leslie reports that the first daffodil opened at her father's house on Wright Street. At Ellis Pond, only four geese. A red maple was in bloom and shedding.

2020: Lilacs leafing, hemlock bushy and spreading, maybe two feet tall, Jill's silver maple shedding, honeysuckle leaves quickly filling the hedge line, algae difficult to control in the pond, two cabbage white butterflies braving today's hard wind (but temperatures in the 60s).

2021: After yesterday's cold wind and occasional sleet: sun and crisp and calm. At the Glass Farm pond this afternoon, a frog was croaking, as well as making a snoring type of call, a little like the call of a gray tree frog. A lone dandelion seen near the water, algae spreading throughout the pond. From Spoleto, Italy, Neysa writes: "The cherries have been blooming. Today is the third day since starting, and they look all the way open now. All three cherry trees at the same time – cool!"

2023: Hard wind throughout the day, ragged cumulus clouds rushing by toward the northeast.. Daffodil count: 150 blossoms. First tulip bud seen. And a long mole mound has appeared in the north yard path. Kitty Jensen reports: "My granddaughter Evadene, 5 years old, spotted a bald eagle today in a sycamore tree between Antioch School and Antioch College. The sighting was confirmed by Kumar, who was riding with her on the bike path."

Here is an unspeakable secret: paradise is all around us and we do not understand.

Thomas Merton

March 30th
The 89th Day of the Year

The world's great age begins anew,
The golden years return,
The earth doth like a snake renew
Her winter weeds outworn.

John Davies

Sunrise/set: 7:23/7:57
Day's Length: 12 hours 34 minutes
Average High/Low: 55/35
Average Temperature: 45
Record High: 85 – 1986
Record Low: 15 – 1887

Weather
Another landmark for spring today: the chances of an afternoon in the 80s jumps from only one percent to nearly ten percent. Seventies come 15 percent of the days, 60s twenty percent, 50s fifteen percent to 20 percent, and cool 40s forty to fifty percent of the time. Precipitation and clouds occur half of the days in my record on this date. Frost strikes one morning out of three.

Natural Calendar
The bright yellow flowers of forsythia bushes always announce the arrival of Middle Spring. This is the season in which the remaining daffodils and grape hyacinths flower and that wildflower season unfolds in the woods with the blossoming of early violet cress, twinleaf, periwinkle, spring beauty, hepatica and small-flowered bittercress. Early meadow rue and May apples (prophets of morel mushrooms) are pushing up out of the ground. Cowslip is budding in the swamp, and leaves grow long on the skunk cabbage. Japanese knotweed, columbine, phlox and lupine emerge in the garden. Ants are building mounds between the sidewalk cracks.

247

1981: First leaves on the raspberries. First tulip blooms.

1982: Dutchman's britches are budding. The first bluebell, star of Holland and scilla blooming in town, first daffodil in bloom, first honeysuckle leaves.

1983: Grinnell Swamp: Buzzards circling, first time seen since fall. New sprouts everywhere, grass begins to return to the swamp flats, growing thick. Male and female mallards walk calmly near me through the cress. Toothwort, Dutchman's britches budding. Toad trillium up. Swamp buttercup in bloom. Large tadpoles found in a pool. At home, peach tree leafing, apple tree buds extending.

1985: My star magnolia blooms at Wilberforce.

1986: First tulip seen. Very first pussy willow pollen forms. Spring beauties open at the corner of Grinnell and Wilberforce-Clifton. At the Covered Bridge, in the middle of a record high of 85 degrees, first bluebell, bloodroot, twinleaf bloom. Toad trillium and May apples up. Buckeyes leafing, winter cress coming on, wild geranium up, hepatica early full, burdock leafing in places. Touch-me-not and ragweed sprouts. In the yard, ferns are starting. Columbine is two inches tall. Bleeding hearts are getting leaves, pussy willow pollen coming out all at once. Magnolias open.

1987: Motherwort grows back now. Viburnum leafing.

1988: A cardinal woke me up at 5:55, second morning in a row. At Wilberforce, the flowering crabs begin to leaf. The north side star magnolia opens just slightly, the south side bursts open. Robins now common in Yellow Springs. Ants are creating their mounds. Some tulips in full bloom, others budding. Iris about nine inches tall, daylily maybe seven inches. Flock of buzzards seen in a field along Wilberforce-Clifton. At the Covered Bridge, violet cress full bloom, first toothwort blooms. Sedum, violets, waterleaf, chickweed, and catchweed foliage becoming prominent, covering the winter brown. Lawns are blue with scilla and star of Holland. Wild rose bushes, lilacs and raspberries are leafing. Carp rolling and splashing in the water near shore.

1989: Black raspberries now leafing. Comfrey three inches, poppies fifteen inches, peonies a foot. Burdock common now, some dock lush and up past my ankle. Periwinkles bloom at Wilberforce.

1990: Hops vines are up six inches to a foot now, but not leafing. Probably emerged at least ten days ago in the heat wave. At the Covered Bridge, the full range of Early Spring: full blooming of bluebells, a few May apples and toad trillium up, twinleaf early full, violet cress late full, bloodroot open, toothwort early full, some ragwort stalks eight inches. Lovers in the nude past the leafing skunk cabbage. At home, the last pussy willow catkins fall in the rain. In the greenhouse, the season of cutting down the mother-of-millions begins.

1991: Cardinal sings 5:42 a.m.

1993: After supper, I found the first comfrey leaf. It wasn't there this morning. Delphinium grew another inch since yesterday. Lupines are multiplying, daylily spears doubling in size overnight. Gingko buds have extended, lilac's bright green now. Windflower full bloom now, crocus season peaking, snowdrops fading quickly, more daffodils budding.

1998: Heat wave: All the pears are blooming downtown. Cowslip wide open along Grinnell. Orange and yellow tulips come in beside the south wall. All fruit trees in leaf. Serviceberry trees flower. First star magnolias. Peach tree full bloom. End all crocuses. American toads call all across the township. First hosta spears push up. Peonies are leafing, almost knee high.

2000: First violet found open in the yard. Money plant has started to send up its stalk. The pussy willow catkins fell yesterday, all decayed. Box elder flowers dangling, falling. The early yellow tulips open in the south garden all at once. Hyacinths and daffodils still everywhere in the village. Along the bike path, more hints of green to the trees, hemlock almost knee high. Vegetable garden digging completed, some garlic transplanted. The lone asparagus stalks are two to six inches, will be ready to eat his week.

2001: Jekyll Island: Cherokee white roses in full bloom.

2007: As this sudden spring continues, all the pear trees downtown are in full bloom, came in almost overnight. All the star magnolias have been in full bloom for days. Pussy willow catkins are falling, willow catkins fully formed, first serviceberry flowers opening, some astilbe up to five inches, peonies unraveling – more than a foot tall, pink spirea leaves coming in, honeysuckle leaves turning the undergrowth pale green and providing a screen for the yard.

At the Gorge, bluebells and first toothwort and toad trillium are open. Hyacinths full. *Trillium grandiflorum* and early meadow rue are up and budded. May apple patches, many plants well developed and unfolded. Hepatica and bloodroot common in full bloom. The first yellow tulip is open in the yard, all the daffodils have come in, redbuds and some crab apples show purple/red buds. Box elder flowers waving in the wind, some peach buds open. One blue butterfly seen along the river.

2008: Spartanburg, South Carolina to Yellow Springs: Starting out the trip at dawn in a light rain, the road through the mountains, even near Ashville, was now full of redbuds in bloom – whereas a week ago, we saw maybe only one or two. There were also more crab apple trees open. North of Knoxville, the redbuds continued, but gradually became less mature until they disappeared a little after the Kentucky border. Pear trees were common in Kentucky, and the first patches of full-blooming dandelions, a shepherd's purse type cress, and purple deadnettle seen near Williamsburg. The past week was clearly a pivotal one throughout the mountains, but arriving in Yellow Springs, we found almost no change at all except more squills up and budded and midseason crocus well budded.

2009: South to Wilmington, 30 miles from Yellow Springs: The change was dramatic in just those few miles: pink magnolias much more open, forsythia in full bloom, willow trees greening, weeping cherry trees flowering, decorative pear buds straining to open. The wheat fields were bright, and the corn and soybean fields had been plowed and seem ready for seeding.

2011: Walking with Jeff at the Indian Mound park area: We saw hepatica, chickweed, bittercress, lots of ramps, lush and tall, and then, on and around limestone boulders, several rare clumps of snow trillium in full bloom. On the way back, we found a dead blue butterfly lying by the side of the path, its color bright. It may have come out over a week ago in the warmth and then perished in the cold spell of the past several days.

2012: More mild weather, sun and showers. Cardinals and grackles singing through the day, crows calling early for the first time in several days. The first golden finch in full color came to the feeder this morning. Great dandelion bloom continuing out of season. Redbuds, Don's pink magnolia and his pie cherry hold strong. At the post office and along Corey Street, Zelcova trees are fully leafed.

2013: I went out to hear birds at 5:40, moon far in the west, and the robins were already in full song. I heard a cardinal at 5:47, and then many more thereafter, and then grackles waking up at 5:50, crows in the northwest at 5:57, doves at 5:55. Leaves are starting on the multiflora rose outside the south bedroom window, just a slight bit ahead of the willow at Ellis Pond. A clump of Peggy's daffodils opened all the way today.

2014: Ed Oxley reported four sandhill cranes flying northwest.

2015: A perfect morning to go out to time birds: clear sky after a little rain yesterday evening, very light frost, no wind, barometer 30.03 rising. First robins at 5:38 – chirping and then right into singsong chorus, first cardinal at 5:44, first crows at 5:52, first song sparrow and dove at 5:58, first grackles at 6:16.

2016: Sun, south wind, high about 70 degrees. I saw the first half-gold goldfinch at the feeder this morning. Grass cut for the first time. August hostas starting up under the east crabapple tree. Don's serviceberry trees are suddenly in full bloom. One of Jill's redbuds is starting to unravel, and the buds of the crabapples at the triangle park are cracking and showing color. At the North Glen, the dominant flowers are only hepatica, Dutchman's britches, and violet cress. The patch of lesser celandine has many more blossoms than last week. A few spicebushes are in flower. Foliage of the tall columbo is six inches high, speckled trout lily foliage is thick, two inches long, wood betony leaves two inches, toad trilliums emerged, some May apples spreading out their tents, wild ginger coming out from under the leaf mulch, some toothwort just opening, most tightly budded.

Delicate white rue anemone is open on the path up from the Cascades, and nodding meadow rue budded. In the yard, the bluebell heads hang down, waiting for a little more warmth. Scilla, grape hyacinth, windflowers and glory-of-the–snow keep several spaces at the west side of the house full of color. By the far west edge of the property, white pachysandra petals stretch out as they age. The circle garden is lush with daffodils, and the north garden tulips are gaining momentum. The pussy willow near the front sidewalk has dropped most of its catkins. Bittercress goes to seed in patches throughout the yard.

2017: Arriving in Sarria, Spain: Full dandelion and plum bloom the most obvious markers of the middle of a Yellow Springs April.

2018: Another day of rain, and now colder. The whole Middle Atlantic region must be sodden. The back lawn is flooded, and when I went out to hoe in the garden a little yesterday, my right boot sunk down half a foot into the mud, and the ground sucked it back when I tried to lift it out. Now the sun comes out for a few hours. I walked downtown past the first forsythia blooming, a few more standard hyacinths open, henbit with tight pink blossoms, a young red maple coming in.

2019: From Spoleto, Italy, Neysa sends a photo of violets blooming in her stone wall. They have been blooming about a week, she said.

2020: Pussy willow catkins falling. Jill's peach tree suddenly with large, pink blossoms. Pears, pink magnolias, star magnolias, forsythia and weeping cherry trees in all full bloom, all the crab apples at the park leafing, the season at least a week to ten days ahead of average.

2021: Grackle activity has increased throughout the past week, dominating activity around my feeders. Pussy willow catkins are full of pollen and just starting to fall. Weeping cherry trees seen partially open. At 3:32 this afternoon, Casey called: a bald eagle had just flown over his house. Jill and I went looking for snow trillium along the river later in the day. The woods was full of violet cress, hepatica, toothwort, Dutchman's britches, Virginia bluebells, lesser celandine and bloodroot; the toad trilliums were up and budded, but the snow trilliums had disappeared. In Dimi's garden, white and purple violets were open and dense as scilla.

2022: The warmest days so far in the year, 80 degrees this afternoon, steady wind. Eighty-four daffodils open throughout the yard.

2023: Jill sends photos of azaleas, flowering crab apples and snowball viburnums from Knoxville, Tennessee. From Warroad, Minnesota, on the Canadian border, nephew John reports two feet of snow on the ground and minus 2 degrees this morning. Here, the glory of the snow and the scillas make the transition from Early Spring into April, interlocking daffodils with tulips.

Then came the lovely spring,
With a rush of blossoms and music
Filling the earth with blossoms
And the air with melodies vernal

Henry Wadsworth Longfellow

March 31st
The 90th Day of the Year

Almost April on the first warm day
when I saw you by the bloodroot
and you told me with your smile:
"It is at the gate of spring alone,
before the wilting of the lilacs and the tulips
and the cowslip and the rue,
there alone my wings are kissed
and I am given license and the grace
to be most beautiful."

"For Ella"

Sunrise/set: 6:21/6:58
Day's Length: 12 hours 39 minutes
Average High/Low: 55/36
Average Temperature: 46
Record High: 82 – 1981
Record Low: 12 – 1923

Weather
Today's temperature distribution: 80s come 15 percent of the days; chances of 70s are five percent, of 60s ten percent, of 50s fifty-five percent, of 40s five percent, and of 30s ten percent. The sun shines 55 percent time. Rain falls a third of all the days, snow flurries are seen once every 15 years or so. Frost occurs on just 20 percent of the mornings.

Natural Calendar
Yin and Yang: Notes on March of 1983 and 1984
The season's potential for warmth grows as the average temperatures rise, but March's averages seem made from greater extremes than February's. Two of the first years in my Daybook, 1983 and 1984, set the recent limits for heat and cold.

Deep winter ended on the 13th of February in 1983, but the weather didn't become unusual until the 3rd of March. Then there were five days in a row in the 70s, one record tied, another broken.

255

Everything seemed to blossom at once. Some daffodils and forsythia opened on the 6th. By the 8th, three weeks ahead of what I later settled on for average, spring beauties, toad trillium, toothwort, bluebells, coltsfoot, periwinkles, violet cress, harbinger of spring were blooming. Comfrey and horseradish were showing new growth.

By the 12th, the raspberries, honeysuckle, mock orange, skunk cabbage, wild roses and lilacs were leafing; peaches, quince and dogwoods, magnolia, box elder, and red maples were flowering. The first new garlic mustard had sprouted. Columbine and bleeding hearts were up. Cabbage butterflies and box elder bugs were out. I saw a tulip on the 14th.

The Early Spring of 1984 seemed to promise a repeat of this warmth. The middle of February had been especially mild: eleven days in the 50s, a new record - 68 degrees - on the 12th. Then an 18 day cold spell began on the 25th. Six inches of snow fell on March 8th, and the next morning set a record at four below zero. More snow on the 10th, the 12th and the 13th. Nothing seemed to grow until equinox. Then the parsnips and dock came back to their February levels, lavender cress and ragwort budded, and a few bluebells pushed out of the ground along the ridge southwest of the covered bridge.

After both the coldest and the warmest Marches, the land came back into equilibrium, finding the pace it always finds by the middle of April, and bringing the green leaves to summer in May.

Sudden Spring: Notes on March of 2007
On the 9th of March, 2007, the harsh cold of late winter suddenly gave way to spring. Highs reached the 60s and then the 70s and finally 80 degrees by the 27th. The month's average ended up being 46.2 degrees, six degrees above average.

By March 25, forsythia and star magnolias were in full flower. The first primroses, puschkinia and daffodils were opening in town, and Mike Triplett reported toads singing and turkeys pairing up along East Enon Road. By the 26th, crocus season had ended, and blue squills were in full bloom. May apples had come up and Dutchman's britches blossomed at Clifton Gorge. By the 27th, pussy willows were heavy with pollen, and cabbage butterflies and bumblebees visited the gardens. By the 28th, hepatica and bloodroot filled the North Glen. Purple cress was blooming along the Little Miami. Skunk cabbage was growing leaves at Jacoby, and plum trees were flowering in the village. On the 29th, the pear trees downtown started to open; they were all out by the 30th. Serviceberry blossoms were emerging along Dayton Street on that date. Peach and crab apple buds were cracking.

Although that March was the warmest since 1973 (the average of which was 48.6 degrees), the hottest Marches on record (with averages between 50 and 51 degrees) took place in 1921, 1945 and 1946. Using phenology and natural history, one can imagine the state of Yellow Springs in early April those years: Redbuds and apple trees and cherry trees were in full bloom then. All the magnolia petals were down. Lawns were long and full of the peak of dandelion bloom. Winter cress overran the pastures. Daffodils were done for the year, and viburnum and bridal wreath spirea flowered along Xenia Avenue. Box elder and maple, ginkgo, pear, serviceberry, ash and mulberry trees were leafing out. It was almost May.

(And, in fact, all that and more came to be in the hot March of 2012, which was three degrees above the warmest in history - March of 1946 - and almost fourteen degrees above normal.)

Final Notes on March of 2012

The statistics for March of 2012 in the Dayton, Ohio, area complement the rapid advance of the flowers and leaves over the past four weeks: an average high of 53.6 degrees, 13.2 degrees above the normal of 40.4 degrees, 2.5 degrees above the previous record of 51.1 in 1946 and 3.5 degrees above a runner-up March in 1945 of 50.1 degrees. Eight afternoons brought temperatures above 70, four days above 80.

After an unusual heat wave in the third month of 2007, I imagined what an extra-warm March might have been like in the warmest years up to that time: 1921, 1945 and 1946: "Using phenology and natural history," I wrote in the *News*, "one might imagine the state of Yellow Springs in early April those years: Redbuds and apple trees and cherry trees were in full bloom then. All the magnolia petals were down. Lawns were long and full of the peak of dandelion bloom. Winter cress overran the pastures.

Daffodils were done for the year, and viburnum and bridal wreath spirea flowered along Xenia Avenue. Box elder and maple, ginkgo, pear, serviceberry, ash and mulberry trees were leafing out. It was almost May."

In fact, it is now almost the first week of a Yellow Springs May. All of the zeitgebers are aligned: Wild strawberries, common fleabane, large-flowered trillium, winter cress, trout lilies, late-season tulips, red-leafed crab apples, pink flowering quince, wisteria and azaleas are in bloom. All of the serviceberry flowers, the star and the pink magnolias, the cherry, the early crab apple, the pear and the peach flowers have opened and fallen. Daffodils are almost gone. Blue squills and the pale puschkinias and the white pachysandras have lost their blossoms. The Great Dandelion Bloom came up from the South when the temperature reached 80 and just has suddenly gone to seed. Mushroom hunters have been finding April morel mushrooms for weeks. The undergrowth has filled in, and the high trees are greening. Honeysuckles and peonies have buds, and the first Jack-in-the-pulpit has been reported.

Daybook

1981: First day in the 80s this year.

1982: First tulip seen in town.

1983: Most grape hyacinth blooming in the yard.

1986: Cardinal sings at 5:44 a.m. First day in the 80s today. First grape hyacinth open in the yard. One magnolia full bloom at my south door. Maples and box elder full bloom, willows leafing, Bradford pear, apple and peach trees start to leaf.

1987: Eight inches of snow, the most of the season, falls in an afternoon storm, high winds.

1988: Rich sweet smell of pussy willow pollen.

1990: Robins twittering by 5:20 a.m.

1992: Late bloom of squills.

1993: One daffodil slightly breaking through this afternoon; beside it a few forsythia buds at the same stage were pushing out. Rose buds extending by the garden wall. Rhubarb grew slowly this week, but put on two inches.

1994: Ants all over my office this morning, awakened by the sun or some body clock. One small ladybug with them. In the south garden, the first daffodil is half open, and snowdrop season is over. First pale blue anemone discovered by the purple crocus. Junco seen.

1996: On the way down Corry Street, I saw the *Cornus mas* was just starting to open. At the Mill habitat, down river from the dam, I found the first wildflowers of the year, four snow trillium, almost a dozen hepatica, a couple of toothwort plants, and a few small violet cress with buds. A patch of toad trillium just up from the ground. The first honeysuckle leaves pushed out, the first wild rose leaves. In front of one house on Limestone, the first daffodil was opening. A red maple was unraveling on Dayton-Yellow Springs Road. In the garden, rhubarb leaves are an inch or so long.

1998: Bleeding hearts 12 inches tall, well leafed. Blue flag iris foliage at least six inches. Purple coneflowers two inches. Hops knee high. Garden rosemary has come back. Pussy willow catkins falling. First violet bloom. Redbuds purple but not full bloom. Buttercup, the bulldog, wakes up knowing that storms will be passing through in the afternoon; she is panting, staying close to me.

2000: First major patches of dandelions seen on the way home from Springfield: their full bloom time begins. Red quince opens now.

2001: Jekyll Island, Georgia to Hendersonville, North Carolina: Between Jekyll and Savannah: late spring/late Yellow Springs May. Wild cherry tree in bloom near Savannah. Between Savannah and Columbia: Middle Spring, still light green tint to the tree line.

Wisteria, redbud, dogwood, the yellow Jessamine vine full. Middle Spring thins between Columbia and Spartanburg, a dramatic shift into mid April.

2004: Driving to school, I saw the bodies of two young opossums run over last night. First worm of the year seen on the sidewalk in Washington Court House, driven out by this morning's heavy rains. At home, the lungwort has produced pink flowers in spite of the cool weather.

2005: Watching some of the warmest and the coldest Marches in local history, one can have a pretty good sense of Early Spring's boundaries and know as much about local March weather as there is to know.

The most unseasonably cold Marches weather in recent Yellow Springs records (up through 2004) took place in 1999, 1996, 1984, and 1960. In those harshest months, nothing except a few snowdrops, aconites, snow crocus, and purple deadnettle bloomed. Pussy willows were only half emerged by the 1st of April. No trees were flowering. Peonies were only an inch above ground.

There have been ten Marches between 2005 and 1883 that have been unusually warm, the most recent being March of 1990. That last mildest March brought out all the middle spring flowers: By the 31st, bluebells, twinleaf, bloodroot, violet cress, spring beauties, hepatica, toothwort, chickweed, Dutchman's britches, daffodils were blooming. Crocus, snowdrops, and aconite were past their prime. Pussy willow catkins had turned yellow with pollen and had fallen in the wind. Peonies were 18 inches tall. Buckeye leaves had unraveled. Maples were blossoming. Butterflies were out.

2017: On the 9th of March, the harsh cold of late winter suddenly

2008: The first blue squill is open in the yard near Janet's redbud. A few forsythia buds are yellow, but no sign of opening anywhere around the area. Several daffodil buds are large and ready. Waterleaf foliage is up and about an inch or so in breadth. Ramp leaves have unraveled. Pussy willows are fully emerged but show no pollen. Robins jostling on High Street as I got set to move the trees cut down last week. The small red tulips by the pond have red buds, would bloom tomorrow if the weather would be warm enough.

2009: Robins began singing at almost exactly 5:35 this morning. In the north garden, purple coneflowers are up an inch, hosta an inch in the east garden. Under Janet's redbud tree, the first yellow primrose is opening, the pink ones full bloom, and the first purple violet.

2010: North from Hunting Island, South Carolina: Wisteria, red clover, garden peas in bloom near Beaufort. A live oak was leafing at Frampton Plantation, and *Leucojum aestivum* (with narrow, long daffodil-type leaves and white bell flowers). Dogwoods seen near Columbia. Pears, daffodils and forsythia in Charlotte. Large patches of dandelions in Statesville. By the time we reached the mountains near Wytheville, Virginia, there were no leaves on the trees, but the pastures and hillsides were glowing bright green. Forsythia was open at the Wytheville campground.

2011: Crows at 5:43 this morning. Don's serviceberry buds are straining to open. Daylily foliage is already a foot tall, peonies four to five inches and unraveling. Puschkinias hold in the south garden, and two of the early tulips there have buds. Grackles, cardinals, titmice, sparrows, doves, steady in the early morning.

2012: All the early flowering trees are done now, and even some of the crab apples are fading. Our red and other red-leafed crabs are coming in, though, the trellis wisteria is reaching full bloom, tulips full bloom replacing the daffodils as foci of color, and the first azaleas and pink quince buds have cracked in front of the house. Red quince flowers are being covered up by the foliage now. Blue eyes and bittercress are almost gone. Don's pie cherry is holding on. Privet and coralberry bushes are well leafed. Rachel's ginkgo is catching up with the larger ginkgoes on Xenia Avenue. Zelcova leaves near the library are almost full size. Mateo's taxus has new growth, maybe just half an inch. In the alley this morning, cardinals, doves, grackles and a red-bellied woodpecker calling, birds flying back and forth, some with nesting materials, the world alive and well, loud and in motion. Along Tecumseh Road to Enon, the tree line is greening, and even some of the oaks appear to be in bloom. Dogwoods, lilacs and redbuds common. Driving past Ellis Pond, I saw two Canadian geese churning up the water in a territorial battle. A mourning cloak butterfly came by as I was paying bills on the back porch

2013: This morning, robins were singing at 5:30, cardinals by 5:45. Casey called with "positive identification" of red-winged blackbirds on his property.

From California, Paul Rea wrote: "Talk about spring flowers. Took a great hike Saturday on Mt. Diablo, which rises as an island, a eco-crossroads between N and S, the Valley and the East Bay. And since it's especially rich in microclimates and eco-niches, the variety of flora is truly amazing. Desert trees such as junipers and gray pines grow near maples, ashes, and of course a great variety of white, blue, valley and live oaks. In places, Diablo's hills seemed as lush as the west of the Emerald Isle.

"Spring flowers included California poppies, brodea, scarlet columbine, lupines and vetches plus, moving rapidly into folk poetry, Chinese houses, fairy bells, and hound's bane. What I called Oregon grape (with the golden yellow flowers) turns out to be Mahonia grape holly. Very handsome plant, tho."

2014: Robins were in full song when I went out this morning with Bella at 5:35. The winds were calm, sky clear in the east, high cirrus overhead, Venus rising above the Danielsons' house. I heard doves at 5:42, cardinals at 5:48, crows at 5:52. Ed Oxley called to say he was watching gold finches at his feeder, and their plumage was almost full gold. He also claimed to have seen red-winged blackbirds at his place on the river three weeks ago. Lori Deal told me she had heard frogs calling at Laramie Lake this afternoon. In the south garden area, one puschkinia is budded.

2016: Throughout the countryside, pear trees are at peak bloom, and the Great Dandelion flowering is well underway, joining the forsythia and the newly gilded goldfinches. Jill reported seeing a red-winged blackbird while she was driving above Columbus.

2018: At the end of a chilly March (36.7 degree average and almost four inches of rain), sun and clouds and light wind, in the 40s, to the Covered Bridge: the rain of the past week had brought flooding up maybe a dozen yards into the woods, but the wildflower growth seemed unhurt, maybe even stimulated.

Along the river, Jill and I found several clumps of lesser celandine with one or two blossoms each, scattered spring beauties, numerous violet cress quite tall and strong, dock leaves were over half a foot long; several ramps leaves fully developed, stalks showing; swamp buttercup had fully developed basal leaves, waterleaf leaves two inches across; chickweed was covering the woodland floor, but no blossoms seen; hemlock was bushy, a couple of feet across now; wild rose leaves were an inch long, branches filling out; skunk cabbage was starting to produce foliage; Jill spied the first bloodroot and once we saw one, we saw many more, and up the hill from them a little ways, a clump of white hepatica; two dandelions; a few small toad trillium lay close to the ground, unopened; we found Dutchman's britches with their first white pantaloons; henbit showed bright pink buds; tiny white bittercress flowers were tucked in the taller grass; a few bunches of large-flowered snowdrops grew in the middle of the fields. In the dry hillsides of the North Glen, only a few white hepaticas showed through the mulch.

At home, the circle garden daffodils were steadily coming in. Some day lily leaves were over six inches. Blue scillas were full in the southwest garden, a few white puschkinias near the dooryard. The bittercress bloomed near the bamboo stand, snowdrops almost gone, windflowers withered, a few aconites and Dutch crocus hanging on, single forsythia flowers open on the old bushes, the high branch pussy willows had pollen, the peony stalks were half a foot and a few were just starting to leaf. From Billings, Missouri, Jeffery Goss reports the first morel.

2019: A cold front brought lows in the 20s last night, more forecast tonight, daffodils drooping. In the porch garden, though, the scraggly glory-of-the-snow flowers that came up a few days ago are holding on. After yesterday's long rain, there are pools of water in the back yard. On Talus Drive, red maples are dropping their flowers. This afternoon, a Cooper's Hawk waited on top of the bird feeder until I went out to move him on.

2020: Average temperature for the month was 46.5 degrees, 6.1 above normal, rainfall 5.75 inches, 2.41 above normal. All the flowering plants following suit.

2021: Now the pussy willow catkins fall in the wind of the approaching high-pressure system, closing out the year the way they did last year, and the red quince at the corner of High and Limestone Streets has started to bloom. Month's average: 46.6 degrees, more than six degrees above normal; precipitation: 3.29 inches, a fraction above average.

2022: After a mild night, 107 daffodils in bloom, up from 84, but now the cold moves back in for tomorrow's new moon. At the corner of High and Limestone, the first flower of the red quince has opened. The star magnolias continue to blossom, having foiled the frost of several nights ago. In the back porch garden, Glory-of-the-Snow (*Chionodoxa forbesli*) has taken over the south end of the plantings. As I sat by the fire looking out the back door, I could see the green glow to the honeysuckle hedge, a change just in the past few days. The month's average temperature was 45 degrees, with four inches of snow and three and a half of water precipitation.

2023: Average temperature for the month: 42.3 degrees. Growing degree days so far in the year: 120. Daffodil count down from earlier in the week: 120 blossoms. Bird song strong throughout the day and into the evening: robins the most vociferous, followed by grackles and blackbirds, song sparrows, cardinals, blue jays, house sparrows and Carolina wrens.

If I should leave off making memorandums of such events as affect, or are interesting to me, I should feel like – what I am, namely, a person that has nothing more to do in this world

Caroline Herschel

Bill Felker has been writing *Poor Will's Almanack* for newspapers and magazines since 1984, and he has published annual almanacs since 2003. His radio version of *Poor Will* is broadcast weekly on NPR station WYSO and is available on podcast at **www.wyso.org**. His three books of reflections, *Home is the Prime Meridian: Essays in Search of Time and Place, Deep Time Is in the Garden: New Essays in Search of Time and Place,* and *The Virgin Point: Meditations in Nature,* along with the entire twelve volumes of *A Daybook for the Year in Yellow Springs,* are available from Bill Felker's website at **www.poorwillsalmanack.com**, as well as from Amazon.